SEXUAL STYLES

Sexual Styles

A Psychologist's Guide

to Understanding

Your Lover's Personality

John Michael Berecz

Humanics Publishing Group
ATLANTA

Sexual Styles

A Humanics Trade Publication

Humanics Trade Publications are an imprint of and published by Humanics Limited, a division of Humanics Publishing Group, Inc. Its trademark, consisting of the words "Humanics Trade" and the portrayal of a Pegasus, is Registered in U. S. Patent and Trademark Office and in other countries.

Humanics Limited, P. O. Box 7400, Atlanta, GA 30357

Printed in the United States of America

Library of Congress Catalog Card Number: 98-86001

ISBN: 0-89334-287-4
ISBN: 0-89334-286-6 pbk.

Dedication

For Deborah: my lover and best friend, who shares my inner life, fills me with joy, and suffuses my spirit with her sparkle.

For my sons Michael, Ryan, Lamont, and Jamison: with heartfelt wishes for much sexual happiness grounded in deeply caring relationships.

A NOTE TO THE READER

The ideas, suggestions, and techniques presented in this book are not intended as a substitute for professional consultation. Individuals who experience persistent difficulties with sexual issues ought to consult a clinical psychologist, psychiatrist, marriage counselor, or other qualified professional.

The cases presented in this book are composites created from nearly thirty years of the author's clinical experiences, and do not refer to specific individuals.

Table of Contents

Overview

Suzette's hand moves slowly, teasingly. She creates small bundles of tactile excitement on Matt's chest with her circles of light touch. As she subtly moves lower, she giggles incessantly. It's both erotic and distracting to him.

Matt vividly remembers his first sexual encounter with Suzette. He thought she was the sexiest woman in the world—vivacious, effervescent, animated, flirtatious—she laughed frequently and seemed to enjoy life more than anyone he'd ever known. Lately however, he wonders if laughing, teasing and flirting are her way of *avoiding* sex. Although they've dated on and off for three years, she never experiences orgasm, they seldom have intercourse and she uses fellatio to "satisfy" him periodically. At the same time, although she claims she loves Matt, she compulsively flirts with any other male within earshot. If Matt understood that Suzette is histrionic, he could save himself a lot of grief and understand her better.

***

While they were dating, Priscilla thought Paul was Mr. Perfect. He was such a gentleman. He always held the door for her, he sent her cards and thank you notes for the smallest things, and he treated her parents with respect. He wasn't always trying to get inside her blouse—in fact he stated that he was a virgin and wanted to remain so until marriage. She especially liked his neatness. She wasn't going to be married to a man who left the toilet seat up! He was meticulous about his attire and hygiene. His car was immaculate inside and out. Paul seemed to do everything perfectly. He even filled his gas tank perfectly! He filled *exactly* to the top—not a drop less. He took this quite seriously, as if he were fueling a rocket to launch a space shuttle. After the pump automatically shut off, indicating the tank was full (at least for ordinary people it meant that), Jim would override this mechanism forcing at least two dozen more "clicks" of gas into his reluctant tank. Finally, almost with regret, he would screw the cap on, but only after the overflow valve had leaked a pint of petro onto the pavement.

Priscilla used to think such precision was desirable and she thought his routines were cute. Now she's worried that his neatness will drive her nuts. On the first night of their honeymoon Paul spent so long in the shower after making love she fell asleep waiting for him to return. Now she simply doesn't count on any "afterglow"—unless, of course, you find the sound of someone showering particularly satisfying. When they married, Priscilla didn't understand how difficult living with an obsessive compulsive could become. Often she still finds it exceedingly difficult. It might be a bit easier if she understood Paul's style and realized how difficult it is for him to change.

***

Ken was kind. He never insisted on having his own way. For Natalie this seemed perfect. Her parents had quarreled unremittingly until they divorced when she was a sophomore in college. Not surprisingly, she had determined that her home would be different. She simply would not live with a man who was like her father—dominant, chauvinistic, controlling. When it came to choosing a restaurant or a movie, Ken always deferred to her. His stock answer was "Whatever you like is fine with me." He seldom disagreed with Natalie, they never quarreled, it seemed too good to be true.

Their sex life seemed OK and they soon had three children. But after about ten years, Natalie found herself in my office saying, "I think I'm going to get a divorce. It's the craziest thing. I know it sounds outrageous but Ken is *too nice*. I have to make *all* the decisions which makes me feel like a controlling bitch. I've lost all respect for him; he doesn't seem like a husband. It feels like I have *four* children."

What had originally seemed like niceness to Natalie was in fact dependency. In the decade following their marriage she had become less and less erotically attracted to Ken and she confessed, "We haven't made love in over a year. When we do, I feel almost like I'm doing it with my brother."

Living with a dependent lover may seem tiring or boring, but if you understand the style, you'll be able to relate without feeling your spouse is one of your children.

***

Sandy had been instantly attracted to Ross. He exuded self-confidence, dressed sharply, and was always up for a party. And Ross knew how to court a woman! Flowers, balloons, stuffed animals, singing telegrams became a regular part of Sandy's life after she met him. It seemed like the UPS truck or some other delivery service was making a trip to her office or apartment almost daily. Sandy found herself helplessly in love with this charismatic character, even though her girlfriends seemed distrustful of him, saying he was "too smooth."

But they had never made love with Ross! There weren't words to describe the exquisite feelings he aroused in her. Sandy felt lucky that Ross paid attention to her, as he had obviously been with a lot of women before and there were numerous others waiting in the wings in case things didn't work out. He seemed to enjoy subtly letting her know that she wasn't the only fish in the pond and that she was lucky to have him.

Ross was the night manager at a posh local restaurant, but he didn't want Sandy to "bother" him while he was at work. He told her to call first if she ever needed to stop by. For the most part, she complied with his wishes, but on a couple of occasions she'd stopped in on impulse. Both times she'd found him having a drink with one of the waitresses and although he assured her it was business-related, she was uneasy. She noticed that he loved to flirt, taking advantage of any opportunity to do so, and creating circumstances where it was easy to "kid around" with someone else's wife. He was an excellent dancer and loved to whirl around the dance floor, typically spending more time with other women than with Sandy. But now that they were engaged, she was determined not to become the "jealous wife" and he had let her know that if she couldn't understand his having women friends, the engagement would be off.

Ross also told her he had sold some of his investments but that it would take two months to clear the brokerage house. He asked if he could use her credit cards just until the cash came in. Of course she agreed—after all, they were getting married and would soon be sharing expenses anyway. He bought her a two-carat diamond for their engagement, even though he had to "max" out two of her three credit cards to pay for it. The remaining charge card was taken to the limit when he purchased some expensive camera equipment to take on their honeymoon.

A week before the wedding, Sandy received an anonymous phone call on her answering machine stating that Ross, was a "cheating a_ _ hole." The voice informed him that in addition to managing the restaurant in San Bernardino, he was married to a woman in Los Angeles with whom he'd had a child. Ross must have sensed the gig was up when Sandy called him on the phone, because all she could do was sob. By the time she arrived at the restaurant to talk with him, he had left—with no forwarding address. Sandy was stuck with a two-carat engagement ring (which she returned at a significant loss in order to begin paying off her credit cards) and a cruel, aching consciousness of what it's like being "loved" by a smooth sociopath.

***

Each of these relationships illustrates the importance of understanding your lover's personality. *Psychological intimacy,* not intercourse, is the epoxy that holds lives together. The secret to great sex is found in deeply understanding and taking part in another person's inner life. Unfortunately, many people view sex as just intercourse. Being a "great lover" means knowing how to push the right buttons—good moves, smooth technique—and racking up conquests. "Making love" is too often a euphemism for casual copulation—sex, devoid of intimacy or caring—just a phrase about joining genitals.

Curiously, the dearth of genuine psychological intimacy is often replaced with a profusion of new techniques designed to make you a better lover. She practices Kegel exercises to tone up vaginal muscles for increased sexual responsiveness, while he searches for the elusive G spot or some other biological button that will transform her into a writhing sex maniac.

Such techniques will only be fleetingly successful unless you can create an intimate inner life with your lover where you both feel safe in sharing your deepest secrets. In this book I will show you that great sex grows out of great *psychological* relationships, not gymnastic maneuvers or fast hands.

You'll never be a good lover if you're not psychologically discerning. Although some well known athletes have boasted about their numerous off-court "victories," it is quite impossible to form meaningful psychological relationships with 20,000 women. Anyone who confuses "number of lays" with being a great lover is seriously deluded.

A patient once described her sex life to me in the following words: "When we do it, I feel like a semen receptacle."

That is as coldly impersonal as I've ever heard sex described, but many persons suffer from milder versions of the "semen-receptacle syndrome." Couples "get off" but hardly talk to each other. Husbands and wives "do it" but can't stop fighting about finances.

We've surpassed our prudish predecessors by recognizing that sex ought to be recreational not merely procreational. But by recasting intimacy as entertainment and projecting intensely private encounters between lovers onto the big screen, Hollywood has shortchanged us. Even the precious phrase "I love you" is often devoid of genuine meaning. Too often words of love are like bounced checks, a sabotaged currency, profuse and devalued. Though sexual words are in ample supply and explicit portrayals of casual coitus Hollywood's bread and butter, genuine caring is in short supply, and intimacy and love too often absent.

I've written this book to help you achieve a better sex life, but it's not another "how-to-have-exciting-sex-by-pressing-all-the-right-buttons" manual. By analyzing personality styles instead of focusing on erogenous zones, I'll help you become more responsive to your lover with your mind as well as with your genitals. You'll discover that the most erotically sensitive tissues are in your brain, not your groin. You'll begin to appreciate the close relationship between everyday life and the bedroom.

Reading this book will help you understand the *personality* of your lover—not only in the bedroom, but in all areas of life. This will aid you in reaching deeper levels of psychological and sexual intimacy with your partner. Instead of settling for mere physical contact, you'll be inspired to understand your lover in a deep psychological sense that is infinitely more satisfying.

On the practical side you'll pick up some information which will enhance your relationships not only with your lover, but with people in general. You'll learn how to successfully relate with almost any kind of personality style. Although we'll focus on sexual issues, much time will be spent in understanding the *person* who is your lover. If you understand the personality of your lover, the positions you assume when making love will be much less important. Psychological intimacy, not technique is what this book is about.

We see something of this kind of intimacy in the relationship between Peter the Great, seventeenth-century Tsar of Russia, and his wife Catherine. Peter suffered from convulsive spasms (tics) when he was under stress. Such spasms often frightened or mystified others around him, but Catherine knew how to relate to him:

"When the first symptoms of these attacks appeared, the Tsar's attendants would run for Catherine, who would come at once and firmly lay him down, take his head in her lap and gently stroke his hair and temples until the convulsions abated and he fell asleep.

While he slept she would sit silently for hours, cradling his head, soothingly stroking it when he stirred. Peter always awakened refreshed. But his need for her went far deeper than mere nursing. Her qualities of mind and heart were such that she was able not only to soothe him, play with him, love him, but also to take part in his inner life, talk to him about serious things, to discuss his views and projects, to encourage his hopes and aspirations. Not only did her presence comfort him, but her conversation cheered him and gave him balance." (Massie, 1980, p. 376)

I don't know precisely what Peter and Catherine did in bed. I'm sure Peter hadn't heard of the G spot, and Catherine didn't practice Kegal exercises. Neither of them read *Cosmopolitan* or *Redbook* for tips on how to become better lovers. But they were *psychologically* intimate, and I'll bet they were great lovers! You can be too.

Introduction

Great Sex = Friendship on Fire

These days, it seems like every where you turn you're served an alphabet soup of diagnoses. On television, at school, even at the office, people like to label each other. Every nook and cranny of your personality is scrutinized and tagged. Tired? Could be CFS. Restless, possibly ADD. Slow in arithmetic? Maybe LD. Did father drink several beers after supper? Maybe you're an ACOA. Like all your ducks in a row? OCD!

So why buy this book? Do you need another label for yourself or your lover? Of course not, but this book isn't about how to be a better *labeler,* it's about becoming a better *lover.* And you can do that best by understanding your partner's personality.

Psychological intimacy, not intercourse, is the epoxy that holds lives together. You won't find the secret to better sex in the latest technique manual. Great sex is found in deeply understanding another person's inner life.

Becoming a better lover isn't just about knowing which buttons to push or which moves to make, it's about becoming a *more intimate friend!* Ideally, *your lover ought to be your soul mate—your best friend. Excellent sex is about excellent friendship.* The joy of sex involves more than joining genitals, making conquests, good moves, or smooth techniques. Joyful sex is *FRIENDSHIP ON FIRE.*

Techniques will only be fleetingly successful unless you share an intimate inner life with your lover. "Good moves"—good techniques may enhance a sexual relationship, but they will never create one. Great sex grows out of great *psychological* relationships, and you'll never be a great lover unless you're psychologically discerning. What your partner *really* desires from you—even more than orgasms—is *understanding.* If you take time to learn about his past, he'll want to share his future with you. If you can penetrate her mind, she'll happily let you penetrate her body.

Too often, couples "get off," but hardly talk to each other. Husbands and wives "do it," but can't stop fighting about finances. This book will help you achieve a better sex life, not by helping you press all the right buttons, but by enlightening you about your partner's personality. You'll discover that the most sensitive erotic areas are in your brain, not your groin. You'll find getting into each others' personalities almost as exciting as getting into each other's pants.

You'll discern the close relationship between everyday life and the bedroom: If she insists on keeping the kitchen decks spotless, it shouldn't surprise you that she wants to shower before you make love. If he's an "on-time freak" and can't squeeze a spontaneous lunch date into his packed schedule, he's not likely to be very accommodating if you're "late in coming" during sex. How she copes with the frustration of forgetting her credit cards or checkbook and being unable to purchase an after-Christmas-sale dress will give you some notion of how even-tempered she might be about failing to climax within the first fifteen minutes of lovemaking.

Reading this book will help you understand the personality of your lover—not only in the bedroom, but in all areas of life. This will aid you in reaching deeper levels of psychological and sexual intimacy with your partner. Instead of settling for mere physical contact, you'll be inspired to understand your lover in a deep psychological sense that will be infinitely more satisfying.

As Ann Landers (1994) aptly put it, "Sex is a good basis for marriage if you can agree on what to do for the next 23 hours and 45 minutes." This book is not only about sex, it's also about the other 23 hours.

And there's another bonus. Your new understanding of your lover's personality will enhance your relationships not only with your lover, but with other people as well. You'll learn to how to cope with various people not only in the bedroom but driving to work, at the office or on the golf course.

To be a successful lover, you might need to know a few basics about technique, but what really counts is how well you understand the *personality style* of your lover. If you can mesh with her mind, the particular positions you assume when making love will be less important. If you touch his heart with your empathy, how you touch his body will be less critical.

Understanding your lover's psychological *style* will do more for your love life than mastering a dozen new positions for intercourse.

What is a "Normal" Personality Style?

Twenty-five years ago, when I first began teaching abnormal psychology to university students, I often found myself involved in an after class discussions that went something like this:

"Dr. Berecz, I like to keep all the things on my desk in order and I sometimes "check" things several times. Do you think I'm an obsessive-compulsive?"

"Probably not," I would reply. "You see, *real* obsessive-compulsives have an inflexible urge to do such things. You might *prefer* to have a neat desk, but I suspect that it's not preoccupying you."

Circumspectly dancing around the issue, I would reassure the anxious student that he or she was *very* different from patients whom I treated in my private practice. Later, as I drove across town to begin a psychotherapy session, I would wonder if I had adequately reassured the student. I would plan how I could make the distinction between patients and normal people more clear in my next lecture.

Now, a couple decades later with a few more gray hairs on my head and several thousand psychotherapy hours behind me, I realize I was wrong. It turns out that "patients" are people just like you and me. Sometimes their circumstances are more trying and often their inner reserves for dealing with problems have become depleted, but underneath it all, they struggle much the same as you and I, to cope with the problems of life. A famous psychiatrist expressed it this way:

"We shall assume that everyone is much more simply human than otherwise…" —Harry Stack Sullivan (1953, pp. 32-33)

Today, after class, my discussions are more brief and more accurate:

"Dr. Berecz I keep all the pencils on my desk in a row…do you think I'm obsessive-compulsive?"

"Probably."

Then, for reassurance:

"Many of us have obsessive streaks in our personalities."

Then I explain—as I'm about to explain to you—the distinctions between *"normal"* and *"sick"* are mostly differences of *degree* not kind. The predicaments that bring people into my office to lie on my leather couch or sit in my overstuffed chair for fifty minutes of psychotherapy are similar to the problems encountered by everyone—more intense perhaps, but similar. Even patients who require hospitalization are more similar to you and me than we usually imagine.

For example, many people experience a "compulsion" to re-check the doors and windows of their homes to see if they are all securely locked before leaving on vacation. However, if you feel compelled to re-check the locks several times before going to work each morning—maybe even turning back after you're several miles down the road to re-check once more— you might consider yourself maladjusted. Should you then decide to talk with a professional about it, your status could suddenly shift—for purposes of billing—from "normal" to "patient". You would likely be assigned a diagnosis, and asked to fill out insurance forms. Nonetheless, *you* would still be *you*—dealing with the same problems.

People seen as "mentally ill" usually experience normal problems, but *more intensely*. This means that as you try to understand what makes "mentally ill" people tick, you can trust your own experience. You're more of a psychiatrist than you thought. Your own wisdom and experience count. In the following pages, I'll try to connect with your inner wisdom as together we look at how people cope with problems.

We'll analyze their *styles* of personality, and as you begin to understand the *style* of your partner, you'll likely enjoy *better sex* because your sexual experiences will be infused with psychological intimacy. As we've noted already, intimacy is what makes intercourse satisfying.

In summary, differences between normal and "sick" are usually differences of degree, not kind. Most of us (presumably "normal" people) share much in common with others in need of psychotherapy or hospitalization. But don't expect things to be simple, because in nature there are no pure styles of personality. Everyone is a mixed bag of tendencies and traits.

As you journey through these pages with me, you will meet people with widely differing *styles* of personality. As you draw on your own experiences, and sharpen your insights about the various styles, you will not only learn more about others, you'll come to understand yourself more deeply.

Recognizing Your Lover's Personality Style

I n this book *style* means *consistent behavior. Style* is similar to *person-ality*—both describe consistent patterns of behavior which character-ize a person over time and in a wide variety of circumstances. I pre-fer the term *style* instead of *personality* because it can be applied to either positive or negative consistencies in behavior. For most people, "person-ality" means *appealing* personality or *charming* personality. If I say "Jessica has personality," it would be taken to mean she's attractive, fasci-nating or in other ways pleasant—someone you'd like to meet.

Style, emphasizes consistency more broadly—positive or negative. Remember your last high school reunion? You likely noticed changes in your classmates—receding hairlines, sagging bust lines, expanding waist-lines—but somehow their styles usually survived the ravages of time bet-ter than their bodies. Personal styles changed very little. The class clown was still the life of the party, the loudmouth could be still be heard above the rest. The "fast" girls were now flirtatious middle agers and the jocks were placing bets on the Super Bowl.

You probably experienced some *deja vu* because although their eye glasses, hair styles, clothing styles, shoe styles had been updated, their *per-sonality* styles had changed very little. And if you attend another reunion in five or ten years, you'll still recognize everyone. They will have changed only slightly. It's like watching a Thirty-Years-of-Johnny-Carson special from beginning to end; he's still "Johnny."

Sexual style is an expression of your total personality. Who you are in the bedroom is consistent with who you are in the kitchen, den or family room. If you like a neat desk, you'll probably want your bedspread neat-ly arranged as well. If you prefer to plan your meals for a week at a time, you'll probably prefer scheduled intercourse over spontaneous sex.

How you treat your sexual partner is similar to how you treat others at the office, on the tennis court or at a traffic crossing. Although you can fake being someone different for a short time, in the long run your lover is going to know who you really are. So as you read the following pages, I hope you'll be as sensitive to your own style as to your lover's. I hope about as often as you say "Ah ha! That's *her!*" you'll also be saying "Oh, my goodness! It's *me!*" I hope discovery will bring you satisfaction and pleasure. Finding out new things about your partner or yourself and revising long-held notions is not always easy, but it's an effort with rich payoff.

Achieving psychological intimacy with another person ranks as one of the truly significant accomplishments of life. More important than life insurance or job security, psychological intimacy is the foundation for mental and physical health. Psychological congruence with your lover not only feels extraordinary, it *is* magnificent. Love, more rare today than multi-carat diamonds, still exists! As you find your lover in the pages of this book, you will discover yourself as well, and in the process you'll sharpen the tools for remodeling your relationship along more loving lines.

Behavior: Inside-Out or Outside-In?—Volcanoes or Tide?

F or most of us, it feels as if behavior moves inside-out, that it flows from somewhere inside ourselves like lava bubbling up from deep inside a volcanic mountain—flowing from an inner core known as *personality*. We believe that somewhere deep inside the brain's central command center, our personality directs traffic much as air traffic controllers guide incoming and outgoing flights. Since we all like to feel that we are the pilots of our own airplanes, that we steer our own lives, this volcano model makes perfect sense, and is widely popular.

This view has been challenged by behavioral psychologists (such as the late B. F. Skinner) who champion an outside-in view of behavior. They insist that people are pushed and pulled about by *external* situations, not by inner forces. That's why, for example, even comedians don't tell jokes at funerals. That's why your heart beats more briskly when a police officer stops you for speeding. In such instances your behavior is being shaped by what's happening outside yourself. So just as ocean tides are brought about the moon's gravity acting on the waters, human behavior can be seen to result from external forces acting on the person.

So who's right? Are the traditional "volcano" psychologists right in suggesting that we possess an inner control center that steers behavior? Are the behavioral "moon-tide" psychologists correct when they insist that the situation powerfully shapes us? You guessed it—your common sense is a good guide—they're *both* right. Behavior is strongly influenced by *both* internal states of mind and external circumstances. In any specific event, *both* internal and external influences form and shape our behaving.

Shapiro (1965) illustrates this blending of internal and external influences in the following way:

"Suppose we observe an Indian, whose culture is unfamiliar, performing a strange dance with great intensity. As we watch, puzzled, we may notice that there is a drought and that this is an agricultural community; we consider the possibility that this is a prayerful dance designed to bring rain and the possibility that this is an expression of apprehension as well. By careful observation, we may be able to decipher certain regular gestures that confirm our guess. There is no doubt that, at this point, we have achieved a significant measure of understanding. But the limitations of that understanding become apparent if we only consider that nearby, watching, is a non-Indian farmer who also suffers from the drought but does not join in the dancing. It does not occur to him to perform these gestures; instead, he goes home and worries. *The Indian dances not only because there is a drought, but also because he is an Indian."* (1965, p. 16)

Style is broad enough to embrace *both* internal and external views of behavior. In seeking to understand various personality styles, we will study persons *and* situations in order to develop a total picture of sexual relationships. Anything less would be incomplete, because a relationship is not a *thing* it is an *interaction*—a dynamic way of relating.

To really understand sexual style we must realize that it is shaped *both* by personal and situational factors. Consider an illustration:

Two middle aged men arrive home Friday evening at the end of the work week. One, a corporate executive, comes home to a suburban home where his wife is fixing chicken stir-fry and has candles and wine glasses on the table. The other, a carpenter, has just put in a long day framing houses. It will be several hours before his wife will return home—exhausted—from her second-shift factory job. Both men might be "in the mood," but while the executive and his wife dine, drink wine, soak in the jacuzzi and make love, the carpenter tiredly takes out a recent issue of Penthouse and apathetically leafs through the pages, wondering if his wife will have to work overtime tonight. Both men have sexual needs, but their situations and their personality styles result in vastly different options for fulfillment.

In all individuals, we see differing combinations of what the person brings to the situation and what the situation imposes on the person. *Style* is always a blend. People "flow" through life in a blended "stream" of behavior, much like the water that flows from the single-control water faucet of your kitchen sink. Just as the stream is comprised of both hot and cold water, your sexual style is a blend of *both* personal and situational influences.

Sexual styles are uniquely personal, and like snowflakes, no two are exactly alike. Snowflakes form into unique configurations based upon laws of crystallization *interacting* with a host of situational variables like temperature, humidity, wind, etc. Most people miss all this complexity recognizing only snow as compared to sleet or rain. But Eskimos, ski enthusiasts, and meteorologists, discriminate among many different varieties of snow. Similarly, I hope to enhance your sensitivity to many different styles of sexuality and to the many nuances within each style. Understanding your partner's style is a very good beginning to understanding him or her more intimately.

In the following pages, you'll learn how your sexual style is shaped by your internal personality and your external situation, and you'll also learn what to do about your present relationships if they're not satisfying.

Personality Style
Determines Sexual Style

D escribing a person as a certain "type" is very popular but very misleading. You hear terms like sanguine, extrovert, driver, lion, or type A freely tossed about to describe hard-driving, achievement-oriented personalities; while terms like melancholic, introvert, shy, passive or type B, are often used to describe depression-prone persons. Book shelves are loaded with books explaining the Peter Pan syndrome, Cinderella complex or advising you—as if you've recently arrived from Venus—how to talk to Martians (the newest stereotype for men).

Such stereotyping may seem like a direct path to understanding people, but behavioral scientists don't accept such simplistic formulations. Serious psychologists carefully study how persons and circumstances *interact.* Human beings are too complex to be precisely packaged into a few simple types. There are many *styles* of behaving and limitless circumstances in which to behave. This results in a nearly infinite number of possible behavioral patterns.

Consequently this book is not about *the* obsessive compulsive type or about *the* histrionic type. Rather, it's about the *many different varieties* of *obsessive-compulsive styles* you'll encounter in the real world. People aren't like car models, rolling off an assembly line with different combinations of the same features. People are thoroughly unique—through and through. It's as if each car were equipped with a truly unique rear view mirror—a single mirror like none in the world—and a one-of-a-kind steering wheel. You get the idea. If cars were like people, your automobile would be equipped with four one-of-a-kind tires, each a slightly different size, each with a different tread design. Even your spare would be hand fashioned and distinct.

People are like fingerprints not Fords, so this book won't enable you to fix every "Ford" you encounter. You won't come away with an exact formula for relating to all obsessives, but you will learn much about the circumstances that promote obsessiveness and you'll meet a lot of obsessive people who, although unique, share some general similarities. This will give you new ideas for relating to your obsessive lover.

In the following pages you'll learn the major characteristics of the obsessive-compulsive style, the histrionic style, the sociopathic style, the narcissistic style, as well as others. This will help you better understand your lover. But in real life you won't find these features in a "pure" form. Instead you'll find obsessive people with several features—like the colors of the rainbow—blending into one another. You'll find people who have a broad streak of histrionic "color" in their rainbow but there may be a band of narcissism, and a bit of sociopathy as well. So although you may not be able to place your lover into a precise pigeonhole, you'll be sensitized to the various "colors" of your partner's sexual style and be able to relate more satisfyingly.

Sexual Myths: "Taking Out the Trash"

Sexual myths are created and perpetuated by romance novels and other media presentations. Sexual myths differ from traditional cultural myths such as Santa Claus, Jack and the Beanstalk, Little Red Riding Hood or Goldilocks and the Three Bears, because no one except a young children believes these stories to be literally true. We don't go to the zoo and expect to see the wolf who threatened Little Red Riding Hood. We're not deeply troubled if Santa's "beard" slips a bit, exposing his shaven face.

However, since sexual myths are acted out on the big screen by "real" people such as Madonna, Sean Connery, or Patrick Swayze, they seem believable, and there is a tendency to accept media portrayals as valid pictures of reality.

It wouldn't occur to the average person to write Jack (of Beanstalk fame) a fan letter, but it might seem perfectly normal to break through police lines to get Jack Nicholson's autograph. And although you would be regarded as mentally unbalanced if you tried to convince your friends you had an autographed picture of Goldilocks, these same friends might "O-o-o and aaah" if you came up with an autographed picture of Demi Moore. Although Demi Moore is undoubtedly real (and Goldilocks, is not) the stories Demi acts out on screen are *myths*—just as Goldilocks encounter with three bears is a myth. And though Jack Nicholson is a real live person who can sometimes be seen at Lakers' basketball games, the stories he portrays on screen are typically no more real than the story of another Jack climbing a very large beanstalk.

In this book common sexual myths will be replaced with accurate information. I have avoided controversial issues and used information which is accepted by the majority of scientists and clinicians working in the field of human sexuality. Kinsey, Masters and Johnson, and other sex researchers have contributed data which can dispel many of the false sexual myths created by media moguls and romance writers.

Learning new information is important, but when it comes to sex, it is also important to *unlearn* numerous things you've been taught. The late Ernie Pyle put it this way:

"It ain't the things you know that make you a fool, it's the things you know that ain't so."

In each chapter some time will be devoted to "taking out the trash" or debunking some of the popular myths about sexuality. In our society there is a lot of misleading "information" about sex. Many articles and books on sexual topics are written chiefly to entertain or titillate the reader rather than to give accurate information. Sexual myths are so much a part of our culture that we're not even aware they exist. In a thousand different ways they're foisted upon us by books, movies, and ever present talk shows. Unconsciously, as if by osmosis, we absorb them.

Sex is exploited by advertisers, movie makers, the media, and even spark plug manufacturers to help sell their products. Since sexuality permeates so much of our culture—especially the media and entertainment industries—it is often difficult to sort out the facts from the fantasies, and sexual myths abound.

But in this book you can be confident that what I share with you comes either from sound research or well-established clinical practice. My first priority is to give you correct information, not to entertain you. Sexual expectations based on fictions are usually impossible to fulfill, and often lead to anger, disappointment,and frustration.

So as an example, let's debunk one of the most prevalent sexual myths: *Simultaneous orgasms are best. The best lovers coordinate their love making so both partners experience orgasms at the same time. thus maximizing pleasure.*

This myth is fostered by erotic books, magazines, and even PG-13 movies. Typically we find a couple entangled in passionate foreplay, which rapidly escalates in heat and intensity until both are writhing in exquisite *simultaneous* orgasmic pleasure. But media portrayals of actors and actresses wildly thrashing about as they reach intense *simultaneous* climaxes often sets real-life couples up for trouble when they try to duplicate this intricate feat in real life.

TRUTH: Significant gender differences occur in arousal patterns. Males usually become aroused quickly and climax quickly. Females become aroused more slowly, but maintain high levels of arousal for longer periods of time. A man usually achieves orgasm within about *four* minutes of beginning intercourse, while a woman typically climaxes after *ten* or *twenty* minutes of intercourse. It's possible to accommodate these built-in gender differences in a variety of ways.

A man can stimulate a woman with his fingers, tongue, or vibrator, bringing her close to climax before he inserts himself. Then they are more likely to experience orgasm together.

However, numerous couples prefer taking turns in giving each other total attention. It is difficult to give your partner undivided attention if you're caught up with your own impending orgasm. For many couples it works well for the male to delay his own pleasure until the female has experienced at least one orgasm. If he then inserts himself, she will still be highly aroused, but able to attend more fully to him. In any event, striving to coordinate simultaneous orgasms detracts from the pleasure of both partners.

Replacing myths with truth will help to revitalize your sexual relationship because you'll be dealing with reality instead of false expectations.

Today many people believe that in long-term relationships, *familiarity breeds contempt,* and starry-eyed brides and grooms promising "For better or for worse" will surely end up "worse." The popularity of books like James Waller's "The Bridges of Madison Country" and "Slow Waltz in Cedar Bend" suggest that many are cynical about the possibilities of lasting happiness within the "confines" of a committed relationship. Most believe the old saw that "Marriage is a great institution...(pause)...if you're ready for an institution!"

In books of the "Bridges" genre, an unfettered male protagonist— Camel-smoking macho photographer or motorcycle-riding professor— preys on a woman who is married to an unbefitting spouse whose provincial ways, leave her vulnerable to a cosmopolitan competitor's charms.

The extraordinary popularity of such books seems to lend plausibility to one reviewer's grim theory that Waller's books have been successful because he understands

"...the *heartland of eroticism lies outside the confines of marriage.* In their puffed-up, clumsy, yet somehow canny way, Waller's novels, sniff out the great valley of discontent between the sexes; his randy, unattached protagonists smugly observe the *slow drip of calcification that occurs in even the best of domestic relations.*"

Such books, contends the reviewer, depend for their effect

"...on the reader's tacit agreement—and there seem to be a lot of willing readers out there—that *marriage is not good for your sex life.* Possession, it seems, is nine-tenths of boredom, and the daily grind will do the rest…One can take this as indictment—or, more simply, as a reflection of the postmodern view of connubial love. *To live with a man or woman on an ongoing, intimate basis is to grow jaded, weary of the imaginative possibilities; at some point, our husbands and wives fail to live up to a long-ago sensed potential.*"2 (italics mine)

I disagree with such a cynical analysis of long-term loving. I don't believe that living with someone "on an ongoing, intimate basis" inescapably leads to calcification, boredom, or loss of passion, but the operative word here is *"intimate."* If life with your lover is "ongoing" but lacks intimacy, the fires of eroticism that blazed early in your relationship will likely burn out, leaving with you with only glowing embers or even lifeless charcoal. This need not happen.

Side-by-side living should not be confused with closeness—coexistence is not intimacy. Unfortunately, many couples exist in non-intimate togetherness—sharing life's journey like railroad tracks—endlessly parallel, never touching.

Regrettably, too many lovers fail to intimately encounter each other: fail to move beyond the narcissism of the neonate, the parallel play of the toddler, or the autonomy of the adolescent. Failing to genuinely share psychological space with another, such people are candidates for "calcification,"—easy customers for the alchemy of our day: instant intimacy through intercourse, closeness through copulation. Sadly, such sexualized attempts to turn the pebbles of loneliness into gold nuggets of intimacy seldom work. Participants typically end up feeling empty and used instead of loved—"Bridges" notwithstanding.

This need not happen to you, and if it has, the process can frequently be reversed. That's why I've written this book. I believe you if you experience psychological *intimacy,* you can maintain the sexual magic over the long haul. You won't find quick fixes or magic solutions, it's not a eat-all-you-want-and-lose-thirty-pounds-in-three-weeks "vundermanual." However, if you thoughtfully read the following pages, you will gain psychological insights about your partner and yourself which will enhance your life together, so that instead of traveling parallel tracks you'll find yourselves moving closer to each other. Occasionally, you might even ride the monorail of profound intimacy.

Gay and Lesbian Lovers

I n this book, the task of establishing psychological intimacy is illustrated with vignettes from the lives of heterosexual couples. However it
has been my clinical experience that gay and lesbian lovers confront
many of the same kinds of challenges in establishing lasting closeness that
straight couples face. In other words, personality styles transcend gender.
Whether you're gay or straight you may have streaks of the histrionic,
obsessive or narcissistic styles. Whether you're lesbian or heterosexual, you
may struggle with codependency, shyness or sociopathy.

This book will be helpful to you whatever your sexual orientation
because it's written with *personality styles* as the central focus. *Sexual styles*
are seen to flow from each person's personality style.

Chapter 1
Histrionic Lovers

*"Do you think anyone will notice my new dress at the
office Christmas Party?"*

HISTRIONIC LOVERS

When Your Partner is an Emotional Bungee Jumper:
From "Absolutely Fantabulous!" to "Grossly Horrendous!" and Back Again

Welcome! You've probably wondered what it's like to be a shrink. Wondered how it feels to talk to "crazy" people, to know what to say. Probably wished you could feel more OK about how you're dealing with your teenager even when she complains to her friends "My parents are stuck in the Dark Ages!' Well you're in luck. Welcome into my brain! Through my word processor I'm going to hook you up to my consciousness and we will travel together. We'll meet, analyze, and understand a variety of different people. Our new acquaintances will include patients, friends, and family.

As you read you'll begin to understand how I think, what sorts of things I look for, what traits catch my attention. You'll learn by watching. You'll get in touch with the psychologist inside yourself. And, to your surprise, you'll discover that you knew more about psychology than you thought.

Professional psychologists aren't magicians. We don't use voodoo or witchcraft. Instead, we're trained to be extraordinarily observant, to pick up certain things about people that others overlook. I especially notice things that happen over and over again. These things are keys to *style*. Not styles of clothing or interior design, but *personality* styles.

Style is what makes people tick. Understanding style is much like understanding the skeleton of your own body. Skin and muscles are draped over your skeleton, while vital-but-vulnerable organs are protected by it. It's your bones that provide structure for the rest of your body and protect your softer components. Recurring behaviors are the "bones" of your style "skeleton." All other behaviors occur around that foundation. As follow me through this book, you'll begin to understand the behavioral skeletons (styles) around which people function. You'll become a bit of a psychologist yourself. Of course, if you plan to make a career of analyzing others, you'll need to go to school and study theories of personality, abnormal psychology, and such things. But if you're mostly interested in understanding yourself or your lover better, you can learn much that will improve the quality of your life just by following me around. It's a little like working with an interior designer for a few months. You might not be qualified to open a public business, but you could sure do a better job of picking out new carpet and furniture for your own home.

Well, enough talk. Let's get started. Time to meet our first patient. I'll do the talking, you just sit back in a quiet corner, and notice how I treat her. Notice what I notice about her.

Suzette

"Suzette" plops onto my leather couch with dramatic casualness. The name on the folder-carefully typed by my secretary—is Susan. I begin:

"You said on the phone your name was Suzette, your chart says Susan, what do you like to be called?"

"Susan is what my parents named me, but I thought it was boring, so when I started a new school in the seventh grade I told everyone my name was Suzette!" (giggle) "By the way what do you want me to call you? Do I have to call you 'doctor?'" (more giggling)

I survey Suzette while I weigh my response. Wrinkles are discernible at the outside edges of her eyelids, though her heavy eye shadow all but obliterates them. When she giggles—with the frequency of commas sprinkled around words—the corners of her mouth produce smile wrinkles, in spite of her heavy makeup. The condition of her facial skin is consistent with her stated age of forty-five on the intake form, but nothing else is.

Her breathy, theatrical, voice has a contrived quality which is rendered the more incongruous by her giggle-while-you-talk nervousness. Her makeup is caricaturely applied—far too heavily—giving her the appearance of a streetwalker. The neon lettering on her tightly stretched black T-shirt screams "Heavy Metal" competing with her braless breasts for attention. Her miniskirt—a throwback to the sixties—barely covers her panties. If one word could summarize her appearance it is *incongruous*. She appears waif-like yet streetwise, childlike but sexual, exhibitionistic yet shy, casually indifferent while hungry for attention. She is sexually provocative but her femininity lacks depth. She seems like a twelve-year-old playing grown up—trying to dress like a sexy twenty-four year-old, but not knowing how.

"What would you like to call me?" I reply.

"Gosh! I'm not sure, (giggles) 'Doctor' seems kind of scary. I was always scared of the doctor when I was little."

"Well, suppose you call me 'mister' Berecz. Does that seem less scary? Does 'mister' seem less scary than 'doctor?'"

"I guess! Well, gee! You're the boss!...Right? (giggle) It's just this place seems so spooky!"

"Spooky?"

(giggle) "Yeah, this big long couch and your chair looks like the kind that shrinks always use in movies, you know real big and expensive look-ing. (giggle) And you! You've got the beard and the whole look. I always wondered what it would be like to go to a head shrinker and now I'm here. (giggle) I can almost feel my head shrinking!" (extended giggling).

"So why are you here, how can I be of help?"

"Gee whiz! I don't exactly know just how to say this, so I'll just blurt it out. I don't have orgasms-at least I don't think I do—but I give great blow jobs! At least that's what the guys say (giggle). I mean, I never had any complaints!"

Her chatter stops for a moment as her tongue sensuously traces the inside of her slightly pursed lips. She seems to be enjoying my attention and carries out this subtle oral maneuver with the skill of an experienced strip tease dancer.

"I guess maybe I try to make up for not having orgasms by giving the best head in town." (laughter)

Although we're less than five minutes into the session, and I've never met this woman before, yet here she sits, expounding her skills at fellatio as if she were telling me about baking chocolate chip cookies.

"Once they've tried me," she continues, "they always come back for more!"

In the weeks that follow, I always know when Suzette arrives—my sec-retary doesn't even have to buzz me anymore. Much as an ambulance siren forewarns you that the driver doesn't intend to stop at the intersection, Suzette's laughter and repartee-on-the-run always precede her down the hallway. She engages in banter—it's never serious conversation—with whomever she happens to meet. Flirting variously with the janitor, UPS man, or security guard, she invariably attracts an entourage of males who are more than happy to return her fire.

The most predictable thing about Suzette's life (and her treatment) is that her consistently outrageous behavior generates continual chaos around her. She doesn't feel anxious, guilty, remorseful, or depressed, like most of my other clients; any negative sensations she feels are immediately flooded by her emotional intensity. She uses her therapy hour as a kind of erotic show-and-tell, regaling me with vivid accounts of the previous week's escapades—reliving more than re-telling the events. She becomes confused and puzzled if I try to analyze her interactions or interpret her behaviors. Simply put, she seems incapable of depth. She isn't mentally retarded, nor is her IQ below average, but her nervous giggling and lack of intellectual focus convey the impression that she is an "airhead."

Although she blithely tells me of numerous weird encounters with "icky" customers at Pleasure Island, a local porn shop where she works part time, she is affronted when I suggest that "selling dildos and inflatable blondes isn't how you're likely to meet Mr. Wonderful." She gloats over her success at winning first prize during amateur night at a topless bar, delighting in the many "fantabulous" guys she's met as a result, but she seems unconcerned by my observation that her relationships with these guys seldom survive the week between our sessions.

Suzette's satellite dish provides fresh fodder for her fantasy life, oscillating mostly between her "soaps" and two adult channels. She sometimes watches censored-for-TV R-rated movies, but complains bitterly that "cutting out the juicy parts is violating my freedom!—This is supposed to be America isn't it?" When I ask her if she subscribes to a newspaper she replies that she gets all the bad news she needs by reading headlines in the newspaper dispensers outside the liquor store. "Besides," she laments, "news is boring! If do buy a paper, I sometimes buy the National Enquirer. At least they have *interesting* news!" Then she fills me in on the most recent Elvis sightings, Martian landings, and two-headed babies, unruffled by my attempts to question the accuracy of such accounts.

One of the challenges of living with a histrionic lover like Suzette is they are so dominated by feelings and overrun by emotions that thinking, planning, or logic has very little influence in their lives. Once, for example, Suzette showed up at the office between her scheduled appointments, insisting that she *had* to see Mr. Berecz *today!* I arranged to see her during my lunch break. The atmosphere in my office all but crackled with the electricity of her excitement:

"O-o-o-o-o-h Mr. Berecz, I...I..."

She stammered as she tried to clear a path through her mental jumble. Her pupils dilated with excitement, and her body quivered.

"I...I just *had* to see you today," she continued, "because our session yesterday was the most important thing that's ever happened in my life! It totally changed how I see things. It's like I walked out of here a new person! I'll never be the same again!"

I was curious, of course, but as I swiftly scanned my notes from the previous session, nothing in particular stood out. Suzette continued.

"This therapy really is working. I feel like I've been born again—not, you know like those religious kooks, but just that I'm a totally changed person!"

Through the months that I had been seeing her, I had become familiar with Suzette's dramatics, seasoned to her sensationalism. Yet now, even I thought some remarkable insight had taken root in her mind. I made several passes through my memory of our previous session—it had occurred only the day before—I was coming up with nothing extraordinary. I was curious, but Suzette seemed to have slipped into a contemplative silence:

"Please," I said, "go on...tell me what made such an impression on you yesterday?"

"But that's just it..."

Her voice trailed off, and I noticed tears moistening her eyes.

"That's why I *had* to come today," she murmured plaintively, *"I can't remember what we talked about!"*

What Suzette remembered from the previous day's session—and for that matter *all* sessions—was not intellectual substance, but rather *feelings.* In histrionic persons emotions override thoughts, feelings wash away cognitions. Whether these emotions flood over a person like a tidal wave, as in Suzette's case, or come in smaller waves as with more ordinary histrionic lovers, *feeling* is king and thinking is minimal or absent. This is why Suzette couldn't remember what we'd talked about the day before, even though it had mightily moved her at the time.

So now you've met Suzette! You'll seldom encounter a clearer example. She embodies most of the characteristics histrionic lovers. Most histrionics exhibit at least *four* of the following:

(1) constantly demands or seeks reassurance, approval or praise

(2) inappropriately sexually seductive in behavior or appearance

(3) overly concerned with physical attractiveness

(4) expresses emotions with inappropriate exaggeration, e.g., hugs casual acquaintances with excessive ardor, uncontrollable sobbing or laughing on minor sentimental occasions, has "fits" of temper

(5) seeks to be the center of attention and is uncomfortable in situations when he or she is not

(6) experiences rapidly shifting and shallow emotions

(7) is self-centered, with behaviors directed toward obtaining immediate gratification; has little tolerance for frustration or delayed gratification

(8) thinking and speaking is excessively impressionistic—lacking in detail, e.g., when asked to describe her father, she might say "He's just great—that's it, just great!" and be unable to elaborate further.

This is the psychological skeleton of the histrionic. These are the recurring themes, the behavioral "bones." Although you seldom encounter people as emotionally intense and intellectually scattered as Suzette, you probably know individuals who are overwhelmed by feelings, often on a moment-by-moment basis. They don't hit you in the face with the kind of intensity you experience being with Suzette; nonetheless, you find yourself asking "Is she for real?" As you discern more clearly what is going on with such people, you'll be able to respond more appropriately—whether at the office, the supermarket, or in your bedroom.

The key point is that a histrionic person engages in sex, religion, or business with intensity of feeling and shallowness of thought. Often flooded with feelings and experiencing an impressionistic mental life, they possess no real cognitive foundation on which to anchor feelings. Histrionics are like surfers—always looking to catch the next emotional wave—always looking for the "big one."

Ordinary Histrionics

Now that you've met Suzette—a *clinical* histrionic—you might ask, "How can I recognize a histrionic lover?" or "How can I tell if my spouse is histrionic?" And, more importantly—"What difference does it make?" "Why should I care?" All good questions.

Most histrionics you meet will not be as breathlessly emotional as Suzette. Nevertheless, you'll hear echoes of her. If you know what to listen for, you'll hear histrionic themes playing—like a movie soundtrack—

sometimes loudly with flash and thunder, but more often as background to what's happening on the screen.

What difference does it make? Well, if your lover or spouse is histrionic and you're not in tune, their emotional highs and lows are likely to throw you off balance. Your attempts to talk things over, plan ahead, or learn from past mistakes will evaporate like dew on a hot summer day. Trying to be logical with your lover will be like beating your head against the proverbial brick wall.

If, on the other hand, you realize that this is your lover's personality *style*, and that it's not likely to change, you may be able to learn new ways of coping which will not leave you frustrated or searching for a divorce lawyer.

In the following pages, I'll share ideas that will help you know where to draw the line—when to put up with something, and when to insist on change. But being wise in establishing your own personal limits requires knowing what kind of person you're dealing with, and that's what the remainder of this book is about. As we encounter many different styles, you'll become more capable of dealing with your spouse or lover's style. Additionally, you'll become more aware of the personality styles of your supervisors, co-workers, friends, and family members.

"Dolly" and Rex

Next, I'd like you to sit with me as I meet "Dolly" and Rex—ordinary histrionics—the kind you'll meet in your neighborhood or at the office—maybe in your own bedroom. Each is mildly histrionic when alone, but when they are together, things escalate with each bringing out the histrionic side in the other.

Rex began playing golf in my foursome. I'd known him casually for a couple of years, but he'd originally started playing because he was a friend of a friend. One September Sunday, he wasn't hitting the ball very well and since we were sharing a cart, we spent quite a bit of time tracking down his stray shots along with my own hooks and slices. By the time we'd played nine holes, I knew why he was so agitated and couldn't seem to keep his mind on the game or his eye on the ball. Dolly had served him divorce papers the previous week.

"Just because I played around a little," he lamented, "I didn't even really screw this babe," he continued, "if I'd known it was gonna end up this way, I would have at least scored!" The slight grin that formed around the edges of his mouth conveyed more pride than penitence, and the tightness in his frame eased a bit.

Rex, a journeyman plumber, had a boyish innocence about him that made him seem more like a nineteen-year-old high school student than a twenty-seven-year-old father of two. He believed that "All work and no play…" was not the way to go. On the job, intermixing work and play meant flirting with "Dolly," (Diane) the receptionist, before work, whenever picking up supplies from the warehouse, and sometimes after work. She'd been dubbed "Dolly" (Parton) her first day on the job because of her blonde hair, Southern drawl, and enormous "jugs" that she slung around with brazen abandon. Her effect on the work atmosphere had been aphrodisiacal. "She can sit on my face anytime!" one plumber chortled. "I'd love to 'suffocate' under those size 40 triple E's!" responded another. And so it would go—much to the delight of the guys and the disgust of their wives.

Dolly developed early and by the time she entered high school she looked more like twenty than fourteen. Consequently she'd became the object of much male attention, collecting better grades (from male teachers) than she deserved, and turning down more dates in a month than many of her friends did their entire adolescence. Dolly knew how to flirt, but Rex was not far behind. They'd begun their erotic exchanges flirt only a week after she started working in the office. Rex had just purchased a new four-wheel-drive pickup. Their coffee-break banter was typical. Rex began with:

"Want to see my equipment?"

Dolly responded:

"Sure! Are you willing to show it?"

"It's bigger than you think," teased Rex.

"Sure it is! When does the show begin?"

"Meet me in the back parking lot, right before lunch…I'm serious. We'll see then who's chicken."

"Ha! you're always big on talk, but no action."

That's what enchanted Rex. Dolly was always ready with a sassy remark. But this time, she would be in for a surprise. And if he didn't pull it off today, by tomorrow, she'd know about his new truck. A new truck made headlines with this group of guys. The 4x4 was a kind of metallic phallic symbol which proved you were really a man. The elevated struts and all terrain tires were necessary equipment, not because anyone really needed to drive through four foot banks of snow, but because in these civilized times, among the species *homo sapien* there were few other ways to establish your territory with the herd.

The next day found them in the back parking lot.

"O-o-o-o-o-o!" she cooed, "It's ... it's fantabulous!! Jeeeeepers! Take me for a ride! Pl-e-e-ease!"

She caressed his truck lightly with her fingers—sensuously—like he imagined she could touch him.

"It came with a winch and 100 feet of cable on the front in case I get stuck and have to hook onto a tree and pull myself out of a rut." Then he added with a twinkle, "Nothing like good equipment with a winch on the front."

This wasn't lost on Dolly who responded, "Did you say winch? Or wench? Are you calling me names? Or just saying you'd like me on the front of your equipment?" She rubbed her crotch against the chrome of the front bumper. "I love chrome," she whispered sensuously.

Dolly had missed his bumper sticker "Well drillers do it deeper," but that would keep for another day.

Most of the guys referred to their wives as "My old lady," but in fact these "old ladies" were mostly in late twenties and were at home managing pre-schoolers. It was no surprise that Dolly was uniformly despised by all the wives of Pipefitters Local 2407.

It may have seemed to Rex as just innocent fun, but Brenda, his wife, knew better. She knew about feminine coyness and understood perfectly well when someone was hitting on her husband. For his part, Rex was more naive. He really didn't see why Brenda was making such a "big deal" about a little flirting at work. Compared to the "playing around" that had occurred during his boyhood, the flirting with Dolly seemed pretty tame.

I found out from Rex's golf course confessions, that his erotic escapades had begun early in childhood, when his alcoholic mother had abdicated parenting to Megan, Rex's teen-aged sister. Megan enjoyed unlimited freedom and minimal accountability and was very interested in boys, and since Rex was her only brother, she devised various erotic games which they played, her favorite being "Doctor" followed by "Getting paddled on your bare bottom by teacher for being naughty in school." Additionally, there were parties with the neighbor kids which occurred in the tall grass of an adjacent meadow. Although Rex didn't recall being forced to participate in sex games, he recalled those "meadow experiences," as times of unbridled sexual acting out with few boundaries.

Histrionic Sexual Style

You're more likely to develop a histrionic sexual style if your early years have been filled with intense or inappropriate erotic experiences. A child who is exposed to sexual experiences too early or too excessively, often responds erotically at the time, but later denies the experience. Such children sometimes become adults who focus excessively on sexual and bodily functions, but fail to blend these with other aspects of personality.

Such was the case with Rex. His life was centered on "earthy" or bodily experiences and he was surprised and puzzled that his flirting with Dolly was so upsetting to Brenda. For him it was just the way things had always been. Like a fish who isn't aware of being wet, Rex was hardly aware that his behavior was improper.

One Friday after he and Dolly had been particularly intense in their flirtatious teasing, Rex said, "After work, the guys and I are gonna stop at TGI Fridays for a couple of drinks…maybe we'll see you there. OK?"

"You're on!" replied Dolly.

That night after several drinks at Friday's and lots of dancing, Rex found himself riding home to Dolly's apartment. He had some second thoughts, because although he'd covered himself by saying he was going out with the guys for a few drinks and might be getting home late, numerous people had seen him and Dolly dancing and in this town gossip moved efficiently. Nonetheless, he was soon climbing the stairs to her apartment and as soon as the door behind them closed, they were into very heavy petting. He buried his face in the ample softness of her breasts while she teasingly unzipped and re-zipped his fly.

His hand moved to the soft skin inside her legs, just above her knees. His breathing was starting to come in short deep swells. He had to have her. You couldn't come this close and walk away. It would be like getting the forbidden chocolate cake out of the refrigerator, cutting a slice, putting the remainder back, and then not eating the piece you'd cut. The half dozen drinks were by now fully into his blood stream, dissolving any residual thoughts of faithfulness to Brenda he might have mustered. For her part, Dolly was doing nothing to discourage his advances.

Suddenly, however everything seemed to change. As his fingers stretched the elastic edges of her panties, Dolly abruptly stiffened. "What if Brenda finds out? We'd better not go any further! Besides Chuck would kill us both if he knew we were thinking about getting it on!"

Brenda! Why was Dolly bringing this up now? And Chuck? She'd barely mentioned his name before. Rex knew she had a boyfriend, but she'd never seemed conscience stricken before. Could she be serious? His groin was frantic for release and Dolly was talking about Brenda! This was weird...really weird. His head was pounding, his passion demanded release, but Dolly couldn't be convinced or cajoled into changing her mind.

"I won't be part of breaking up a marriage!" she sniffed theatrically. "God knows I've had plenty of opportunities, but it just isn't right."

Rex was bewildered, his mind in turmoil. Suddenly the shop seductress had turned Church Lady. What was going on?

In fact, what happened between Rex and Dolly is not particularly unusual. It was simply the hysterical "climax" of an emotionally intense, but psychologically shallow relationship. There is likely a Rex or a Dolly in any assortment of persons numbering over two dozen. You're not likely to encounter the intensity of a Suzette very often, but many people, like Rex and Dolly, are dominated by feelings and live their lives as a kind of daily soap opera where shallow drama is everywhere present.

Things between Dolly and Rex were never the same again. The banter which had occupied so much of their time ended as suddenly as it had begun, and Jim, one of the other plumbers, became the happy heir to Dolly's titillating teasing.

Brenda found out about Rex's escapade the same night. When he arrived home around two a.m. with his pride damaged and half a dozen beers under his belt, it wasn't long before he was sobbing and confessing in response to Brenda's questions. Although deeply hurt by this tryst Brenda could see the shallowness of Rex's involvement with Dolly and offered to drop divorce proceedings if he would agree to go for counseling.

Brenda had grown up with two highly conflictual alcoholic parents. As an adolescent, she had equally divided her time between keeping her parents together and rescuing her drunk father—often driving to the bars at closing time to pick him up and bring him home. Since her father had died of cirrhosis of the liver two years before she married Rex, it wasn't hard for her to "take care" of her husband instead of her father. His involvement with Dolly allowed her to now focus her "saving" efforts on her own marriage. She didn't really want the divorce, but filed papers in order to, as she put it, "Get his attention."

Like most histrionics Rex never got very deeply into counseling. One day on the golf course, he confided to me that

"It was kind of over my head. This broad (female therapist) kept trying to make a big deal out of every detail of my life. The first time it was kind of spooky...her fancy office and stuff, but I got bored real quick."

He halfheartedly went a few times, reporting to Brenda that he'd gotten things figured out, and would never flirt with Dolly again. Since Brenda was the adult child of alcoholic parents, and since Rex's histrionic streak wasn't too severe, they were able to work things out with Brenda taking care of the relationship and Rex keeping his trousers zipped. Rex kept me updated whenever we played golf together.

So...you might ask, "Where does all this leave us? We've met Suzette, Rex, and Dolly. How is this going to help me in my own life?"

The Three R's of Improving Your Love Relationship

I will help you to utilize the *Three R's* to improve your love relationships: **R**ecognize your lover's style, **R**eorganize your expectations, and **R**evitalize your relationship. Let's start with the first R—*Recognizing* if/when you're involved with a histrionic lover or if *you* have histrionic tendencies yourself.

RECOGNIZING the Histrionic Sexual Style

It probably doesn't come as a news flash that choosing a spouse or deciding to move in with a lover is far from an exact science. In fact if you ask people how they first met and what attracted them to each other, you get such an assortment of answers that it soon becomes clear that personalities and proximity came together in largely unpredictable ways. After over thirty years of marriage counseling, even I'm not sure if opposites attract or repel. My guess is that although opposites initially attract, they often have a hard time living together. On the other hand I've seen some very successful marriages between spouses who seem to have worked their "oppositeness" into a fulfilling relationship.

I'll avoid a theoretical debate and simply suggest that two common patterns occur: (1) birds of a feather flock together, and (2) opposites attract. You will have to figure out whether you were charmed by your "Soul Mate" because the two of you were so similar, or because you felt she made up for certain of your deficiencies ("I'm shy, he's talkative" or "She's assertive, I like to follow someone's lead.") In any event, whether you're attracted to someone like yourself or very different, it's important to *recognize* the personality styles which meet in your bedroom. Once you understand your partner and yourself, you can begin to *reorganize* your thinking in a way that enables you to *revitalize* your sexual relationship.

When You First Met

First impressions by histrionic lovers often leave you reeling, maybe breathless for a moment. Like Suzette, most histrionics make a splash. Maybe not as big a splash, nor as flirtatious, but nonetheless a splash. Vibrant and vivacious, they get your attention. Remember when you first met your spouse or lover? Recall how her effervescent emotions entranced you? You found your own emotions—like champagne—hissing out of control to meet her. She popped your cork and you were a goner! You noticed her thinking was a bit superficial, but you chose to ignore it because your reservations were outweighed by her emotional aliveness—her passionate, if exaggerated style. Or, recall how he seemed to electrify everything and everyone around him? Although you noticed within minutes, that he wasn't "deep," it didn't seem to matter. You were magnetized by his intense, colorful aliveness.

Immediate contact is what histrionics seek to evoke. They are hungry for contact, so they bypass the tedious-for-them process of getting to know someone in depth. In bed, at work, at play, in all aspects of life, histrionics seek immediate connection.

Recall Suzette asking if she had to call me "Doctor." She wanted to call me "John" because this felt closer. But we've seen how such intense hunger for closeness sabotages real intimacy, because it bypasses getting to know the unique individual. Histrionics create for themselves the illusion of intimacy by substituting stereotypes and daydreams for reality and by mistaking contact for relationship.

In summary, histrionic lovers are enthusiastic but superficial. They are headline readers of the news, channel-flipping soap-and-game-show watchers of TV, and, if they read at all, romance novel devotees. Some people search for things in the world—ideas, goals, meaning. Other people actively *create* things—careers, families, causes. Histrionics, however, are *struck* by things. Flamboyantly traveling through life, bombastically bouncing about, they remain ultimately shallow in their cognitive comprehension the world.

Victims more often than perpetrators, their shallowness of thought and hunger for excitement make them fair prey for a variety of exploitive or calculating persons. But, of course, this quality is what attracted you to your partner—that sparkling pizzazz! That effervescent chutzpa!

Self Quiz on the Histrionic Style

Now that you recognize the histrionic style in others, you might also wonder if there's a histrionic streak in yourself. It's always useful to know how your own personality interacts with your lover's. Are you together because you're alike, or because you're different? Do you find yourself together or at odds on many issues? These are important issues when you try to **R**eorganize and **R**evitalize your relationship.

So how about it, are you a bit histrionic? Try answering the following questions. Uh uh! No cheating! Be honest. It won't do you any good if you try to give the "right" answer. Tell it like it really is. Answer how you really feel. Only you will know.

1. Do details bore me? Do I find myself attracted to things exciting, dramatic, or spectacular?
2. Do I often find myself a "victim" of some person I thought was wonderful, but who turned out to be a real jerk? Or, do I find myself often "rescuing" people who turn out to be just taking advantage of me?
3. Am I often flooded with emotions? Do my feelings "run away" with me?
4. Do I enjoy being the life of the party?
5. Do I read exciting newspapers such as National Enquirer instead of USA Today or the local paper? Do I like People Magazine much better than Time or Newsweek?

6. Do I enjoy outlandish, almost bizarre clothes?—the kind that get a "I-can't-believe-it!" look on the street?

7. Sexually, do I actually prefer cuddling or hugging to intercourse?

8. Do I usually forget details?

9. Do I often find myself overreacting?—screaming when startled, laughing until I cry, or becoming so angry I "lose it?"

10. Do I like colorful language using "jillions" of dramatic words like "scrumptious," "nauseating," "gorgeous" or "fantabulous?"

11. Do I enjoy shocking people by using words like "shithead?"

12. Do I enjoy flirting? Seeing if I can turn on someone of the opposite sex, but usually not following through? Have I been called a teaser?

13. Do my moods change rapidly? Do I often find myself laughing one minute and crying the next?

14. (female) Do I often wear a ring on each finger?

15. (male) Do I wear three or more rings.

16. (female) Do I wear two or more earrings in each ear?

17. Do I prefer brilliant lipsticks and heavy eye makeup?

You can probably guess from taking this quiz that histrionics tend to over do things—especially clothing, makeup, jewelry, and hair. If you answered "Yes" to many of these questions, you probably have a histrionic streak in your personality. It doesn't mean you're sick and in need of treatment, it merely indicates that your view of the world is romantic, flamboyant, impressionistic, less detail-oriented. It suggests that you're guided by your feelings and that you don't get involved in problem solving—figuring out details. You simply trust that problems will take care of themselves.

Early Roots of the Histrionic Sexual Style

The histrionic's intense need to be noticed, the hunger for contact, and their provocative ways of fulfilling such needs, all suggest some deficiency in early life. The histrionic *child* often grows up in a home where the parent(s) may have been depressed, excessively busy or absent. Failing to receive sufficient mothering, a little girl sometimes turns to Father, but if her needs are too intense and his boundaries not good, the nurturance is sometimes permeated with coy or flirtatious behavior between father and daughter. Analogously, a little boy who finds his father absent or unavailable as a role model, may become overly involved with Mother in an eroticized relationship—a relationship that doesn't have the healthy counterbalance of father's role modeling for the son. If mother is emotionally absent, the little boy seeks to find (or create) mother in all the women he meets. You will see this illustrated in Carl's case, which we will discuss shortly.

The histrionic *adolescent*, like some of your friends in high school, carries this hunger for closeness into the high school years where she tends to oversexualize relationships with boyfriends, becoming known as "easy" or a flirt. However, in spite of apparently high levels of sexual activity, histrionics tend to be sexually shallow and sometimes gain the reputation of being a "tease." It is really a pseudosexuality without psychological depth or intimacy.

Histrionic sexuality in *adults,* the kind you have seen in Suzette's case, is really a caricature of sexuality, but this is not limited to females. The overly feminine female histrionic has a counterpart in the hypermasculine caricature of sexuality known as the Don Juan, seducer of women. As in Suzette's case, such frantic efforts to be attractive to numerous members of the opposite sex bespeak a deep insecurity regarding sexuality rather than a hyperabundance of hormones.

Thus, although histrionics seem at first glance to be oversexed, this is only a facade. Erotically teasing and provocative, they typically engage in cat-and-mouse flirtations with members of the opposite sex. Such behaviors compulsively occur not only during culturally sanctioned occasions such as the office Christmas party, but occur in virtually all situations including grocery stores, banks, and work settings.

Histrionic women are sensuously provocative in dress, cosmetics, posture, and attitudes. More generally, they are exhibitionistic about almost anything including medical problems, physical defects, or psychological needs—whatever it takes to pique the interest of the opposite sex.

Men, though culturally expected to be more macho also sometimes employ victim roles, especially if it's likely to result in rescue by an attractive female, or financial rewards in the form of workman's compensation or insurance benefits.

Upon close scrutiny, the histrionic female's sexual provocativeness invariably has a little girl, pre-adolescent quality about it. Such women seem genuinely surprised when males misinterpret their friendliness as sexual. A common complaint from histrionic women is "I just want to be held and cuddled, but he always gets turned on and wants sex." Such statements, betray the histrionic's childlike hunger for holding and touching. While most women enjoy the caressing and fondling that accompanies sex, what distinguishes the histrionic is not the *inclusion* of touching and holding with adult sexual needs, but the *avoidance* of genuine sexuality.

Colored by Culture. You ought to note that *all* sexual styles are shaped by culture and the times. Indeed the gracefully fainting histrionic ladies of the Victorian period were expected to perfect swooning into a socially acceptable skill. Today, due to different upbringing and changing sex role expectations, such behaviors would be unacceptable, and consequently the skill of fainting gracefully has all but disappeared.

Similarly, society requires male histrionics to express themselves differently than females. Culture doesn't allow them to directly manifest dependency needs through helplessness or frailty as is often seen with females. Consequently they often seek soothing through alcohol or drugs. Frequently such needs are denied by maintaining a tough hypermasculine facade.

What remains consistent, across both sexes, is that histrionics typically present a *caricature* of the sex role. Whether seen in the helpless fainting of females, or the hypermasculine conquests of "Don Juan" males, the sex roles are exaggerated to the point of travesty. This results in a fragile facade which dissolves under pressure. Macho men, for example, easily become little boys when illness or other trauma cracks the shell of bravado. Flirtatious women become frightened little girls when confronted by a male interested in a deeply involving sexual relationship.

You have seen a blazing histrionic female in Suzette. You encountered significant, but less intense histrionic trends in Dolly and Rex. Now, as a final illustration, I'd like you to meet Carl, a male histrionic. At first, you wouldn't think of him as histrionic because his style isn't bombastic or dazzling. He's no Suzette. But if you look carefully, you'll notice that he seeks instant closeness by surrounding himself with "victims" to whom he can quickly become the knight in shining armor.

Among male histrionics, industrial accidents resulting in chronic disability are common. Such men overreact to pain, injury, or illness. This is obvious to family members, yet difficult to escape. These men exploit others through dependency. A typical histrionic role reversal is that of "disabled" Dad staying home and watching TV, while Mom shoulders the responsibilities for keeping the family afloat. But male histrionics can also switch roles from being victims to rescuers. This was the case with Carl.

Carl

Carl and I met on a transatlantic flight. Imagine you've joined us and we're sitting three abreast in the plane. You've got the window, I'm on the aisle, Carl is between us. You seem to be engrossed in reading a novel, but you can hear every word of our conversation. Even if you were obviously listening, Carl doesn't seem to mind because he talks in a voice that's loud enough for others around us to hear.

I'm on my way to professional meetings and he's attending a public relations convention. A handsome man in his early fifties, we barely taxi to the end of the runway before he introduces himself, finds out I'm a psychologist, and with sparkling eyes announces:

"Wow! Now I have my own private shrink! And it's free!" He begins by telling me that he and his fifth wife are about to break up.

"I don't like being a five-time loser!" he insists, but his words are too matter of fact and there's a hint of a grin on his face as he begins to share his "audiobiography." Intelligent, intuitive, and very caring toward his employees and clients, Carl works on the periphery of the entertainment industry as the CEO of a small but respected public relations agency. Many of his clients are famous or nearly-famous actors, actresses, and musicians.

He is vaguely aware that his emotional style contributes to his business success. Carl is something of a con artist, but he's a con artist with a heart. Unlike a sociopath, or an unscrupulous car salesman, Carl has a strong histrionic streak that tempers his manipulativeness. He really does care about his customers.

"I can smooth talk a broad into almost anything," Carl grins, "because I take the time to listen, and out there, in that dog-eat-dog world, nobody else listens. Everyone just wants to tell someone else what to do. But I listen, and that's what keeps my clients coming back and telling their friends about my agency. 'Carl listens.'"

His manipulativeness is not exploitive in a financial or business sense. In fact, he prides his himself on being scrupulously honest with clients. But his "I-really-care-about-you" attitude invariably has a hidden angle. Largely because of his sensitivity to the feelings of others, he is very effective in maintaining harmony within his organization as well as with clients.

However, Carl is irresistibly drawn to intelligent, beautiful women with needy personalities. He has married a succession of them. In each instance the matrimonial bliss has always been short lived. Tensions build up, there is a lack of reciprocal nurturing—both partners demanding that the other "take care" of them—and separation invariably follows. Even before divorce proceedings are well under way, Carl forms a new relationship with another beautiful woman who is already waiting in the wings.

I learn that when Carl was eight years old, his mother—a beautiful woman who had once been her high school's homecoming queen—ran off with another man, leaving him alone with his depressed father. It is apparent that Carl's relating to a series of beautiful women has more to do with his mother than with sex:

"I always remain friends with my exes," he states, "I don't see any reason to be mad just because you've been married. In fact three of these women still work in the company, and we get along great."

Carl cares for his ex-wives much like he did for his mother, to whom he frequently sends flowers, and other gifts, in spite of the fact that he remains bitterly angry about having been abandoned as a young boy.

Carl's sexual style has more to do with pleasing women—as he tried to please mother—than it does with genuine sexuality. Although he often seeks and engages in sex with various beautiful women, he is compulsively concerned about whether they have been satisfied. After a while however, in his attempts to be super sensitive, empathically attuned, and completely caring for the women in his life, he eventually burns out, and then blames the woman for expecting more than any man could possibly provide. This cycle had been replayed numerous times in his life—not only with the five women he has actually married, but with nearly all the numerous women with whom he becomes seriously involved.

The "Fasten Your Seat belt" light is on and I can feel the plane begin its slow final descent. Carl insists that we keep in touch, but since I'm not a beautiful female, I doubt he will really follow through.

Later: In spite of flamboyant exchanging of business cards, I never heard from Carl again, except for a postcard he once sent me from Hawaii a year or so later when he was honeymooning with wife number six.

Sexual themes for histrionic lovers include victim-aggressor, rescue-rape, or child-parent motifs. Quite often this is carried out with overdone flamboyance leaving you wondering "Is she (he) for real?" And you're never quite sure. The caricature-like roles these people assume for themselves and project onto others seem contrived to most of us, but they are consistent with the histrionic's blurred, impressionistic, romantic view of life. However, it would be wrong to get the impression that all histrionics are all scatterbrained airheads with no ability to think. You've just met Carl, an intelligent, successful business person. While it's clear that he is very competent, it is equally apparent that his life is primarily shaped by powerful histrionic undercurrents.

Short circuited thinking leaves histrionics particularly vulnerable to a variety of scam artists who happily sell them everything from encyclopedias and vacuum sweepers to sex. Some histrionic women are unconsciously drawn to dangerous or abusive men. Such men bring excitement and danger with them. They have "pizazz" and the histrionic finds this irresistible. Typically such interactions include strong sexual components, but for the histrionic, it is the excitement and intense emotionality of the relationship which attracts. Since many histrionics see life in romanticized themes of dominance and submission, victims and villains, they easily become involved with unsafe or exploitive persons and hardly sense any danger. These interactions allow them to act out their own dramatic fantasies.

Ted Bundy, for example, while on Florida's Death Row, received the following letter from an exceedingly histrionic woman named "Janet," after responding to only one of her many letters:

"I got the letter you sent me and read it again. I kissed it all over and held it to me. I don't mind telling you I am crying. I just don't see how I can stand it anymore. I love you so very much, Ted...I adore you and I just can't stand not hearing from you. It's absolutely tearing me apart. You are so precious to me. I want you so much I can almost taste it. What I wouldn't give to have an hour alone with you. There's nothing I wouldn't do (Michaud and Aynesworth, 1983, p. 278)."

This letter is all the more remarkable when you realize that this woman had *never met Bundy!* Nonetheless, like a little child clutching her favorite Teddy bear during times of distress, she *held* the letter, *kissed* it, and *cried* over it. This is histrionic hyperbole. The romanticized exaggeration of love, adoration, faithfulness, and distress are emotionally intense yet psychologically shallow. Such lack of analytic thinking is why histrionics participate in and encourage patterns of *repetitive* abuse. They *participate* in becoming victims because it fits their world view. Remember how unaware

Suzette was of why men "hit on her?" This lack of insight is why she repeatedly entered relationships with marginal men.

Although such relationships occur most often between female histrionics and male sociopaths, similar dynamics can be seen with male histrionics who often lead drifting and marginal lives while attempting to bolster self esteem through clothes, automobiles, and sexual conquests. Just as Carl flaunted his five marriages and many women, most male histrionics take pride in their conquests and seem proud to be known as "heartbreakers" or "womanizers."

In women, the histrionic need to be the center of attention, often includes, coquettish sexual flirtations. Additionally she sometimes engages in dramatic displays of helplessness, detailed accounts of victimization, or socially unaware insistence that her wishes be met.

Histrionics solve sexual problems by emotional blurring or mental fuzziness. When things become complicated, they get "confused" and just move on. By now, you're beginning to understand them at a deeper level, and you know that beneath the veneer of giggles and emotional vivacity there is an emptiness of spirit that is opposite to what appears on the surface. The hypersexed histrionic turns out not to be genuinely sexual at all, but rather a frightened child seeking emotional nurturance. The bravado of the Don Juan barely conceals his poverty of self esteem.

REORGANIZING Your Expectations

Suppose you're convinced that your lover is histrionic. What if you find strong histrionic tendencies in yourself? Now what? Where do you go from here? The next "R" involves *Reorganizing* your expectations. Most people—especially histrionics—fall in love with a dream more than a real live person. It's a bit like lying in the grass with a friend watching puffy white clouds drift overhead and talking about what you see. Chances are, you'll see very different images. Where he sees dinosaurs or polar bears, you might see cotton candy or fireworks. Where she sees an elephant slowly lumbering across the horizon you might see an apple with a worm hanging out the side.

Being in love is a bit like that. You see all kinds of things which are creations of your imagination more than replicas of reality. Histrionics are especially prone to believe that what they feel or see is real and will never change. But after marriage this often changes and he laments "She's not the girl I married," or the woman complains "He's changed so much!" Probably each saw in the other positive things that weren't there and missed negative elements that were, because clearer perceptions might have destroyed the romance.

People in love usually have difficulty seeing their lover's true personality. You probably did not realize that your lover was histrionic. Instead of seeing her as an emotional bungee jumper, you saw vivaciousness and effervescence. Instead of shallowness, you saw spontaneity. Impetuousness was perceived as passion, flirting as attractiveness, and self-centeredness as assertiveness.

Most lovers minimize faults in their beloved, but when one or both members of a couple are histrionic, the romantic glossing over of distasteful details is more extreme. As we've already noted, histrionics romanticize relationships. This allows them to easily overlook faults, but also allows them to easily dump the partner when the going gets tough. They can swing from "Mr. Right" to "The Creep"—from "Fantabulous" to "Dickhead" with the same disregard for details that caused them to become involved in the first place.

Staying connected to your histrionic partner is like whitewater rafting or bungee jumping! It requires quick reflexes, elasticity and courage. It requires *reorganizing* of your relationship so that it is based less on romance and more on reality. As you lie on the grass gazing into your sky you'll need to exchange the romance of swans drifting across the sky for the reality of rain clouds building up a thunderhead.

Histrionic lovers resist such a nudge toward reality: "You're never romantic, you're always spoiling my plans by asking about money!" However, if the relationship is to endure over time, the "spoiler" (non-histrionic partner) needs to maintain a sense of creativity and playfulness even while balancing this with reality considerations. Thus you might agree with your spouse that it would be "exciting" to quit work and sail around the world on a small yacht, but you wouldn't cosign to purchase a boat, and you wouldn't be encouraging him to quit work. As a compromise you might agree to purchase a small catamaran and sail it on weekends.

Your histrionic lover isn't out of touch with reality in a psychotic way; he doesn't literally see pink elephants, but he may be out of touch in a more subtle, yet pervasive way. They live in a world of make believe, where no one ever plays marbles "for keeps."

Living happily with your histrionic partner means understanding that he/she is wired differently than most people. You are now able to recognize some histrionic traits almost immediately—the intense emotions, the shallow thinking, the "splash" they make at any gathering of people. But what is it like to live with a histrionic partner day after day? In a word, the relationship remains *shallow*. Even after spending months or years with such persons you might be surprised by the bombastic breeze-in-breeze-out, attention-seeking behavior. Much like Suzette, though less intense perhaps, your partner is dominated by emotions. Feelings ride up front, cognitions are in the back of the bus. Quiet contemplation, introspective analyzes, deep thinking are not seen.

This shouldn't surprise you, because as we've already noted, histrionic "thinking" does not consist of clearly-formed ideas, based on factual data; rather, histrionics live in a world of *impressions*. This is why they're sometimes described as suggestible. How could it be otherwise? Suggestibility means you are looking to someone else for answers. You are willing to follow someone's advice without questioning it. It is somewhat the opposite of doing your own clearheaded analytic thinking. The scholarly study of a problem, or a careful analysis of a situation is simply not possible for someone who lives in a world of impressions.

This is why histrionics are so prone to instantly idealize—they hold little in memory aside from the immediate and thus have little with which to make mental comparisons. Alongside blurry impressions of current realities exist romantically colored recollections of the past and capricious plans for the future. One writer put it this way:

"Hysterical people, we know, are inclined to a Prince-Charming-will-come-and-everything-will-turn-out-all-right view of life, to nostalgic and idealized recollection of past figures and places, and to a sentimental view of the present. Nostalgic or idealized recollection, leaving aside once again its specific content, has exactly the sort of impressionistic quality that I have described. Typically it is conspicuously lacking in factual detail and indeed one sometimes has the impression that objective facts or factual detail would spoil the story." (Shapiro, 1965, p. 118).

Such impressionism however isn't only about happy, exciting things such as sex or romance. The positive histrionic judgement "He's wonderful!" has its negative counterpart in "He's yucky!" and the switch between emotional states occurs glibly and rapidly, uncomplicated by attention to details or facts. Consequently the impressionistic world of the histrionic is populated by villains as well as heroes.

When, for example, I asked a histrionic patient why she had married a man whom she knew to be an alcoholic and a drifter after only two evenings of dating, she replied:

"He just had so much pizzazz!—I guess he put a 'hex' on me!"

When I persisted in trying to get more details, she could only respond:

"It was his pizzazz that hooked me!"

My attempts to elicit further elaboration only brought puzzlement. She hardly seemed to understand the kind of data-based information I was seeking.

Although we've talked much about sexual style, it is clear that histrionic people are dramatic, emotional, and impressionistic in *all* areas of their living, not just in their sexual behavior. They delight faith healers and hypnotists by quickly volunteering for stage demonstrations. Among the religious they are the believers who respond to "altar calls" at evangelistic meetings, are "healed" at faith assemblies, or have the "devil cast out" by exorcists in deliverance meetings. Meanwhile other parishioners sit quietly and observe such happenings.

The histrionic style can be seen in the snake-handling religious cults of the South, the glossolalia of Pentecostal believers, and even in the high levels of emotionalism generated within satanic cults. Where an emotionally-laden experience is to be found, a histrionic will be nearby. What is common to all is a frenzy of emotionalism, unaccompanied by reflective cognition.

To summarize, I suggest that you *reorganize* your expectations along the following lines:

1. You have to learn to live with "fuzzy" thinking and not waste a lot of time or energy using logical reasoning with your partner. Their lives are dominated by feelings not reasoning. They are influenced by impressions, not data. So if you argue or try to convince your partner, remember that *feelings* are more important than *facts!*

2. Your partner will probably always experience rapid emotional shifts and you may as well learn to go with the flow. When she or he is emotionally energized, there will be little tolerance for your attempts at logical reasoning. It's a bit like trying to play chess with an intoxicated

alcoholic. It doesn't work. Better to "Yes dear" it until the emotional flood waters recede a bit.

3. If you're prone to jealousy, your histrionic partner may drive you up the wall, because flirting is almost as addictive for him or her as drugs for the substance abuser. Instead of quarreling about it, you might be comforted to know that such flirting is really seeking affirmation and reassurance and is not primarily sexual in nature. As a partner, you have a right to insist that such flirting *not* result in actual sexual encounters, but most histrionics can live with that because they're more interested in the teasing and game playing than sexuality anyway. Try not to get upset with the flirting, but remember you *do* have a right to negotiate limits within which you both can live: e.g., "No honey, I don't think you should wear your see-through top without a bra to the office Christmas party!"

4. You're likely to tire of your partners constant seeking to be the center of attention when you're at a party or with others. You might feel like a wallflower by contrast, and you may also sense that others tire of your partner's attention-seeking as well. Nonetheless, remember it was this vivacity that first attracted you to her (him), and though it wears thin at times, others find it tolerable in small doses. It's you—not others—who must live with it every hour of every day and are likely to be worn down at times. When these times come, just take a break by going away for an afternoon of golf, shopping, or whatever "floats your boat" as your partner might say.

5. Don't try to correct your partner's exaggerations. When a histrionic is recounting (more like *re-living*) an experience, it's designed to impress or entertain, not to give accurate information. Don't spoil the story with facts.

6. Instead of trying to "put the kibosh" on everything your partner wants to do *Now!* avoid squabbles by asking "Can we discuss this again tomorrow morning?" Then follow through with your promise to discuss it. This will sidestep numerous quarrels, because although histrionics have little tolerance for delayed gratification, they have even less for the word "No." But time will be on your side because of your partner's rapidly-shifting moods. By tomorrow morning, it may be "no big deal," maybe not even worth discussing.

7. Be generous in your compliments. Even though your partner may at times seem like an emotional black hole, soaking up affirmation, reas-

surance, and admiration, it helps to realize that this isn't sheer selfishness, rather it's a hungering for affirmation that was missing during childhood years.

8. Finally, you should realize that good sex with a histrionic lover requires that you pay attention to creating the right "atmosphere." This means that *foreplay* and *afterglow* are as important as intercourse, maybe more important. Your partner will likely share with you what kinds of sexual pleasuring are most enjoyable, but you will need to be quite sensitive to—as Barry Manilow croons—*"Feelings."* Be generous in your compliments. Foreplay and afterglow should be saturated with "You're so beautiful." "That was the greatest." "I love holding you." "You've got to be the sexiest there is!" and other such reinforcing confessions. While all lovers enjoy hearing that they are the best, for the histrionic it is essential.

REVITALIZING Your Sexual Relationship

You're now in an excellent position to rejuvenate a relationship that may have gone sour. Or, if things aren't all that bad, you can still use your new understanding of the histrionic personality to enrich and enhance your relationship with your sexual partner. Now that you understand this style, it will be easier to avoid those cycles of agitation and emotional intensity which leave both of you upset and thinking about breaking up.

You'll be able to separate your partner's problems from your own frustrations, and you won't expect vast changes in his/her style. Histrionic lovers sometimes change a little bit, but the basic style remains in place, so the sooner you give up your fantasies about changing your partner, the better you'll feel. Also when you quit hoping, praying, or nagging for change, it sometimes gives your partner a sense of freedom and modest shifts style sometimes occur.

You probably have noticed that the 3 R's apply mostly to *you*, not your partner. If *you* can recognize, reorganize, and revitalize, this empowers *you* to feel better even if your partner is unable or unwilling to make substantial changes. By understanding what makes your histrionic partner tick and by reorganizing your expectations in line with that, you can begin to enjoy him her as never before. Take a moment to remember how her vivacity and sparkle once attracted you? Reminisce about how turned on you were by his awareness of feelings.

Don't try to strike a bargain about important issues. "If you quit flirting at parties, I'll quit hassling you about the time you waste watching soaps," doesn't work. You won't get anywhere if you think she'll stop flirting because you've begun mowing the lawn. These sorts of bargains don't work because histrionic people live in the moment and have a difficult time carrying through on contractual agreements.

By now you probably realize that what has been killing the relationship is not so much the kind of person your partner is, but rather the extent to which she has failed to live up to your wishes, dreams, or fantasies. Since many of your hopes and expectations were acquired from non-histrionic people, they probably don't work with your partner. It isn't that your expectations are faulty for most people, but your sexual partner—like Suzette, Dolly, or Carl—marches to a different drummer, whistles a different tune. You have to learn to "speak their language." Talking to a histrionic as if she were an obsessive compulsive gets you nowhere! Speaking articulate Armenian won't buy you a bagel in France. Fluent Portuguese won't purchase you a taco in Mexico. You've got to speak the language of the people interacting with.

Now that you've learned the language of the histrionic and adjusted your expectations accordingly, it will be easier for you and your partner to mesh—to feel loved and accepted by one another. This will enable both of you to feel better and a positive "snowball effect" can occur.

Taking Out the Trash

Before concluding this chapter I'd like to discuss several sexual myths. Although these particular myths are believed by many people, they are especially popular with histrionics. Like most sexual myths, they are misleading and often sabotage a good sexual relationship. Falsehoods set you up for frustration, because what you expect of your sexual partner or yourself is profoundly influenced by what you believe is true. Since expectations based on fiction are impossible to fulfill, the final result is anger, disappointment, and defeat, instead of happiness and fulfillment.

Sexual myths are promoted by erotic magazines, romance novels and ordinary media presentations, and they differ from traditional cultural myths such as Santa Claus, Jack and the Beanstalk, Little Red Riding Hood, or Goldilocks and the Three Bears. Everyone understands that cultural myths aren't *literally* true. You don't go to the zoo and expect to see the wolf who threatened Little Red Riding Hood or the three bears who chased Goldilocks!

However, since sexual myths are acted out on the big screen by "real" people such as Madonna, Sean Connery, or Patrick Swayze, they seem believable and many people uncritically accept media portrayals as valid pictures of reality. Thus while it wouldn't occur to the average person to write Jack (of Beanstalk fame) a fan letter, it might seem perfectly normal to break through police lines to get Jack Nicholson's autograph. Although you would be regarded as mentally unbalanced if you tried to convince your friends you had an autographed picture of Goldilocks, these same friends might "Oooh and aaah" if you came up with an autographed picture of Demi Moore. Demi Moore is undoubtedly real (and Goldilocks, is not) but the stories Demi acts out on screen are myths—just as goldilocks encounter with three bears is a myth. And though Jack Nicholson is a real live person who can sometimes be seen at Lakers' basketball games, the stories he portrays on screen are typically no more real than the story of another Jack climbing a very large beanstalk.

In each chapter of this book, we'll scrutinize several sexual myths, point out the errors, and replace the fallacies with accurate information. Even professionals sometimes disagree with one another, so I have carefully avoided controversial issues and used information which is accepted by the majority of scientists and clinicians working in the field of human sexuality. Kinsey, Masters and Johnson, and other sex researchers have contributed data which can dispel many of the false sexual myths created by media moguls and romance writers. As the late Ernie Pyle put it:

"It ain't the things you don't know that make you a fool, it's the things you know that ain't so."

Histrionic Sexual Myths

Please take note. These myths are believed by many persons—not just histrionic lovers—but they have a special appeal for histrionics, so I'm including them in this chapter.

MYTH # 1: Men who are good lovers are *always* able to create powerful, explosive, earth-shattering orgasms in the women they love.

TRUTH: Since orgasm is a total body response, it varies with your physical condition at the time. If you're tense, tired, or suffering from a sore throat, the pleasure and intensity of your orgasm will be reduced. Like other bodily events such as eating, drinking, or sleeping, much depends on your needs and moods at the time. Orgasms vary from mild: ("It left me feeling relaxed and warm.") to moderate: ("There was a warm rush of feeling with a strong pulsating rhythm. Then everything was warm and quiet like a yellow sunset.") to intense: ("When I came it was like an explosion—I felt like I was flying, like a rocket soaring into the sky with wind rushing by with incredible force and heat.")

MYTH # 2: It is a man's responsibility to provide the woman a good orgasm.

TRUTH: Although histrionics (and our culture) tend view the male as the "orgasm provider" sex is always an *interaction*. Each person must *share* responsibility for the interaction. This means providing your partner information about what feels especially good or what is unpleasant. Good sex is characterized by mutuality, reciprocity, equality. It takes two to tango!

MYTH # 3: Planned sex is always boring.

TRUTH: Histrionic lovers, drawn as they are to excitement, seek dramatic, vivid, electrifying partners. They think it would be "n-e-e-e-to" to have sex in thrilling circumstances (e.g., on the steps of the Capitol). Nonetheless, in a marriage or long-term relationship that kind of Let's-do-it-while-we're-skydiving attitude can sabotage a more realistic, healthy attitude towards planned sex. I'm not suggesting that spontaneity has no place in a love relationship, but when both persons are working and raising small children, they might regularly be more relaxed on weekends. Because a couple has sex every Friday night—regular as clockwork—doesn't mean it's necessarily boring.

MYTH # 4: Sex with the same partner inevitably becomes boring and having an affair can add spice to your marriage.

TRUTH: Having an affair—typically a euphemism for "betrayal"—seldom brings a couple closer. The damage done to trust and intimacy never completely heals and it often takes years for the pain to subside. Although some cultures have permitted polygamous (more than one spouse at a time) marriages, these arrangements have typically been carried out with responsibility and the full knowledge of all persons involved. This differs significantly from today's affairs in our society where deception and betrayal are key elements.

Group marriages, consisting of four or more partners who consider themselves married to each other, are not legally recognized in this country. There is a limited amount of research that has been carried out on this topic, but it is known that group marriages do not survive very long. Sexual jealousy is fairly common, and figuring out who sleeps with whom can be not only psychologically but mathematically challenging. For example in a six-person group there are nine possible heterosexual pairings and fifty-seven different relationships of two to six people.

The highest levels of intimacy are achieved in one-to-one couples relationships or in family relationships where long-term commitment assures each participant that this is no fickle impulse. In such circumstances love deepens with the passage of time and although the exciting getting-to-know-you stage passes, it is replaced with deeper levels of love and intimacy. Boredom is a symptom of problems, not a necessary ingredient of long-term relationships. Just as an elevated temperature indicates you're fighting an infection, boredom signals something is wrong.

MYTH # 5: If romance dies, you may as well throw in the towel because romance is the basis of love.

TRUTH: Histrionics overvalue romance. Since their mental lives are dominated by dramatic, exciting, and emotionally charged issues, so their sex lives are based on overly romantic notions. Often their ideas of romantic love are derived from media stereotypes as seen on soap operas or in the movies. Many persons forget that marriage for *love* is a recent historical development, most highly developed in our own time. For centuries most civilizations have viewed marriage as an arrangement between families, not as the end result of a couple's heated romance.

Because romantic love is so intensely pleasurable, many people are propelled into marriage by it. However, unless love is more than romance it is unlikely to provide a lasting basis for relationship. Yale University psychologist Robert Sternberg has suggested that genuine love is like a triangle composed of three sides: intimacy, passion, and commitment. The histrionic is often drawn to a one-sided kind of love that emphasizes passion at the expense of intimacy and commitment.

MYTH # 6: Aphrodisiacs can add zing to your sex life.

TRUTH: Although people for centuries have avidly searched for substances that increase a person's sexual powers or desire, the truth is that none has ever been found. There is a long list of exotic mixtures, including powdered rhinoceros horn, oysters, animal testicles and turtle eggs, which have been extolled as aphrodisiacs but modern medical science recognizes none of them as effective. If, however, a person suffers from a certain *deficiency* or is in some way malnourished or in poor health, *any* substance which corrects the deficiency or improves health will also increase sexual desire. In truth, the best aphrodisiacs are adequate rest, good nourishment, and an intimate psychological relationship with the partner. Good health and good conversation, not powdered testicles, provide the basis for sexual desire.

Summary

Well here we are, at the end of the chapter, and I trust that you've enjoyed getting better acquainted with the histrionic style. These people are by turn tempting, tiring, demanding, seductive, overemotional, but *never* boring! Actor-manipulators extraordinaire—their quest for attention and emotional intensity can be wearing, but this is often balanced by an exquisite sensitivity to their audience. Sometimes the histrionic's ability to make perceptive observations is uncanny, and if they aren't too emotionally wrought up themselves, they can alternate between entertaining you and demanding your attention.

Sexual theater, sexual display, is their bailiwick. If female, she'll likely have bleached blonde hair, wear the kind of tops that display her breasts and nipples to best advantage, and be parading about in a profusion of bright yellows, reds, pinks, or other colors designed to dazzle. If he's male, he is more likely to be gay than heterosexual—enjoying the flash, display, and sexual theater that are intrinsic to this style. Heterosexual male histrionics are less frequently encountered, but, as our case example of Carl illustrated, do exist in significant numbers.

In addition to learning about the histrionic style, I trust you now have a better idea now of how a shrink's mind works. As you've followed me around—into my clinical office, on airplanes, and on the golf course—you've become acquainted with a variety of different kinds of histrionic lovers, and have likely learned much about this entertaining and emotional style. Now you can recognize histrionic streaks in yourself and among your family, friends, and acquaintances. Hopefully, the distance between "patients" and ordinary people has lessened and your understanding of the Suzettes, Rexes, Dollys, and Carls in your own life has increased. Living with a histrionic partner can be challenging, but the lively emotions and the effervescence are usually worth the effort.

In the next chapter we'll meet a variety of obsessive-compulsive persons. This could be seen as learning by contrast, because in many ways the obsessive-compulsive style is the polar opposite of histrionic. Whereas histrionics are dominated by feelings, obsessives don't feel enough. They're more like computers, dominated by logic, order, and perfection. They strive for errorless living and consider emotions "soft" and unreliable. Whereas histrionics feel too much and think too little, obsessives think too much and feel too little. One writer described them as "living machines." A frustrated woman described her husband in the following terms:

"Being married to Doug is like living with a computer."

Another woman described her husband (who had been making good progress in therapy) as a "recovering engineer."

Chapter 2: Obsessive-Compulsive Lovers

"With or without the metronome this time?"

CHAPTER 2: OBSESSIVE COMPULSIVE LOVERS

When She Can't Climax if There are Dishes in the Sink

T hese days we seem immersed in an alphabet soup of diagnoses, every nook and of your personality is labeled. Are you tired? Could be CFS. Restless, possibly ADD. Slow in arithmetic? Maybe LD. Dad likes several beers after supper? ACOA. Like your ducks in a row? OCD! Maybe you've how to tell if you're *neurotic* or simply *neat*. After reading this chapter you'll know whether your obsessive ways simply tint your sexual life with a bit of orderliness or taint it with neurosis. In any case— even if obsessiveness is a broad streak in your personality—it's not a fatal flaw.

First impressions by obsessive-compulsive lovers don't have the "splash" of hysterics. The grand entrances and the life-of-the-party effervescence of the histrionic are not seen in obsessive styles. Contrast Suzette with the people you meet in this chapter and you'll sense the difference. Suzette seeks comfort through physical contact—hugging, cuddling, fondling— whereas James, Megan, Ted, and other obsessives try to create security with repetitive rituals and perfect performances.

This is typical, you won't find obsessive-compulsives making a scene. In the most intense forms they tend to be the nerds or geeks, often bright but socially out of synch. Obsessive-compulsive lovers are often worriers, collecting data in order to make "perfect" decisions, but still unable to make up their minds. They often appear intense, data oriented, and serious. Being in control is high on their agenda and manifests itself in ways that are obvious even in brief social interactions. For example they like to arrive unannounced. This way, *they* know when they're arriving, but *you* are off guard, scrambling with surprise.

The better you understand obsessiveness, the easier it will be for you to live in today's highly structured world, and the better you'll be able to relate to an obsessive lover. So relax, take the quiz, and let's get started.

RECOGNIZING the Obsessive Streaks in Yourself and Others

Self Quiz on Obsessive Compulsive Style

1. Do I prefer dining in Chinese restaurants, with a group of friends where everyone orders a favorite and shares, so I don't have to decide which is *the* best item to order?

2. Do I set my watch to "beep" every hour?

3. Do I frequently attend time-management seminars? Do I adopt practically all the suggestions?

4. Has it been more than three years since I've taken at least a two-week (non-work-related) vacation?

5. Do I find I'm never really satisfied with a job because I know it could always have been done better?

6. Do I find it aggravating to quit in the middle of a job? If, for example, I'm three-fourths done mowing the lawn and it begins to rain, will I mow in the rain rather than finish it tomorrow?

7. Does commitment scare me? Does it feel dangerous to be dependent on others?

8. Do I brush my teeth three or more times a day?

9. Do I teeter-totter about decisions, balancing pros and cons, back and forth, again and again, finding it almost painful to tip the balance and choose one instead of the other?

10. Do I suffer "buyer's remorse" after a purchase?

11. Do I love lists? In addition to shopping lists do I have a things-to-do list, a books-to-read list, an important-birthdays list, a ways-I-need-to-improve-myself list, a movies-to-rent list, to *list* but a few?

12. Do I floss my teeth more than twice a day?

13. Do I have *every* periodic maintenance done on my automobile according to the schedule outlined by the manufacturer?

14. Did I enjoy building model airplanes, cars, ships, or other such structures when I was growing up?

15. Do I have a *collection* of any kind—stamps, postcards, scrimshaw, spoons, bells, Civil War weapons, etc.

16. Do I have head covers for my iron golf clubs—including my putter?

17. Does my car wear a bra?

18. Do I use an edger on my lawn?

19. Have I ever been in a family portrait where everyone is wearing matching clothing?

20. Am I part of a family where all the children's names start with the same letter—Kim, Kevin, Kelly, and Kirk?

21. Do I find it difficult to throw things away and therefore end up collecting all sorts of things which have little real value—torn movie stubs, old shampoo bottles, rubber bands, strings, newspapers, mayonnaise jars, broken bicycles?

22. If my neighbor cleans his garage, do I have a secret urge to rummage through his street side trash for valuable things he's put out for the disposal truck?

23. Do I make the bed when I stay at a motel?

24. Deep in my heart do I believe there are only two ways to do everything—*my* way and the wrong way?

25. Do I frequently turn around, go back home, and check to make sure I've locked the door or turned off the stove or TV?

26. Do I like to fill the gas tank of my car clear to the top? Do I keep clicking the handle after the automatic shut off in order to make sure it's really full?

27. Do I sometimes stop my car several miles down the road in order to check if I have put the gas cap on after fueling?

28. When creating in the kitchen do I follow recipes *exactly?*…precisely measuring each ingredient?

29. Do I enjoy high tech hobbies like photography, stereo, computers, electronics?

30. Is it upsetting to me if sandwiches don't have their peanut butter and jelly or mayonnaise spread to all four corners?

31. When reading, do I *carefully* highlight important paragraphs? Do I have a file of magazine articles?

32. Would I *never* under any circumstances use my lover's toothbrush? i.e., if we were staying overnight in a motel, would I go out and buy another toothbrush rather than use one belonging to my lover?

33. Do I notice this quiz has thirty-four questions instead of seventeen like the one in the previous chapter? Does it bother me?

If you or your lover answer "Yes" to many of these, you have a substantial streak of obsessive-compulsive style in your relationship. This chapter is for you, because it's not always easy to live with an obsessive partner. They can be like computers—seldom wrong, infuriatingly methodical, and sometimes impersonal. It's like you're on a Star Trek mission, married to Spock. They strive to create a perfect world while dreading disorganization. Prodigious workers, they gravitate towards professions that require high degrees of precision and avoid "artsy" careers. So you'll find more obsessives among scientists, accountants, engineers, dentists, and financial planners, while histrionics are captivated by more touchy-feely careers such as art, music, social work, massage therapy, or what are generally known as people professions.

Psychologists consider someone obsessive-compulsive if their *perfectionism* is inflexible and pervasive. In this chapter we'll meet people who illustrate each of the following characteristics:

(1) preoccupation with details, organization, order, rules, lists, or schedules to the extent that the major point of the activity is often lost

(2) difficulty expressing affection

(3) decisions are avoided, delayed, or prolonged while the person teeter totters back and forth trying to find the "perfect" solution

(4) perfectionism that interferes with completing projects because overly strict standards are not met

(5) difficulty discarding worn-out or worthless objects even when they have no sentimental value.

(6) stubborn insistence that others submit to exactly his or her way of doing things

(7) extreme devotion to work and productivity to the exclusion of leisure activities and friends—even when not economically necessary

(8) overconscientious scrupulosity and rigidity about morality, ethics, or values (beyond what is accounted for by religious or cultural identification)

Since there are no 100% cases in the real world only streaks of different styles in everyone, you'll find some people who *blend* both histrionic and obsessive styles into thinking *and* feeling. Although your dentist probably loves precision and might even become obsessive when he drills your teeth or builds bridges in your mouth, he must also be able to build communication bridges with you as his customer. He must successfully soothe your fears as well as polish your teeth. Similarly, the professional musician might obsessively practice difficult scales for hours each day, but in the end, she must "feel" the music in order to achieve eminence as an artist. The crucial issue is not whether you're histrionic or obsessive, but whether you can remain in touch both with your thoughts *and* emotions.

Enough theory! I'd like you to meet James. He is more extreme than most obsessives you're likely to meet at your job, health club, or Little League game, but he vividly illustrates one of the primary traits common to them all.

Preoccupation With Details

James

His appearance is peculiar. Attic-like. Rumpled suit, un-ironed white shirt, too-narrow tie, and scufftoed wingtips created a curious miscarriage of fashion. But this is only the beginning of numerous incongruities emerging from his small brown frame house.

Fidgety, white-haired, he sits rigidly on the edge of what should be a comfortable lazy boy recliner. His eyes scan my face while he divulges his inner turmoil by alternately clutching and wringing his reddened, washed-too-often hands. It's more than nerves. James is comprised of contradictions. His appearance is pathetic even while he attempts a facade of dignity. His behavior is agitated yet rigid, his mood intense but brittle.

Stacks of four-by-six note cards held together by thick red rubber bands and small piles of paper clips clutter the kitchen table. The kitchen counter is strewn not with dishes, eating utensils, or an occasional paring knife, but with numerous three-ring binders, several Bic pens, a stapler, and other office paraphernalia. However, in spite of what appears to be Herculean efforts at organization, tell-tale indicators of disorder ooze out everywhere. This is why I sometimes make house calls when doing an assessment; information seems to seep out of the walls.

"What do you like to be called?...Jim?" I ask, trying to establish a bit of rapport.

"A *gym* is where people exercise and get sweaty."

His eyebrows raise almost imperceptibly and I detect a slight tremble in his hands which are, for the moment, hanging limply at his sides. He seems affronted that I had suggested "Jim," but continues in a controlled monotone.

"My name is *James* Alexander Marshall and I like to be called James. Whenever Mother was mad at me she used to call me 'James Alexander,' and *nobody* (there is a slight inflection in his voice for the first time) has ever called me 'Mister' Marshall, so I just go by James."

I turn toward the kitchen table.

"James, can you tell me about these cards? What is all this writing about?"

"Those are my records. I keep careful records."

"Mind if I look at them?"

"No, it's OK."

I roll the rubber band off a bundle of four-by-eight cards and casually began trying to decipher the carefully penned notes that fill both sides of each card. Although he has given me permission to look, he is clearly distressed by the casual way in which I shuffle through his cards. His controlled uneasiness reminds me of how I feel at the office while evaluating a hyperactive child who spins my world map, pushes the intercom buzzer, yanks at the drape, and plunges both hands into my aquarium before I've had time to ask him to please not spin the globe so violently. My tropical fish don't eat for days after such episodes. James seems almost as disturbed by my casual handling of his cards, so I carefully band them back together, fuss with the edges, making sure everything is carefully aligned and replace them on the table close to the spot where they had been. It is obvious that I have disturbed the fragile order of his world, and I sense that James appreciates my efforts at restoration.

"I don't mind if you look at them."

He manages to get the words out, but with a tense, concocted quality—like conversation on a first date.

"Thanks," I respond, as I carefully begin to reexamine his revered records. The cards, I discover, provide a moment-by-moment record of everything James does throughout the day. Like a court reporter, whose rapidly moving fingers translate every audible word into legal copy, James carefully records everything. He loses few details. Not only does he "card" weddings or county fairs, he conscientiously chronicles what others would regard as trivial. "Events" such as bringing in the mail from the mailbox, walking the dog, answering the phone, eating lunch, all receive the same meticulous consideration. There is no hierarchy of importance, no ranking of priorities, all details are accorded equal attention.

To improve his "efficiency" sorting mail, James has a custom made rubber stamp with the following words:

"I, James Alexander Marshall, took this item out of my mailbox on:_____,
at:_____.
I read this mail at:_____,
while located:_____."

After bringing the mail into the house he first stamps all envelopes and circulars and then fills in the blanks with date and time. Later, when actually reading his mail he fills in time and location for each item as he comes to it. For James, there is no such thing as "junk" mail. All pieces are examined with equal care, each is treated with respect. I notice an envelope from the power and light company, and turning it over I find the following information:

"I, James Alexander Marshall took this item out of my mail box on: 8/18/85/A.D., at: 1:22:34 P.M., E.D.T. I read this mail at: 4:17:21 P.M., E.D.T while located: *in the easy chair approximately 2.25 feet west of the north-south wall and 5.75 north of the east-west doorway of the living room.*"

James stamps everything that finds its way into his mail box, carefully documenting the how, when, and where of each article. Through his intense ritualizing he transforms trivia into something meaningful—nuisance into significance. Each piece of junk mail is treated as if it were a certified letter, each circular handled as if it were a diploma. This intense documentation serves to keep his mind occupied with trivia instead of anxiety, and infuses his drab days with significance. He states that going through his mail takes "about an hour and a half" each day.

If James makes momentous events out of sorting mail, you can imagine the significance he attaches to walking a friend's dogs or attending a wedding. Carol, one of his friends, has been out of town for several days, and he has been caring for her dogs. This is carefully documented on two sides of a 4x8 card entitled "Walking the Dogs."

Surprisingly, I find that James attended a wedding over the weekend. He kept his social anxieties in check by busying himself with record keeping. No less than both sides of *five* 4x8 cards are used to document this event:

"WEDDING OF ALLAN, JOYCE & BALTZMAN, DANIEL, IN FOURTH LUTHERAN CHURCH OF DENVER, 9/14/85/AD BEGINNING APPRX. 3:18:27 WITH ORGAN MUSIC.

(Support beams of arches laminated natural wood) Approx. 3:20:44 bridesmaids (5) & men (5) walked down center aisle to front. 3:25:16-3:26:49 Joyce A. walked up the center aisle and onto the rostrum. 3:27:39 the minister prayed. 3:29:15 the minister talked. 3:40:37 the minister prayed. 3:42:16 A N.F.P. (a Negro female person—James explained) approx. 20, app. 5'4", app. 120 lbs., sang 'Entreat Me Not to Leave Thee' and 'Love Divine.' 3:48:37 songs ended. 3:49:38 Joyce A. said marriage vow to Daniel B. 3:50:27 Daniel B. said 'I do.' 3:54:53 the minister pronounced them husband and wife. 3:52:17—3:54:36 A C.M.P. [Caucasian male person] app. 40, app. 5'11", app. 180 lbs., prayed for them while they knelt. 3:56:10 he introduced them as Mr. and Mrs. Baltzman.

The remaining four cards record the wedding reception in deadening detail, making a light-hearted social occasion sound like an ordeal. Celebrants are converted into lifeless codes, preserved, mummy like, under pyramids of particulars. Instead of "Connie sat across the table, laughing and enjoying the refreshments." we read "She is a C.F.P. app. 30, app. 5'4", app. 130 lbs."

I've now spent nearly three hours with James and I can see he is relieved that I'm about to leave. Thanking him for his cooperation and assuring him that I have all the information I need, I turn and slowly walk to my car. Driving to my office, I feel tired. Like a survivor. Like I've almost drowned in a sink hole of details. But I'm also energized. Who could have guessed the secrets lurking within that small brown house? That's why I still make house calls. I contract with a state agency to evaluate people who claim they are unable to work. Usually they come to my office, but sometimes because of physical or mental problems they are unable to travel, so I go to them. Now you can see why.

Many of your acquaintances, coworkers, friends, and family members also have significant obsessive streaks in their personalities. It should come as no surprise that many people experience sex in an obsessive way; not, perhaps, in the rigidly mechanical style used by James to collect and sort his mail, but in a style that drains sexuality of spontaneity and joy. They're able to "do it,"—go through the motions—but they derive little pleasure from what ought to be playful recreation.

In the bedroom James is no Casanova. In fact, he's still a virgin. Not surprising is it? How could someone like James ever feel safe enough to undress in front of another person? He is clearly dysfunctional and, at the age of fifty-seven, his chances of changing are almost nil. So why have I taken all this time to introduce you to James? He's not likely to become your sexual mentor! I wanted you to meet James in order to reassure yourself a bit. Just because you prize neatness, or like all your ducks in a row, doesn't mean you're neurotic. James illustrates how *preoccupation* with details becomes dysfunctional.

For James ordinary activities such as washing hands, reading mail, or attending social functions became transformed into time-consuming, but anxiety-allaying rituals. His rigid rituals began early in childhood. His father and mother argued violently and frequently about money, his father's drinking, and other women. Although James has no personal recollection of this time period, his mother later told him that he was "very frightened" by the ensuing divorce, and constantly asked "When is Daddy coming back?" Sadly, his father moved to another state and never again visited the children. James recalled very little else from his childhood except that "None of my brothers or sisters ever wanted to play with me...I was always a loner."

Clearly, losing your father following violent arguments predisposes you to anxiety, especially if your mother is unable to comfort and soothe you. James described his mother as "...not a loving person—she would never kiss me."

"Ouchy Ouchy Ouchy"

Parental soothing is important to children because that's how they learn to take care of themselves. If a child's parents naturally and easily comfort their young, such children will subsequently learn from Mom and Dad how to sooth themselves.

Last summer, I happened to be looking out the window when the three-year-old across the street took a nasty spill on her tricycle. Almost immediately, Mom came streaking out of the house, picked up the screaming child, held her closely, kissed her skinned knees and soothingly repeated "Ouchy, ouchy ouchy! Poor baby, how that must hurt!...Ouchy, ouchy, ouchy! Let Mamma kiss it."

After a few moments of such comforting Bethany was again happily riding her tricycle—skinned knees notwithstanding—and had developed some new vocabulary for dealing with such disasters. Some weeks later, I noticed she'd again spilled, but this time, instead of screaming, she sat down cross-legged, kissing her own knee, while quietly murmuring "Ouchy, ouchy ouchy!" Then, without further ceremony, she got back on her tricycle and began to ride.

James had never received "ouchy ouchy" soothing, so he wasn't well equipped to deal with the dangers and stresses of adult life. He attempted to keep his anxieties at bay with records and rituals. His sexual experience was shriveled because a key element of good sex—playfulness—was completely missing from his life. You would hardly expect someone so grim in the living room to become a playful lover in the bedroom.

Now that you've met James, one of the most severely obsessive people I've ever met, let's balance it with Deb. She's mildly obsessive, but definitely in the normal range. I probably wouldn't have married her otherwise!

Deborah

Deborah looks splendid sitting on the sun porch with the late afternoon sun streaking her blonde hair. At the moment her wide-set blue eyes are intensely focused on reading and one leg is sensuously draped over the side arm of the sofa. When I say "sensuously" this is a private opinion. She doesn't even know I'm voyeuristically ogling. She's a third-year law student intensely underlining one of those tedious encyclopedic volumes having to do with property settlement and contracts. Boring stuff. We'd rather be making love, but she's got exams next week so I've been "cut off."

I'd like you to notice her *style* of study—how she's underlining her book. She uses five different high lighters. Yellow is for text underlining, orange for headings, blue for definitions, pink for statutes, and green for case names. She says this helps her keep things straight when she reviews for exams. Everything in the room is orderly. Even Cinder, her gray cat is comfortably stretched out on the antique rocker which in turn has an antique shawl symmetrically draped across its seat.

Deb isn't really rigid, she just likes things in order. She can't study if things are messy in the room. I have loads of fun teasing her by "forgetting" to put the rocker back in its place after watching football. Scrabble is great fun because she doesn't like the crooked way I make my words with the wooden letters. But Deborah understands that my gentle kidding about her obsessiveness is really an affirmation of who she is. My wife knows I love her deeply—even when she notices fingerprints on the toaster or spots on the ceiling when we make love. There is much to her personality besides an urge for orderliness so her streak of obsessiveness isn't something most people even notice.

The obsessive compulsive style is widely encountered. We've already seen that obsessive style begins as the infant's early efforts to cope with anxiety. Human babies are born in a completely helpless state. Although this gradually changes as you mature physically and psychologically, you're never totally in control of forces which act upon you. Children often use magical routines to create a sense of safety. Sometimes this involves avoiding walking on cracks or touching certain things. Other times it's evident in the child's love for hearing the same bedtime story night after night.

Nearly everyone relies on routines to simplify life and trusts in certain spiritual or magical rituals. For example, most of us go through our individual morning routines with little variance, habitually arranging all the details of showering, shaving, dressing, eating, etc. with little conscious thought. I didn't know my sequence was "incorrect," until Deborah informed me one morning that I should put on my socks *before* I put on my trousers. I'd been putting on my pants before my socks all my life and had never suffered any dire consequences as a result, but she informed me that it would wrinkle my trousers less if I didn't shove the cuffs up while putting on my socks. So there you are. Now I do it right! It's not a big deal for us because I don't personally care if my pants go on before or after my socks, just so they get on, but for Deb it's important to do it in the right order.

Next we'll see why feelings—even positive feelings like affection—seem so dangerous to obsessives. Anything "out of control" worries obsessives, and since our emotions seem to rise like steam from the boiling cauldron of our viscera they are very difficult to control. That's scary! Even if they're *pleasant* emotions it's scary. Butterflies in your stomach are more worrisome than thoughts in your head because they're harder to catch.

Difficulty Expressing Affection

Megan

Back at my office, I'd like you to meet Megan. Although she's made an appointment for therapy, she's not a severe case (like James) of obsessive compulsive style. In fact you probably know several people like Megan in your circle of acquaintances and friends. She's the kind of person who is at first distant and aloof. She seems unfriendly, but as you gradually get to know her, your opinion changes and underneath you discover a warmer, friendlier person. But it's well guarded. Megan sits in a far corner of my waiting room conspicuously engrossed in her study of *Better Homes and Gardens*. She seems hardly to notice me when I first greet her and ask her to come into my office. Typically people leave the magazine they're reading in the waiting room when entering my office, but not Megan! In fact it becomes, as therapy continues, a kind of "defensiveness thermometer" indicating to me how trusting Megan is feeling on a particular day.

Julia, another obsessive patient, used to provide me Xeroxed copies of a prepared agenda in order to feel more in control of what occurred in therapy. Megan, however, carries her security blanket with her in the form of this magazine. And it works marvelously! She hardly looks at me for most of the first session, responding only to direct questions, and then a bit irritatedly, as if I were interrupting her important reading.

I know that if this had happened early in my career as a clinical psychologist, I would have been offended at playing second fiddle to *Better Homes and Gardens,* but by now, I knew better than to take such affronts personally.

"What brings you here, Megan, how can I be of help?" I begin gently.

"I don't know! You're the doctor!" she snaps from behind the flower-splashed magazine cover.

Now I begin to understand the experience of people who complain that they have breakfast each morning with the *Wall Street Journal.* Her response is not only abrupt—it is anonymous. How am I supposed to converse with a magazine cover? That "You're the doctor!" phrase is never a show of respect or admiration, it's always a set up. She's saying "You're the smart ass!" "You're the genius!" "You tell me, if you're so intelligent!"

"I'll try to help," I say, "but I need some idea of what brought you here."

"What brought me here is my work supervisor said she thought I could use some counseling, also my husband and I have been arguing a lot lately."

Hmm, I think, *now I know she's in trouble at work, and things aren't great at home. But that's about all, and she doesn't seem inclined to tell me more.*

And so our first session shuffles haltingly along with long periods of silence, interrupted only by the polished whisper of glossy pages turning as $800,000-homes and gardens and prize-winning recipes strut their stuff in front of Megan's intensely focused eyes. When she responds to my occasional questions, her answers are brief and precise—neatly clipped, like the green hedges she spends her time scrutinizing. At the end of our session I'm tempted to quip "I'm sorry I had to interrupt your reading with my questions," but of course I don't.

The next session isn't much better. Once when I fail to understand one of her rapid-fire replies and ask, "Could you say that again?" she replies, "I only chew my cabbage once!"

After two or three months pass, she softens and the pain within her becomes more apparent. She slowly begins to trust, letting me into her world a bit at a time. She recalls an incident which took place when she was about four-years-old, and I begin to understand why she has tried so hard to maintain control over her life ever since.

"My sisters and I were in the kitchen one Sunday morning," she confides. "My oldest sister was fixing pancakes, we were just eating and having a good time. Daddy came downstairs and—thinking about it now—he seemed upset. He looked like he had been crying, but Mom was still upstairs. He told us 'Mommy is sleeping in late this morning, she's not feeling well.' About an hour later, when we were cleaning up breakfast dishes, Mom came downstairs with a suitcase. Said she was leaving for a short trip."

As her story unfolds, she begins weeping, softly at first, just a few sniffles, but as she recounts the details, her sobbing becomes increasingly intense until her entire body shakes as she tells me, "We never saw her again. She just walked out of our lives."

After this, she no longer brings magazines into the sessions. Her answers are less rat-a-tat-tat and she talks about her feelings without much prodding on my part.

In the bedroom Megan and her husband Chuck are experiencing little joy and a lot of frustration. Chuck blames her, saying she's "cold." She counter attacks with "You're only interested in my body...you never talk to me." Both charges are true but shallow. For Megan, not talking to Chuck when they make love is a way of wanting him to reach out for her without her having to ask—a safe way to feel cared for, but hardly a stimulus for good sex.

As I get to know Megan over the next several months, she begins to slowly warm up. Having disclosed her family secret, she feels the worst is out and she now can talk about why she finds it so difficult to say "I love you" to Chuck. Not surprisingly, when you've been abandoned by your mother, it leaves deep scars in your self esteem. You subconsciously vow to never again be vulnerable to loss. One way of doing that is to not let people know you care. The scariest words in the world become "I love you." Or, even more scary, "I need you."

Chuck is a nice enough guy and he really does love Megan, but it baffles him that although she claims to care about him, she is always so aloof in bed.

"She's so 'careful' about everything," he says, "it's like making love to a porcelain doll. She seldom climaxes and then only after what seems like hours of clitoral stimulation."

Chuck's voice oozes with frustration, and I learn that it's been this way from the beginning. Time hasn't helped. As the early months of marriage faded into years and two children came along to add complexity, they made love less and less often. Now, nine years later, they're lucky to make love once a month and both prefer it that way. It's just too much hassle. Not worth it.

Fortunately, they never sink into name calling or other destructive tactics. Chuck never calls her "frigid" or a "cold fish." She never accuses him of ignoring her because he is having an affair. This makes it possible for me to help them re-discover each other. I spend most of the therapy hours with Megan, and she becomes quite comfortable telling me of her daily stresses, anxieties, and joys. And, as often happens, she also begins sharing her inner life with Chuck. Their love life improves and they begin enjoying each other more than ever before.

One day, however, I sense something is very wrong because Megan is sitting in a far corner of the waiting room appearing intensely interested in *Better Homes and Gardens.*

"You seem upset today," I say.

"Well, I am! How did you know?…Chuck's been promoted. His company wants him to move to New York City…I guess we'll be moving in sixty days."

"Surprises" always upset obsessive-compulsive persons, and this one deeply troubles her. She's lost a little ground and feels the need for familiar defenses against anxiety. This time, however, the hide-behind-the-magazine protection is short lived, and she puts down her *Better Homes* within the first five minutes of our session, looks directly at me, and begins talking about how she hates change.

I'm able to recall with her how much progress she's made in therapy. How when she first came, she felt lonely at her job and distant from her husband. We both know that she had made considerable progress in therapy, slowly growing to trust me, and using the sessions to experiment with being more open about expressing her feelings. Reviewing her progress is reassuring to her. Chuck's job transfer comes at a good time because she had pretty much completed her work with me in therapy.

During our last session, I feel genuine regret about having to conclude. Megan hasn't entirely learned to trust, nor does she fully fathom how profoundly her mother's leaving has affected her life. Nonetheless, she had made excellent progress, and promises to seek further counseling with someone in New York City if she feels it necessary.

At her last session Megan brings me a couple of her favorite recipes as a parting gift, asking me to promise that I will "At least try them once." As the hour draws to a close, she begins quietly sobbing, saying she appreciated my patience with her and that she'll really miss "these sessions" (she can't quite say that she'll miss *me,* but I know what she means).

Megan illustrates how an obsessive tries to cope with stressful emotions by sitting on them. After her mother left, she learned to muffle her feelings—even good ones. As an adult, Megan appeared aloof, cold, and uptight, but behind her well-fortified defenses was a warm and caring person, a frightened but kind lady. Here the adage "Don't judge a book by its cover," is worth remembering. I'm not saying that behind every obsessive-compulsive style lingers a Mother Theresa, but whomever the *real* person is behind the "I've-got-to-be-in-control" defense, it always takes awhile to get past the "early-warning" defense systems.

This is especially true in sexual situations. Since sexual matters are intrinsically private, obsessive people often feel exposed or vulnerable when they find themselves in a sexual situation. Your partner may subconsciously feel that you're invading her space—intruding. As with Megan, trust takes time, but it is worth the wait. If you proceed patiently in a gentle way, you'll probably find a caring, emotionally alive person behind the exterior aloofness.

Perfectionism: Difficulties in Deciding, Finishing, & Discarding

Ted

Malcolm & Alexi

Arthur

I'm going to discuss deciding, finishing, and discarding together, because in real live lovers these traits are intertwined and all driven by the search for perfection. "Nothing is ever good enough" makes it difficult to choose anyone, discard anything, or finish a task.

Decisions are difficult for obsessives because they involve *risk*. Even decisions which appear to others as trivial or the simplest of choices become weighty with life or death importance for obsessives. Thus whether to wear a burgundy-colored tie with black stripes or a navy and gray paisley becomes an agonizing mental tug of war. As soon as the decision seems to move one direction, there is a compulsion to consider alternatives yet one more time. When this is done, the entire process recycles again...and again. Many an amorous lover has lost the mood while she struggled to choose the "right" negligee. This can drive you nuts when you're trying to get ready for a party or concert. It'll drive you nuts whether you're obsessed or waiting on the obsessor.

In the bedroom suppose you're waiting for her to join you for some adult games, but she's having a difficult time picking the perfect peignoir. Then she decides she simply must shower, shave her legs, and mask her face before coming to bed. Your mood changes from amorous to irritated, tension replaces passion.

It might help if you could see beyond the frustration of the moment to realize she not trying to irritate you. As you know by now, deciding is difficult, and looking perfect by wearing the right outfit is how she prepares for all important events. Without the perfect outfit, she feels like a toddler without his blanket. Sometimes the inability to decide—to risk being wrong—has far-reaching consequences. Such was the case with Ted.

Ted

Ted lived across the hall from me in college and I got to know him quite well. In those days, I used to feel sorry for Ted, because he never could find the right woman to date, let alone marry. He went out with numerous women, but always returned to his room bemoaning their various shortcomings. I didn't know much about obsessive styles back then, so it puzzled me that the very same qualities he claimed to be searching for in one woman would turn him off in another. His dates would variously be either too smart or too dumb, too beautiful or too ugly. If they were beautiful he felt unattractive by contrast, if they were homely, he felt he hadn't made a good choice.

Once, when I was reading about IQ tests in one of my texts, I asked Ted what he thought would be the ideal IQ for his wife. He thought about it and replied that 135 was too high—he didn't want her to lord it over him and make him feel dumb. But, of course, 95 was too low, he didn't want to be married to someone of only average intelligence. Half jokingly, I told him he needed to find a woman with an IQ of exactly 114—a bit above average, but not too smart. He agreed, but of course never found the right one.

Even if a woman had met all Ted's specifications with respect to intelligence, there were dozens of other considerations as well, and it seemed all but impossible for him to find precisely the right mix of qualities in a single woman. This was especially true of the more nebulous qualities such as charm, sex appeal, or charisma. Here it was hopelessly impossible to even devise a measure of where she might rank on these features. It was some years later that I finally understood Ted. Like other obsessive persons, Ted was ostensibly searching for the "perfect" wife, but in fact he was so afraid of lifelong commitment—of making the wrong choice in such an important matter—that his standards guaranteed that he would never make such a decision.

There is a happy ending to Ted's tale. Unlike James, who never married, never even came close, Ted did *finally* find the "right" woman. Well, he didn't find the perfect woman he had been hunting, but at the age of 47, he decided life was passing him by and he entered psychotherapy. Fortunately for Ted, his therapist was experienced in working with obsessives and soon they began discussing why Ted was still single. It quickly became apparent that Ted's "list" was not really a shopping list but a shield.

After some months of work, Ted began to consider marriage to the woman he'd been dating for five years, but he still felt uneasy—not ready. His therapist encouraged him to take the smaller step of purchasing a house. (Not surprisingly, Ted had rented for twenty years because he hadn't found the "right" house.) Ted experienced severe "buyer's remorse" immediately after signing the mortgage agreement, but with his therapist's help, he was able to live with the anxiety and even enjoy his new place—after several months.

Finally, he took the ultimate step and asked Delores to marry him. His psychologist helped him work through his pre-engagement jitters, post-engagement remorse, and early marital anxieties during the first few months of marriage. When I talked to Ted at our class reunion he was happier than I'd ever seen him before. It hadn't been easy for him to break the obsessive see-sawing and take the risks involved in committing to a long-term relationship but he happily reported that it was "worth it all!"

Ted's difficulty marrying illustrates how the quest for perfection interferes with the obsessive's ability to decide about important issues, but even minor decisions can become crises. Sometimes when ordering dinner, Ted would like to try steak, stir fry, and lobster, but feels he really *should* get salad. He wants the perfect meal but can't decide without changing orders twice. Only embarrassment prevents him from changing yet another time.

Ted isn't alone in having difficulties deciding. Saltzman, (1985) tells of a severely obsessive young man who studied the specifications of all the new cars in order to make the best purchase possible:

"This process was so involved and became so prolonged that by the time the survey was finished the new model arrived and he had to begin his survey all over again (1985, p. 67)."

In order to break this mental see-sawing obsessive persons often resort to rituals, rules, formulas or procrastination in order to avoid responsibility for the decision. They may resort to a "color wheel" and a weekly "menu" to schedule what kind of necktie to wear or food to eat. Often if you procrastinate long enough, decisions will be pre-empted by circumstances, as when failure to act before a deadline automatically "makes" the decision, while allowing you to disown it. Such was the case with Salzman's patient:

"This sequence continued for a few years until need finally forced him to make a choice. He then purchased the first car he saw on a used-car lot, a car which lacked all the engineering qualities he had until then considered absolutely essential. He took no responsibility for this choice, claiming that he was forced into the decision by the automobile industry and the therapy (1985, p. 67)."

Often obsessives allow circumstances to decide. With this trick they subconsciously circumvent the incessant seesawing of their thoughts. That's how Malcolm "chose" his mate!

Malcolm and Alexi—Deciding by Default

Malcolm had been dating Alexi for three years while they both worked on graduate degrees. He had finished his Ph.D. and she her Masters. It seemed like the right time to get married, but Malcolm couldn't make up his mind and each time Alexi talked about setting a date, he seemed to withdraw even more, and if it hadn't rained so hard they might still be "just friends."

Alexi lived in an area of student housing where a high water table and torrential spring rains brought flooding to her basement apartment. She and Malcolm hurriedly moved all her furniture to his place, where it remains to this day. They've been married over thirteen years now, a decision made by the great, muddy Mississippi.

If you live with an obsessive lover, you better not hold your breath while you wait for him to *decide* anything. If you think a getaway weekend would brighten your relationship, call your travel agent and book it. Sure it might be more romantic if he surprised you by deciding to go somewhere, but it might be your golden wedding anniversary before that happens.

If you're breathlessly waiting for him to finish those shelves, or redo cupboards, you're going to be short on oxygen for a long time. Better hire a carpenter.

Obsessives place such a high premium on *perfection,* they find it almost impossible to *decide* something is *finished.* I've known numerous obsessive graduate students whose writing of the perfect dissertation took the better part of a decade to complete—if it was ever completed. Some gave up completely, not because they weren't intelligent enough to complete the task, but because, like the man who wanted to buy the *perfect* automobile, they wanted to include all the very latest studies in their research. This attempt, when perfectionistically pursued, makes finishing a dissertation impossible, because each day new data is published somewhere in the world.

In the bedroom this sometimes means that your lover waits for the perfect occasion—when the dishes are done, the phone's not ringing, the kids are at camp, and her parents are in Florida—in order to get passionate. Unfortunately since such perfect occasions seldom occur, sexual frequency is likely to be low. You can help by gently initiating less-than-perfect sexual encounters, and then reflecting how much fun it was, even though *everything* wasn't just so!

Arthur

Art is a hoarder. His "collecting" goes beyond what you would consider reasonable because he collects everything. Car parts clog his garage. Massive antique tractors, rusted reapers, and grand threshing machines stand silent guard over the back yard. Spare bathroom fixtures and sundry small pieces of plumbing accessories occupy various containers spread about the bathroom floor.

I won't even try to describe Art's basement except to say that *everything* clutters his basement! Since Art simply can't decide what to throw away and what to keep, he keeps nearly everything.

In the bedroom it feels like a cave. Disheveled columns of cardboard boxes, like drunken stalagmites, reach nearly to the ceiling. Papers protrude from between them like lettuce and lunch meat. It feels like a spelunker's nightmare where you're trapped among endless columns in a large elevator like room with no way out.

An accountant, Art somehow manages to do people's taxes in addition to his regular job. He began using the bedroom as an office nearly seven years ago, promising his wife it would only be temporary. However the columns of paper seem to be metastasizing and the cancer of collecting threatens to choke out Arthur's already-meager sex life.

If you've ever been in a long-term relationship with an obsessive collector you can appreciate why Janet, his wife, felt like she was drowning in the mess they called home. She used to feel totally helpless and left him on numerous occasions. However after several trial separations, both Art and Janet realized how much they cared for each other and decided that they would each seek therapy. I've been working with Janet and Art has been seeing someone affiliated with the EAP at his work. She reports that in the last month she's noticed significant improvement in Art's mood. "He seems less depressed," she reports "more alive." I see new hope in Janet's face. "He hasn't moved the boxes yet, but his mood has changed," I reassure her, "give it a little time, things seem to be moving in the right direction."

I hope that from looking over my shoulder, you will notice *less* not *more* pathology! When you see someone with a large collection of coffee mugs, you won't automatically assume they suffer from obsessive hoarding. Instead you'll be sensitive to the fact that healthy collectors differ from compulsive hoarders not primarily in *what* they accumulate but in *why*. As we've seen, the obsessive-compulsive hoarder collects to feel safe and to avoid *deciding* to toss something. Their compulsion to *keep,* derives not from an interest in the objects, which are often worthless, but from a fear of throwing away something *might* someday be of use. "After all, you never know when this might come in handy!"

The healthy collector, on the other hand, collects objects for their sentimental value, emotional significance, or financial worth. Philatelists collect stamps, phillumenists collect matchbooks, and numismatists collect coins because they are interested in the objects themselves. Such collectors are motivated by an interest in the "collectible," not by fears about throwing something away.

Now we'll look at how some obsessives take a completely different route to keeping anxiety in check. Whereas many obsessives try to avoid anxiety by not deciding, others strive to control everything.

Needing to be In Control

Christopher & Sheila

Human infants arrive in this world totally helpless, entirely dependent upon others for survival. Most survive this state of helplessness and gracefully comprehend that even as adults we have only limited control over our lives. Many obsessives however, engage in a futile lifelong struggle against early helplessness. They seek through various rituals and maneuvers to deny *any* helplessness or *any* dependency on *anyone!* They seek to avoid vulnerability by always being in control.

Often obsessives come to the first session with a prepared list of items to be covered, one client even provided me a Xerox copy—so that we could both be "on the same track." Such planning and organization usually turns out to be an effort to stay on top of things, i.e., to remain in control.

The following conversation with Christopher, at the beginning of his first therapy session illustrates yet another way in which obsessives strive to maintain control:

Chris: "Well, what do you want me to tell you about?"

Me: "Oh, just talk to me about whatever is troubling you."

Chris: "Do you want to know about my childhood, or my parents, or what?"

Me: "Whatever seems most important to you will be fine."

Chris: "Why don't you ask me questions? I'll answer your questions. Whatever you ask me, I'll tell you about it."

Even while trying to "cooperate," Chris finds it anxiety provoking to "go first," and ultimately waits me out, refusing to talk unless I ask him questions. When I ask open-ended questions he still remains withholding:

Me: "Well, suppose you tell me what it was like when you were growing up?"

Chris: "What do you want to know?"

Me: "Tell me something about your family."

Chris: "I had one older sister and two younger brothers. My dad was a carpenter and my mom stayed at home."

Me: "Can you tell me what the psychological 'climate' was like at home—how everyone got along?"

Chris: "My dad worked a lot. Us kids all did OK in school. My mom kept real busy."

Notice that Chris wasn't trying to be uncooperative, he simply wasn't accustomed to thinking in terms of emotions or feelings, and in a new situation he wasn't going to take any risks.

In the bedroom control and perfectionism don't work very well together. As you might surmise these two concerns have a fire-plus-gasoline kind of effect. Chris was anxious be the perfect lover and turn on his partner like nobody else could, yet he felt it was perilous to let go. He was unable to maintain an erection long enough to "do the job" as he put it. He described how he and Sheila easily got "hot and heavy" just so long as he kept his trousers on. However the moment he (or she) unzipped his jeans to "get down to business" his penis "went soft."

Chris suffered from fears about *performance,* or what is called "spectatoring." This is one of the most common sexual problems encountered, and although we hear more about rape, incest, and exhibitionism, it is anxiety about performance that troubles most males. After several weeks of relaxation training and practice in "sensate focus" (a technique in which partners learn to experience and communicate pleasure in touching without having to sexually perform) Chris reported that he'd "finally got the job done!" He was ecstatic to finally "feel like a man."

As I've said, performance anxiety is probably the number-one sexual problem for males, and you can see how obsessive-compulsive males would be especially prone to such problems. Some of the core components of good sex—mutuality, trust, playfulness—are difficult for obsessional lovers to experience. Spontaneity seems unsafe and lack of perfection feels like a felony. So like mariners of Greek mythology, obsessionals find themselves sailing precariously between the Scylla of perfectionism on the one hand and the Charybdis of control on the other. Circumspectly navigating the perilous waters of sexual interaction, they discover little joy, spontaneity or laughter. Such was the case with my neighbors.

"Prissy" & Paul

You'd like Priscilla and Paul for neighbors! When they moved in across the street I was delighted. They're the picture perfect couple. They met while working at a brokerage firm where she's a program analyst and he's a financial planner. They have no children so they focus their love on their dogs. They jog each morning precisely at 6:30 a.m. I can't help thinking that the nickname "Prissy" has stuck all these years not only because it's a shortened version of her name, but because it so accurately describes her. Prissy is proper, and so is Paul.

They edge their lawn, spray their dandelions, rake their leaves, and—most importantly—take their adored Afghans (Anthony & Cleopatra) running in the morning so they engage in toiletries along the roadside, not on my lawn. These people are excellent neighbors, the variety you'd send away for if catalogs existed for such things. However in spite of their apparent flawlessness, all is not well.

Two peas in a pod often have difficulty finding happiness if they're both obsessive compulsives, and such was the case with Prissy and Paul. Yet, this is a fairly common coupling, because obsessives initially feel most comfortable with other obsessives. Such relationships are characterized by mutual restraint and caution which pleases both partners. As I learned from Ted, the guy across the hall from me in college, marriage is not something an obsessive enters into easily, and if *both* partners seek to avoid risk by requiring perfection in the other, it usually takes a very long time for obsessive couples to feel safe enough to risk such a long-term commitment as marriage.

Once married, they often experience a seesaw relationship punctuated with periodic power struggles in which each partner seeks to establish control. Sometimes these intense power struggles and the subsequent making up afterwards, provide the only real emotions such couples feel.

They often have elaborate bookkeeping systems (if only recorded in private memory). They carefully track who last did the dishes or how recently their partner cleaned the house or bought groceries. This extends to personal items as well. Thus, who gave the last back rub, or who initiated sex last time become sources of conflict if not carried out on a 50–50 basis. Forgetting your partner's birthday is almost unforgivable.

Fairness and equality are paramount in such relationships, but this isn't based so much on a moral sense of fair play, but rather on the fear that one might be taken advantage of. Love, affection, and gifts are all handled with the same "fairness" which really means *symmetry* or *same number of times*. Such tug-of-war relationships between partners who each insist on equality might seem tiring or cheerless by many standards, but for obsessives there is safety in such "computerized" relationships.

"In the bedroom," Paul confides, "we don't have much fun." He confesses that their sex life is joyless, and as he shares, I can see why. Their sex has evolved into a complicated game in which neither he nor Prissy comprehend the rules. They seldom talk about it anymore, because it seems pointless to quarrel about something neither understands. Marriage counseling is for people with "real problems" and though there isn't much bliss in their bedroom they feel their marriage is better than most they know.

The cycle begins with both Paul and Prissy waiting for a signal from the other before initiating sex. Neither wants to risk rejection by making the first move. After an adequate period of waiting following the previous sexual encounter, Paul feels increasingly hurt and neglected. He lets this show, hoping to force Prissy into giving out some positive signals which would allow him to initiate sexual activity again.

For her part, Prissy delays any positive gestures until Paul's sadsack expressions and poor puppy behaviors cause her to feel guilty. Eventually she gives a sign by taking a shower and going to bed early. Paul, who has been preoccupied with whether or not he can get Prissy to agree to sex, now worries about whether he'll be able to completely satisfy her. In this cycle, Prissy usually plays the role of martyr, agreeing to give Paul sex in order to please *him* more than herself. Paul sees himself as the considerate husband who never forces the issue. Specifically, it works as follows:

Upon arriving home from work Paul scrutinizes Prissy for any gestures of friendliness that he might interpret as a sexual invitation. In order to avoid alienating her with "pressure," he is careful not to be direct. Prissy is likewise careful not to be overly congenial because she worries that he will interpret *any* friendliness as a sexual invitation. Usually she reports some physical symptom ranging from the proverbial headache, to being "totally exhausted" from her day at work. This puts everything on hold for another day, but after several such evasive maneuvers, tension builds and Paul becomes visibly annoyed. Prissy then accuses him of being angry with her, or uninterested in her physical problems. Paul verbally denies this but communicates through body language that he is in fact annoyed and well on the way to getting angry. At this point, sensing that sex is necessary to forestall further problems, Priscilla signals her availability, clearly communicating to Paul that she will accept his advances. Sounds like a lot of work doesn't it?

Well, after all this dancing around, intercourse finally takes place, but by this time Paul's needs are so urgent that he ejaculates too quickly, leaving him feeling like a failure for not holding out longer or achieving simultaneous orgasms. Since sexual interaction occurs only when one or both of them feels annoyed, guilty, or sexually starved, it's little wonder that they find it less than satisfying.

Over the six years we've been neighbors, I've pieced this information together from back yard "counseling sessions." Often when Paul and I have been out at the same time spraying dandelions, mowing lawn, or raking leaves, he comes across the street and shares the latest episode in the saga of their marriage. Although I've listened more as a friend than a psychotherapist, I've been able to help Paul to re-think some of his favorites myths (simultaneous orgasms, perfect sex act, I am responsible, etc.) and to "take a chill pill" and quit worrying about who is in control. Instead of all the indirect dancing around, I've encouraged him to be more open with Priscilla about his needs. He reports a noticeable improvement in their relationship.

Obsessive compulsives worry about sexuality because erections and orgasms, like heart beats and digestion, cannot be consciously controlled. Sexual responding is governed by the autonomic nervous system, so any conscious efforts to direct or regulate sexuality are doomed to fail. You simply can't *make* love in the same way that you can decide to take a walk or ride a bicycle. Every male with erectile difficulties knows you can't *make* an erection happen by trying harder to concentrate. If you try too hard, you virtually guarantee it will *not* occur. Similarly the female cannot directly think herself into having an orgasm. Most adolescent males also know you can't stop an erection by trying either!

Mental effort, which is one of the obsessional's mainstays, typically thwarts sexual responding. You can sometimes embellish your sexual experience by *indirectly* using fantasies to enhance the who, when, or where of your sexual encounter, but seldom will directly thinking about your erection or orgasm increase your arousal.

Now you can understand why obsessive lovers are uneasy about sex. At the very core, sex is about letting go. Good lovers are able to relinquish control and simply trust their autonomic nervous systems. For a person who finds it difficult to trust the lesser emotions such as laughing or crying, sexual orgasm can be frightening.

Optimal sex requires letting go of psychological control issues as well. If your main concern is to remain on top, if you're afraid to "give in" to your partner, good sexual relations become almost impossible. If only one person is obsessional the problems may be less, especially if the other partner is secure enough not to be overly concerned about power and control. However if both partners are afraid of letting go or losing control good sex becomes very difficult.

Now you understand why making love with your obsessive partner sometimes lacks vitality and seems more like a dutiful prayer than a festival. Good sex is playful. Like other games, it means letting go, changing some rules, but this feels dangerous to your lover, since he constantly guards against losing control. You can sometimes help by reassuring him how much you care about him and how safe he is in your arms.

If you understand that his need to be in control (maybe literally "on top") is not really a wish to dominate you or to make you feel inferior, but rather a way of feeling safe, it may become easier to work out a good sexual relationship. Realizing that such preferences are not really power struggles but security maneuvers may allow you to compromise without feeling you're giving in.

Time management is high on the obsessive compulsive's agenda, because time, like everything else for the obsessive, represents something that needs to be planned and managed (i.e. controlled). Time is pervasive yet it moves relentlessly on, seemingly uninfluenced by human forces. As such, it presents great difficulties for the obsessive-compulsive person, eroding his sense of omnipotence. Obsessives usually spend significant efforts in managing time and becoming more efficient, but paradoxically, they sometimes discount it because they can't manage it. In such cases, time is ignored or minimized. Time may be organized poorly, and is almost always *underestimated*.

Time has contradictory meanings for the obsessive. On the one hand she invariably tries to cram too much into a short time, defying the limits that time puts on us all, and typically being late for appointments or deadlines. On the other hand, he expects *others* to be punctual, efficient, and accurate in their time estimates so that they do not "waste" his time with tardiness, etc. Thus the obsessive-compulsive's relationship to time is ambivalent.

For obsessive lovers, this sometimes translates into scheduled sex with carefully timed components comprising the sex act. Although he doesn't actually use a stopwatch to measure foreplay or orgasm, his brain is partially focused on issues of time. "How long is this going to take?" "Do we have time?" "We'll have to hurry!" are the kinds of internal conversations he has with himself. Needless to say, this kind of sex isn't very much fun. Trying to enjoy intercourse following the principles of time management is a little like taking a shower when you're running out of hot water. It just isn't very pleasurable. Antidote: Convince your partner that you've got all night if necessary, and that you love sex at a leisurely tempo. Set the tone with some slow dancing or slowly sipped wine, and begin before, not after, the eleven-o'clock news.

We've seen how various obsessive lovers try manage anxiety by avoiding decisions, never completing projects, failing to discard anything, or trying to control everything. Some, however, sidestep all of these routes, managing instead to bury themselves in work. Commonly known as "workaholics," they are sometimes difficult partners. Tony was one such guy.

Devotion to Work, Neglect of Leisure

Anthony

Most obsessive tend towards workaholism, investing extraordinary amounts of time and effort on the job. Work achievement is highly valued, while social or recreational pursuits shrivel. It's not usually because they're socially inept or lack refinement, rather they are simply too busy to "waste time" socializing.

Since opening his own restaurant, Tony was seldom home. He never took the family anywhere. It was always his wife who took the kids to their ball games, the beach, and dance lessons. No one could remember when Tony had taken a vacation. He proudly talked of starting to work at eight years of age doing a paper route, and working ever since.

Somehow, the family—even the restaurant staff—ganged up on Tony and insisted he take a two-week vacation. Everyone ended up regretting it, because when an obsessive-compulsive person takes a "vacation" it becomes a pressure cooker for everyone else. Vacation-planning conversations with Tony took the following form:

"Okay, the first day, if we drive for eleven hours, and take no more than ten minutes for bathroom stops and thirty minutes for lunch and supper stops—we can eat breakfast in the car—we ought to be able to make it to Mt. Rushmore by late Monday evening. Then we can be at the Monument by the time it opens in the morning, shoot a couple rolls of film and be on the road by ten-thirty. If we drive most of the day we can make it to..."

If you've ever vacationed with an obsessive lover or spouse, you probably arrived home as Tony's family did—exhausted, but relieved, having covered six thousand miles in ten days, while shooting fourteen rolls of 36-exposure film, all for under four hundred dollars by eating in the car and camping along the way.

This shouldn't be surprising when you consider that the obsessive people always try to maintain productivity. Enjoyment, *per se* is not a worthwhile use of time and thus never sought directly. Consequently, even a vacation must be made into a some kind of learning experience. Obsessives who are professionals solve this dilemma by planning vacations around professional meetings. They cite tax-deductible travel and accommodations as the reason, but the real reason is they cannot "waste time" by only vacationing.

In the world of work obsessives at first seem impressive, often accomplishing prodigious amounts of work in a short time, but they do not fare well *over the long run,* because obsessives differ significantly from genuinely creative persons. In both there is a capacity for intense, concentrated focus. But the creative person is motivated by the positive pleasures of discovery and the satisfaction of using her skills, while the obsessive compulsive is dominated more by the need for perfection and the search for absolutes in order to achieve security. Although both kinds of activity may benefit humankind, nonobsessive persons are more likely to achieve creative solutions at the office and in the laboratory, because they are concerned with exploring the unknown and transcending boundaries—something which provokes anxiety in the obsessive-compulsive. Obsessive people often have meager social lives because work and career swamp everything else.

In the bedroom Tony is not part of any "Anthony & Cleopatra" combo, primarily because he is so seldom there! It's hard to discuss techniques or timing with a vacuum. Workaholic spouses are often replaced with soap operas, self-stimulation, or tragically with other lovers. His wife laughingly bragged "Tony's great in bed...whenever I see him...on Christmas eve and Easter...the only two times the restaurant isn't open!"

Some obsessive lovers, instead of being absent, simply bring their work ethic with them into the bedroom. Obsessed with concerns about productivity and doing a good job, they mistakenly assume that more is better, quantity is what counts. They think that if you engage your partner in inter-course a certain number of times each week, you have a good sex life. It often takes considerable time and creativity to help them realize that in matters of sex, quality is far more important than quantity.

Scrupulosity

Kathleen

She wasn't perfectionistic in the way many obsessive-compulsive lovers are, she didn't worry about cleanliness, orderliness, or punctuality. She did-n't wash, count, or alphabetize. Her enemies weren't germs or bacteria, and she didn't particularly care whose name preceded or followed hers in the phone book. What *did* concern her was being right with God.

Hers was a devoutly religious family, and much of her psychological development had taken place within their nearby church. She'd attended pre-kindergarten classes there, vacation Bible school during the summers and never missed Sunday school or mid-week prayer meetings. She had attended the school operated by the local parish for all of her elementary and high-school years. She was exceedingly diligent in trying to live per-fectly each day.

Kathy told me she'd been trying to be morally perfect for a long time, but admitted she'd been less than successful. She recalled a time in the fourth grade when her church was holding revival meetings. These were old-fashioned revival meetings conducted in a tent that had been erected on the football field of the parochial high school. The preacher was fer-vent, and of the old-fashioned pulpit-pounding variety. His sermons were vehicles for ever-present calls to repentance and revival. Late one Sunday evening, when the preacher's fervor had reached a particularly high pitch, and Kathy's memory of her many childhood pranks and misdeeds had cor-respondingly raised her sense of guilt to unbearable proportions, she hit the sawdust trail. Finding herself at the front of the church, she was prayed over by the preacher and felt thoroughly cleansed from all her sins.

"My mother was weeping with joy," she recalled, "and for a few glori-ous moments, I felt as pure as I've ever felt in my life. I remember think-ing before I fell asleep that night, 'If I have to die, this would be a good time...I *know* I'd be in heaven.'"

She forlornly confessed that it was the *only* time in her nearly thirty five years that she'd felt perfect enough. In clinical terms we would say her *real* self and *ideal* self were congruent that night. I wanted to help her feel more together on a regular basis, less torn apart by the gap between her ideal and real selves. She had already expended enormous amounts of psychological energy trying to close the chasm by becoming more perfect, and it hadn't worked. Subsequently I began to gently challenge the necessity of living a perfect life. We spent a lot of time talking about how it's possible to be *inspired* by someone without *copying* them.

"If each time I played golf," I suggested, "it were my goal to *exactly replicate* the playing of Greg Norman or Jack Nicklaus I would *never* enjoy a single round of the game. I would fail on each of the eighteen holes." She smiled and agreed that it was appropriate for me to be *inspired* by the way Nicklaus plays, without being obsessed with copying him.

PRs Instead of Grandiosity. Kathy was a runner, and this provided me a useful metaphor. She was able to see that the notion of *a* single winner of a race has been significantly expanded by the many runners who participate. We agreed that although in the strictest definition of the word, there is *a* single winner of the New York marathon, this really fails to grasp the spirit of the race. It doesn't account for age and sex differences, which race officials recognize by awarding separate trophies by gender as well as by age. Most of the fifteen or twenty thousand runners compete with *themselves,* trying to achieve a PR (personal record). For some this simply means *completing* the 26.2 miles. If it takes 5 or 6 hours, no matter. Other more experienced runners attempt to better their previous marathon times, and so it goes, each runner setting appropriate personal goals and measuring success according to that.

In the bedroom things began to improve. As Kathy became less morally scrupulous, less harshly judgmental of herself, she began to impose less strenuous standards for her work performance as well. With this softening of her impossibly-high ideals came a lot more comfort and spontaneity. Happily this spilled over into the bedroom. Much to the delight of her husband, Kathy became more sexually adventurous, even daring to make love with the lights on or when the children weren't asleep. For the first time ever, she began purchasing sensuous underclothes and nightwear. Victoria's Secret made a killing!

Perpetual Worriers

Worrying is *the* primary pastime of obsessives. If they're not working, they're at least worrying. By now, you understand why worrying is so vital an activity for them. It gives them the illusion they are *doing something* about controlling the world *even before it happens!* It combines their need for control and risk avoidance with their proclivity for hard work. After all, since you can't really do anything about the future, you owe it to yourself to at least worry! This tendency, present in all of us, reaches its zenith in obsessives, who tend not only to about the future, but about the *past* as well. Again, providing themselves the illusion that they're doing something about controlling it.

Ogden Nash aptly catches the flavor of the obsessive's worrying in a poem entitled "If a Boder Meet a Boder, Need a Boder Cry? Yes." Nash, who likes to invent new words, creates the term "aftboding" to describe how obsessives worry about things after the fact:

"I haven't much faith in bodings;

I think that all bodings are daft bodings.

Forebodings are bad enough, but deliver me from aftbodings."

In the bedroom "aftboding" often takes the form of "Did I please him?" "Were we too much in a hurry?" "Should I have showered first?" "Would he have preferred being on top?" "Did she fake that orgasm?" "Did I have bad breath?" "Why didn't she come more quickly?" "Have we lost our romance?" Such questions, though seemingly based on real happenings, reflect instead the obsessive lover's anxieties.

REORGANIZING Your Expectations

Suppose after reading this chapter you Recognize that you or your lover has an obsessive compulsive streak. It might be that his obsessiveness bothers you because you struggle with many of the same issues yourself. Or it could be that her obsessiveness bothers you because it's so different from how you operate, she's always worried about little nit-picky details and you couldn't care less. Now what? Is there any hope? The answer is a definite "Yes!"

Much about how we get along with others depends on our *perception* of them—our *expectations.* Now you have an entirely new understanding of what makes obsessives tick, you'll be able to reorganize your thinking and change your expectations so they'll be more in line with reality. This will ease a lot of tension.

You'll begin to see that most of those arguments about sex aren't really about sex at all. When she insists on cleaning the kitchen counters or putting dishes in the dishwasher *before* making love, she's not really rejecting you as a lover, or suggesting that doing dishes is more fun than doing you! It's just part of her personality to want everything in order. If he showers *before* and *after* intercourse it doesn't mean that he thinks sex is dirty or that you've polluted him with your bodily fluids, it just shows he's mildly obsessed with cleanliness.

REVITALIZING Your Sexual Relationship

If you're having trouble adjusting to an obsessive compulsive partner, or you recognize that obsessive streaks in your own makeup interfere with good sex, don't be discouraged. You can Reorganize your thinking along the following lines:

(1) Lighten up! Perfection is an illusion. No one is perfect, not you, not me, not your partner, not anybody. Perfectionism is an *attitude* which sabotages all accomplishments by whispering, "But it's not perfect!" "If only you'd tried a little harder, you might have gotten it right." As long as you have this outlook you'll never be satisfied with anything your partner does, and worse, you'll know that you yourself can't do anything perfect enough either. Then why do so many of us suffer from this carrot-that's-always-just-out-of-reach attitude? I think it comes from two sources, parents and "perfect" people seen in the media.

Perfectionistic parents encourage their children to try harder with phrases like "That was good...maybe next time you can get an A." Or, "Thanks for mowing the lawn, but you missed that little section in back of the tree house." Because of their own perfectionism, such parents find it difficult to praise less than perfect productions. This leaves the ill-fated child with a chronic sense of failure which she attempts to overcome by trying even harder. This establishes a cycle of perfectionistic striving followed by a sense of failure which sometimes persists throughout life.

Movie stars, athletes, and other "perfect" people provide unrealistic role models for us. We're constantly comparing ourselves to athletes or movie stars we have no hope whatsoever of replicating. I'll never play golf like Arnold Palmer, shoot hoop like Michael Jordan, or pass like Joe Montana.

My wife will never play tennis like Chrissy Evert, or run like Jackie Kersey-Joyner. But because the media puts these people up for us to use as the yardstick, we chronically feel inferior.

Movies portray a flawless world of fantasy in which the stars live lives of lust, leisure, and perfection. Ever notice how few flies or mosquitoes you see in movies? When was the last time you saw your favorite movie star pass wind, burp, or urinate? Although you've probably observed numerous "perfect" sexual encounters I doubt you've ever seen a constipated Tom Cruise laboring to defecate or Kathleen Turner popping a zit. Movie stars are always young, beautiful, healthy, and totally perfect—especially when they're advertising soap, toothpaste, deodorant or douche—in which case they emphasize how perfect you'll be too if only you use the right brand of personal hygiene products. All of this leaves you and me, by comparison, feeling like we just don't measure up.

Obsessive compulsive sexual partners try to achieve "perfect" sex but end up feeling ashamed for failing to meet this impossible standard. Either your or your partner might feel like a sexual failure for a variety of reasons. It appears that the shame is based on actual realities—"She didn't have an orgasm," "I wasn't able to get it up," "We've lost the excitement." In fact, most of these apparent failings have less to do with sex and more to do with your mental outlook. We'll discuss this more in the following section dealing with myths.

(2) Don't sweat the small stuff! Worry about *details* drowns the delight of any activity. Whether it's having sex, cleaning the garage, or taking a vacation, there is not *one* right way to do it (i.e., *your* way!) You think too much! You design, plan, and worry too much. This occurs before, during, and after nearly all activities, making it impossible for you to really enjoy yourself. You worry incessantly about the stereo's volume or speaker balance instead of enjoying the music. Similarly with sex, instead of worrying about all the details, you *can* learn to enjoy it, even if you haven't followed all the steps outlined in the latest sex manuals. You don't have to push all the right buttons each time, or compulsively find new ways to arouse and excite. You can just enjoy being with your partner. Your goal is mutual enjoyment, not world record performances. Relax, have fun, you're not choreographing a world premier performance of Phantom of the Opera—OK?

(3) "There's more than one way to skin a cat." Or, if you're a cat lover, "All roads lead to Rome." Since obsessive partners really believe "There's

only one way-my way-to do it," complications arise if each of you has a strong obsessive streak. Sex is very personal and each partner usually has particular preferences regarding what is pleasurable, which is the best position, or when is the best time. If your partner insists on something which seems ridiculous to you, ask yourself if it *really* matters. Is it something you can live with? If so, do!

It might seem foolish that she insists on lighting all ten candles in the room before you make love, or you might be annoyed that he insists you both shower first, but if it helps one of you to feel more comfortable, what's the big deal? Why let little rituals rile you? Instead think of them as part of foreplay. Think of them as small signals that good times are on the way.

(4) "All work and no play makes Jack a dull boy." But since work offers more predictability and safety than leisure time, obsessive compulsive lovers are drawn to it. However this doesn't work well in sexual interactions, because *good sex is playful!* If it becomes too predictable, too organized, too mechanical, too work like, the joy will be lost. You should think of your bedroom as the adult playroom, complete with "toys" such as mirrors, perfumes, candles, vibrators, stereo, and possibly even a fireplace or hot tub. Even without a lot of expense it can be a fun place, a kind of massage parlor or pleasure palace in your own home. Whatever it takes, sex ought to be fun. Workplace efficiency has no place in your bedroom.

(5) Just do it! Gamble! Be Rash! Be impulsive! Be Hasty! Take a chance! Instead of always protecting yourself from risk, allow yourself the luxury of *not* planning something for once. An over planned life—which is the obsessive's specialty—can be a real drag, especially when it comes to sex. Remember, a spontaneous sex isn't life threatening! Try it, you'll like it! Make love not *plans!*

If your partner is obsessive, slowly encourage her to become less planful. But take your time, because if you pull out the rug (of rituals) from underneath her, she'll feel more anxious and things could become worse. Sometimes a bit of gentle humor—make sure you're not laughing *at* her— helps to lessen the obsessive seriousness. Be gentle, be loving, but take some risks.

(6) Don't be so straitlaced. While not *all* obsessives are prudish, there is a tendency towards stuffiness. As we've seen, obsessives are susceptible to scrupulosity and other forms of overconscientiousness, which makes it difficult for them to experience or express feelings. Now that doesn't sound

like a fun person does it? Furthermore, since most sex education is caught not taught, most of us have "caught" the notion that sex is somehow dirty, indecent, or immoral. Much of this is passed along without much thinking, as the following story illustrates:

A bride served baked ham, and her husband asked why she cut the ends off. "Well, that's the way mother always did it," she replied.

The next time her mother-in-law stopped by, he asked her why she cut the ends off the ham. "That's the way *my* mother did it," she replied.

And when grandma visited, she too was asked why she sliced the ends off. She said, "That's the only way I could get it into the pan."

(James & Jongeward, 1971, p. 102)

Your tastes in sex are much like that, often passed on from Grandma to Mom to you. I hope that as you read this book this book, absorbing new ideas, some of those deeply held attitudes will shift a bit. But change doesn't come quickly, so be patient. Continue to re-examine, re-think, and reform your ideas about sex. Hopefully, our discussions will help you loosen up a bit and become more spontaneous. You'll be less stuffy! Won't that be great?

(7) Don't be so *tight!* I'd like to encourage you and/or your partner to be more generous, more affectionate, and less tight-fisted. Obsessive compulsives find it difficult to *give*. The natural tendency is to be miserly, stingy, tight. And this really has little to do with finances—it's about your mental attitudes, not money.

You've probably heard of billionaires who owned half the city, but wouldn't use a pay phone because it cost too much. You've also read about hoarders whose homes were so jammed with collected trivia that it took a dozen trucks to haul it all to the dump when they died. They were, of course, extremely obsessive—afraid to let go of anything—afraid that a dime spent in a pay phone might start the collapse of their financial fortunes.

So remember, it's not about money. it's about your attitude. This is why people describe intensely obsessive people as "uptight," "tight ass," or "anal-retentive." You can see the common element—tightness. Tight can mean stiff, tense, rigid, or inflexible; but with obsessive people it describes *excessive holding on.* It entails a fear of letting go, a phobia of spontaneity. It takes time, and it takes practice, but learning to let go is key to overcoming obsessiveness.

Usually this happens indirectly. You can't—although the obsessive invests immense energy trying—*make* it happen with your brain! When you try directly to be less "uptight," you're still thinking about it. Instead, you've got to take the risk of trusting by letting go. Try *wasting* some time and money, go out to eat before making love. Maybe you can let a new client or contract go and come home from the office an hour earlier. In giving to others and in sharing your resources you'll generate some positive feedback. Others enjoy receiving and will likely tell you so.

Implementing my suggestions to "loosen up" will not always be easy, but as your mental attitudes change, your behavior will slowly follow. I know it isn't easy to just let go and go with the flow, but let me share a personal example from golf. Sorry to disappoint you by talking about golf just when you thought you were going to hear about my sex life, but there are important similarities.

When I first started playing golf, I concentrated on technique—all those "fundamentals" about how to grip the club, address the ball, start the back swing, pivot shoulders and hips, initiate the down swing, snap the wrists through the hitting zone, follow through, etc. Sounds complicated, doesn't it? Well it was kind of like putting together a five-hundred-piece puzzle each time I tried to swing. It won't surprise you to find out that I wasn't being very successful.

Then a friend suggested, "John, forget about all those details and think *rhythm.* Before trying to hit the ball just swing your club back and forth a few times in a nice smooth arc. Set up a rhythm and everything else will fall into place." He was right, I began hitting the ball much more consistently and my brain wasn't cluttered with all the details of how to swing. So that's how *you* can put it all together too. Whether you're trying to revitalize your golf game or your sex life, *rhythm* is a key ingredient.

The rhythms of sex—back and forth, in and out, up and down, constriction and relaxation—are as important in the emotional realm as they are in the physical act. Without physical rhythms coitus is impossible. Without interactional rhythms communication is impossible. Relaxing, opening up, letting go, begins in the brain not the groin. In extreme cases (a condition known as vaginismus), a woman is so anxious that her vagina reflexively clamps shut making sexual intercourse impossible. This is vivid physical metaphor of how physical tightness makes biological intercourse impossible. Less obvious, but nonetheless true, mental tightness makes psychological intercourse equally impossible.

Most obsessives tend towards tightness, but I hope as you've read this chapter you've begun to understand the sources of your rigidity, because this will allow you to relax and develop new ways of coping with your anxieties. Now as part of that new slackening I'd like you to reconsider some of the sexual myths that keep you tied in knots of mental frustration and tightness.

TAKING OUT THE TRASH

Always lurking in the background are those pernicious media sponsored sexual myths, so much a part of our culture that we're not even aware they exist. In a thousand different ways they're foisted upon us by books, movies, and ever present talk shows. Unconsciously, as if by osmosis, we absorb them. Let's look at some of the sexual myths most likely to appeal to obsessive compulsive persons.

MYTH # 1: Flawless *technique* is the key to being a good lover.

TRUTH: Good sexual technique can enhance your expression of love but it is only a *tool* to communicate caring, it is *not* the core substance. Obsessive compulsives need to remember that sexual intercourse is not a gymnastic feat, not a tug of war, not an event that requires constant laboratory like experimentation. Rather it is a mutual encounter involving an endless variety of techniques designed to enhance love.

As in the field of music, how you stroke your violin strings is important, but it doesn't make you a musician. Rather it's a way of conveying the music that is in you. Great performers are first musicians and secondly technicians. Some excellent musical technicians never achieve greatness because although they have near perfect mechanics, they don't creatively interpret the composer's dream. Obsessive lovers (and musicians) are in danger of spending so much time perfecting technique that they never really hear the music.

MYTH # 2: If you are willing to *work* at it, do your research—you can become a great lover.

TRUTH: Great sex cannot be achieved solely through effort. You can't improve your sex life by simply reading more sex manuals or trying thousands of new positions. Obsessives feel most comfortable when they're working hard, expending effort, being productive. However in sexual relations this backfires. As we've already noted, trying too hard stifles spontaneity, transforming playful interactions into ponderous rituals. The obsessive lover is in danger of intellectualizing and planning excessively. This can destroy the vibrant center of a sexual relationship leaving behind only tedious rituals.

MYTH # 3: There is a *perfect* way to make love. This myth is close to the heart of all obsessive compulsives, because it is built on the bedrock of perfectionistic striving.

TRUTH: Sexual perfectionism—like all forms of perfectionism—destroys pleasure. The perfectionist always hears a whisper saying "But you could have done it better...if only you had tried harder!" As you know, obsessives strive for perfection in all areas of their lives, so it comes as no surprise that they carry extra baggage when making love as well. In the bedroom as elsewhere, they need to let go of the false notion that there is always a more perfect way.

A British psychiatrist used to encourage mothers with the notion of "good enough" mothering. Perfectionistic parents, worry that they're not perfect. They also worry that their children aren't perfectly behaved, attending perfect schools with perfect teachers in the midst of perfect peers. Being a good parent doesn't mean you have to be perfect. You only have to be *good enough!*

It would be reassuring for all lovers to recognize that sex can be *good enough* without being perfect. This would be especially heartening to obsessive lovers who grimly go about trying to be more efficient, productive, and perfect.

MYTH # 4: Regular douching is necessary to keep the vagina clean.

TRUTH: By now it won't surprise you to discover that some obsessive people focus their attempts to create perfection in the realm of hygiene. For some, enemas and douches become a purification ritual that helps them feel more squeaky clean, but alas, this was never intended by Mother Nature! Clean yes, obsessively scrubbed no! Douching is unnecessary because the natural secretions of a healthy woman keep her vagina clean.

MYTH # 5: Douching is an effective method of birth control.

TRUTH: Wrong! Some believe that douching can flush sperm out of the vagina before they have a chance to enter the cervix and begin traveling up the Fallopian tubes where fertilization occurs. Actually the sperm travel so quickly that even if the woman springs out of bed and begins douching almost immediately, she is likely to be too late. In fact, douching might even have the opposite effect, pushing sperm more quickly toward the uterus than they might otherwise travel.

MYTH # 5: You can have a good sex life without divulging secrets. Sharing too much about your self is dangerous.

TRUTH: Deeply satisfying sexual relationships are built upon intimate psychological relationships. But this involves being vulnerable. You can't be intimate while at the same time keeping secret selected portions of yourself. That kind of "selective intimacy" is really not intimacy at all. Real intimacy is difficult for obsessives, because it involves risk. It means sharing feelings and affection without first considering safety. In a word, it means becoming vulnerable.

For obsessive lovers "safe sex" doesn't mean taking precautions to prevent the spread of sexually transmitted diseases, it means inhibited, careful, predictable sex where the other person doesn't find out too much about you. It means trying to have *physical* sex without sharing feelings or secrets. Obsessives feel safest with sex that doesn't involve psychological intimacy. To disclose one's secrets is to feel exposed. "Unprotected" sex for the obsessive doesn't mean sex without a condom, it means sex without the usual defenses. Although it's scary, intimacy consists in sharing our vulnerabilities with a significant other. The risk is intimidating, but the payoff immense.

When Harry Met Bessie

Harry grew up on the farm surrounded by cousins, herds of cattle, and an abundance of food. There were dried apples, candy, peach butter, preserves, and cookies. In the autumn after hog killing time there were homemade sausages. As Harry grew older, Mother noticed he was "blind as a mole," and took him to the city to get a pair of double-strength wire rimmed glasses.

When he wasn't working on the farm, one of the most important activities of Harry's young life was playing the piano. He would often practice for two hours each day beginning at five o'clock in the morning. In addition to his music he loved to read, especially history.

Harry met Bessie when they were in the fourth grade together. Bessie was his "ideal." She was popular, stood out in class, and always dressed in the finest clothes. Her family was well to do, Harry was a simple farm boy, so when years later he wanted to marry her, it wasn't surprising that Bessie's mother said, "You don't want to marry that farmer boy, he is not going to make it anywhere."

Only after Harry had enlisted in the army and came home with the rank of captain did opposition to their marriage soften. Still, it wasn't until he was thirty-five that Harry was able to marry his fourth-grade sweetheart.

Harry was what some might call a "string saver." Thrifty and hardworking, he was determined to get ahead. Particular about his appearance, he was always particular about his shoes, ties, and suits. His car was washed every few days, had the oil changed every 1,000 miles and the upholstery was regularly vacuumed and cleaned. He wouldn't allow anyone to smoke in his automobile, since he didn't smoke himself, and didn't want his car to smell of cigarettes. But Harry Truman wasn't all seriousness and business. He loved Monday night poker games with his pals, and he loved Bess - with enthusiasm. So much so that one night two of the slats in their White House bed broke and had to be replaced.

Summary

As you've now seen, there are many different kinds of lovers who are obsessive and they engage in many varieties of ritualistic behavior. But anxiety about being perfect is a common element in all. Obsessive persons try to create predictability in order to reduce anxiety. They believe there is but *one* correct way things ought to be done—or the world should be— and this can be known ahead of time. In other words, obsessives mentally construct a precise future world, then try to *fit the present into those pre-constructed categories!*

Obsessives always want to improve—tomorrow they *must* be better, and the world must be cleaned, tidied, purified and improved. Then, surely, happiness will follow. Unfortunately, in sexual matters, more scouring, more precision, more perfection seldom helps. Quite the contrary, erections and vaginal lubrication like an some elusive elixir of youth seem to fade farther away, the more persistently they are pursued. Ironically, the frantic effort to achieve excellent erections or "perfect" orgasms precludes the very product that is so relentlessly pursued. Erections, like happiness, disappear when too directly chased.

In our culture, there are more male obsessives than females. More hard-driving "Type A" men trying to grind out perfect products—whether at the office or in the bedroom—than females. But female obsessives do exist in a variety of styles.

Offit, a female psychiatrist, contrasts two quite different obsessive styles in women: one, a genteel cosmopolitan, hides her concern about cleanliness and perfection behind an ambiance of culture and serenity. The other, more a Molly Maid kind of scrubber, is far less subtle. Yet, for all their differences, they both share the obsessive's concern with perfection and cleanliness in common. First, let's look through Offit's eyes at the urbane obsessive:

She beckons with a promise of restfulness. Evoking memories of new notebooks, sharpened pencils, freshly scrubbed classrooms, she promises reward for all work carefully done. She invites our fantasies of sheets whitened in the sun and softly ironed, flowers on the table, spotless glass and silver. She transports us to a polite, dustless world where roses grow untrampled at the far corners of the tennis court.

She seems so bland, quiet, charming; so effortlessly efficient, so well ordered. The unfortunate price is that, in bed, she may mainly be concerned with the folding of blankets, precise ventilation, and tomorrow's menu.

Everything finally arranged to ultimate perfection, she may lie down next to her waiting partner, stretch tentatively, and start to worry. The anxiety that hangs on the bedposts aborts most attempts at sexual relating. (Offit, 1995, pps. 70-71)

Contrast this with the cleaning-woman:

Many women do not camouflage their obsessions with housework and ritual so politely. We recognize the obvious compulsive, the more open variety of valkyrie, far more readily than her civilized sister. She never really looks clean, yet hygiene concerns her constantly. Rollers twist her hair into a plastic palace covered with the same daily square of Japanese chiffon while she services the household gods. Only on formal occasions, like weddings, does one get to see her entire head. She wears a "housedress," a garment frequently cut so as to reveal the armpit and it's owner's apocrine abilities. She eats and cleans, sweats, and gets fat. She uses a lot of Lysol in the bathroom. When her husband joins her in bed at night, the hair rollers present an insurmountable barrier against comfortable relations, not to consider her dissatisfaction with the way he has disposed of his dirty socks, his undershorts, his competitors, and his money. He often goes rapidly to sleep in self-defense. (Offit, 1995, p. 71)

If you live with an obsessive lover or are one yourself, I trust this chapter has helped to sharpen your understanding. You already knew that obsessives distrust feelings, but you probably didn't know how much! And you didn't know what to do about it. Now that you understand that their rituals and strivings for perfection are defenses against feelings of insecurity, you can look behind his rituals and find the fear. Once she lets you past her barricade of compulsive cleaning, you'll find an anxious little girl.

Now when you feel your blood pressure rising because she can't decide which dress to wear, you might realize how important it is for her to appear perfect, and this might enable you to soothe and reassure her without becoming enraged. Now when he dictatorially insists you do it *exactly* his way, you may be able to keep your cool because you realize this rigidity is an attempt to keep things predictable and not driven by a need to control you or to put you down.

This concludes our discussion of the obsessive-compulsive style. In the next chapter we turn to dependent and codependent styles. These are lovers who have a need to take care of someone or to be taken care of themselves. Just as the histrionic pursues excitement and the obsessive seeks control, the codependent lover searches for someone to rescue while the dependent lover waits to be rescued.

Chapter 3:
Dependent and Codependent Lovers

"You Decide"... "Anyone you like is fine"... "I'll see whatever you want to see"..."I don't have a preference"..."I don't care"... "Whatever"..."Okay! Okay! I'll decide! Let's try number 6."

DEPENDENT & CODEPENDENT LOVERS

When "I Love You"
Really Means "I Need You"
or
"I Need You to Need Me"

Dependent persons have a psychological "center of gravity" which lies outside themselves. They reflexively look to others for permission, help, and support. They have difficulty making decisions, however, unlike obsessives, it's not perfection they're seeking, it's *approval* and *reassurance.* They are devastated by criticism, feel uncomfortable or helpless when alone, and typically agree with others (even when they privately disagree) to avoid risking loss of the relationship.

The most notable characteristic of dependent lovers is their lack of self confidence. Their voice, posture and body language all tell you "I'll be nice, cooperative, and even submissive if you'll like me and promise not to abandon me." This clinging helplessness and search for support translates into the fact that you can always count on them to be "nice." Dependent persons are usually skilled in obtaining the support of others.

Dependent lovers are usually self-effacing, agreeable and docile. They seldom offend anyone or if they do, the other person feels terribly guilty for being irritated because the dependent person was only "trying to help." In long-term relationships however, dependents become a "drag" because of their clinging closeness, but this is not usually evident in the beginning.

Codependent lovers are dependent in a different sort of way. Their dependency takes the form of *facilitating* or *accommodating* a significant other, who might take advantage of the codependent's efforts, but who does little to change or improve. The term "codependent" was originated by therapists working with spouses of alcoholics and other addicts. It became apparent that the spouse of the addict often supported the addiction (by working extra jobs, taking care of the family, bailing the addict out of jail, etc.) while at the same time protesting how awful it was being married to a drunk.

In this chapter we will discuss dependent and codependent lovers somewhat interchangeably. Although there may be slight differences, *dependency* is the core characteristic seen in both styles, and it is this quality which we will discuss at some length.

Dependent/codependent people invariably lack self-confidence, often belittle themselves and often find themselves dominated or exploited by others. They often volunteer to do things that are demeaning or distasteful in order to get others to like them. In the long run this usually backfires because others find it difficult to respect someone who is insecurely dependent, although they often seem willing to exploit them.

As we'll see in a moment, Ken and Natalie illustrate the complex cycles of dependence and domination which often occur when dependent or codependent people marry. Such cycles are seldom apparent in the beginning however, because dependency is easily mistaken for love. Young lovers typically fail to differentiate between "I love you" and "I need you."

Such was the case with Ken and Natalie. He was dependent ("I need you."), and she codependent ("I need you to need me."). At first it worked, but soon their marriage began to sour as each felt overwhelmed by the dependency or codependency of the other.

Dependency, like drugs, is addictive—at first it feels so good to just be able to let someone else take care of you—but in the long run it doesn't work because filling one's voids through another person instead of developing one's self is really a kind of slavery for both, and the end product is invariably resentment instead of respect.

Ken & Natalie

At first his voice trembled only occasionally, between phrases and the trembling of his hands was scarcely noticeable, but as Ken continued talking his tenuously held "composure" quickly gave way, and he began sobbing uncontrollably.

"She's gone!" he wailed, "And I don't even know where to start looking for her!—or if she's ever coming back!"

His sobbing voice communicated grief while his eyes reflected stark desperation.

"I can't live without Natalie, I just can't live without her! If she doesn't come back, I'll kill myself. I really will. I won't go on without her."

He limply held out the note he'd found when he got home from work that evening. My reaching out and taking it from his hand induced a slight easing of his taut facial muscles, as if some of the terrible weight had been shifted to me. I unfolded the rumpled paper and began reading:

Ken,

I just can't go on living like this. I'm not sure anymore whether I love you. I'm just not sure about anything. So I'm going away for while. Don't try to track me down, you won't be able to find me, because I don't know where I'm headed. I bought one of those Travel America passes from Greyhound, so I can go anywhere I decide for the next ninety days. Right now I'm not sure where I'm going or when I'm coming back or even if I'm coming back.

I know this will be very hard for you to understand, but I feel like I'm suffocating, slowly strangling. There's got to be more to life than waxing floors and making pizza, and before I come back I've got to figure out what that "something" is, or I'm not coming back.

Natalie

P.S. Please tell the kids that "Mom's taking a vacation for a few days." I'll send them a postcard every day, so they'll have a general idea where I'm visiting. But don't come looking for me or try tracking me down because if you do, I'll never come back.

I'd never met Natalie, although I knew Ken owned a successful insurance business, employing half a dozen people. I'd seen him around town—at the post office, bank and such places. He was a large-framed man with a little-boy quality about him. Nervous, pacing, talking almost incessantly with a slight stutter, he seemed to know everyone in town on a first name basis.

Now I was about to become acquainted with the real Ken. It still amazes me, after over thirty years of testing, evaluating and doing psychotherapy with individuals, how different people are on the inside—when they feel safe enough (or desperate enough) to trust you with their real selves. That's why AA has a slogan that goes "Don't compare your insides to other peoples' outsides."

Ken, the quintessential salesman, the lustrous local citizen with two BMWs and a ski boat, was at heart a frightened little boy, whose greatest fear was displeasing his Mommy (or wife).

His parents' relentless bickering had worn down his young psyche like a dripping faucet. They had the kind of shrew-milksop marriage that often keeps people enmeshed for a lifetime of misery. They were good, church attending Baptists, so Dad never utilized alcohol to dull the pain, and Mom had Bible texts to back up her demands for perfection. There were no midnight shouting matches, scenes of violence, or breaking of furniture; only the dreary drone of daily unhappiness, seldom even verbally expressed.

Only Dad's ulcer, hypertension, and migraines (which they conveniently attributed to "the pressures of his job") hinted that all was not well in this "model" family. When Mom wasn't complaining about Dad she was busy with church activities—teaching a Sunday school class, playing the organ every other week, and functioning as assistant treasurer.

Dad spent weeks, even months at a time, on the road as an auditor, leaving Ken and his two younger brothers alone with their chronically resentful mother.

His parents finally did split up, but only after Ken and his brothers had all graduated from college—too late to remedy the chronic anxiety which Ken would experience for the remainder of his life.

He had learned that men "with balls" get into serious trouble, but boys who please Mommy earn smiles. Consequently his psychological "testes" never developed while his need to please grew to gargantuan proportions.

Although his obligatory joviality brought him success in the insurance business, his marriage was a gloomy echo of his parent's failed relationship.

Ken was the oldest son, in the middle of four other siblings. His two older sisters, Esther and Estelle, formed with Mom a kind of matriarchal triumvirate that no male—including Dad, if he were ever home—dared defy. Not surprisingly, both sisters married dependent passive men. Of the three boys, only Ken had risked marrying. Chuck, the youngest, lived with a gay lover in New Orleans, and Ted, the middle son, was a handsome womanizer who compulsively flirted and became sexually involved with numerous women, but who always broke their hearts when they would began to get serious. He showed no signs of settling down.

Ken had resolved *never* have a marriage like his parents' and had tried hard to make Natalie happy. Now, in spite of his best efforts, she was gone and he was devastated. Ken's plaintive voice was an amalgam of puzzlement and pain that barely covered his anguish.

"We just got back from a *great* vacation two days ago! We went to Disney World and had a great time. Why would she leave now?"

For Ken it was truly a bolt out of the blue. He'd come home that evening, expecting to eat supper, watch the evening news, play some computer games with the kids, read the paper, go to bed, have sex, and fall asleep like he did most other nights. Now Natalie was gone with not even a promise to return.

About a week later Natalie returned home and at Ken's distraught insistence, she came to see me. Her version of the "great" vacation to Disney World differed significantly from Ken's:

"It was 'great' alright! In order to save money, we drove our camper. Ken and the kids had a great time, watching the scenery, listening to tapes, and generally relaxing and enjoying themselves. I cooked three meals a day, just like at home, except in our camper it was like trying to wash dishes in a coffee mug! Everything was so cramped, everyone was in my way, I thought I'd go crazy trying to make a simple breakfast our first day on the road. I made scrambled eggs and bacon, but then everyone was still hungry, so Ken suggested we have some pancakes and hash browns to round out the meal.

"Well that was easy enough for him to suggest! All he had to do was drive, and I had to try to mix up pancake batter and fry hash browns while we were winding through the Smokey Mountains. Meanwhile Josh and Jessica kept whining that it was "taking forever." I would have put them to work, but a five-year-old and a seven-year-old aren't always the biggest help in the kitchen, and besides there wasn't room for all three of us in the cooking area.

I finally got breakfast finished but then the kids begged for hot chocolate, so I made that too.

"By the time I finished cleaning up and ate a little something myself, it was 11:30. Almost time to start lunch! After that, I made Ken stop for at least one meal a day. Usually we ate breakfast at McDonald's, so I only had to fix lunch and dinner.

"When we *finally* got to Florida I was so exhausted from all the cooking and tension that I just wanted to stay in the camper and rest. That was fine with Ken. He and the kids did Disney World and Epcot Center. Each morning I'd fix breakfast and send them off. They'd be gone for several hours, and eat snacks at the park. Then they'd come back about dark—expecting supper of course!"

The resentment in Natalie's voice wasn't even disguised. She was quite aware of her anger—of how she felt taken advantage of—yet she saw no alternatives, stating that women were expected to do most of the household chores.

"Men," she complained bitterly, "have it made."

During the entire week they spent at Disney World and Epcot Center, she only toured the facilities on two occasions, preferring to stay in the camper sleeping or reading Harlequin Romances—when she wasn't preparing or cleaning up after meals. She poignantly described her feelings upon returning home from Florida:

"I was completely drained. I felt so tired, I didn't even have the energy to water my plants. And I was so tired of sex, I didn't ever want Ken to touch me again. On vacation he was horny all the time, and in that little camper, I just know the children could hear us. After awhile I just felt like a semen receptacle."

Natalie's departure by bus, two days later, seemed to her the only way out, short of suicide. She traveled to Las Vegas, where her reckless younger sister lived. They spent a week doing the casinos and night clubs. Although Natalie never became sexually involved, it was reassuring to have men hit on her, heartening to know she was perceived by others to be something besides a floor-waxing, pizza-making housewife. She did however experience some resentment about being wanted as a "semen receptacle" again. "I wouldn't have to travel to Phoenix for that," she murmured, "I wouldn't even have to leave home!" Adding, "but what else can you expect of men? Their brains are in their balls."

Ken and Natalie ended up in marriage therapy with me, but they are by no means extreme cases. Many couples who never seek professional help are enmeshed in similar patterns with one another. Before proceeding, let's clarify what constitutes the dependent style in its more extreme forms.

There is a pervasive pattern of submissive and dependent behavior in a variety of situations as indicated by at least *five* of the following:

(1) is unable to make daily decisions without excessive reassurance or advice from others

(2) allows/encourages others to make most of his or her major decisions such as where to live, what kind of job to take, etc.

(3) almost always agrees with people even when he or she believes they are wrong because of fear of being rejected

(4) experiences difficulty starting projects or doing things on his or her own

(5) volunteers for unpleasant or demeaning tasks in order to get others to like him or her

(6) feels uncomfortable or helpless when alone, often going to great lengths to avoid being alone

(7) feels helpless or devastated when close relationships end

(8) frequently preoccupied with fears of abandonment

(9) is easily hurt by disapproval or criticism.

I would like to note that when we characterize someone as a "glutton for punishment," "masochist," or "saint," we are likely talking about someone with a significant streak of dependency/codependency.

"I Love You."

When a *dependent* lover says "I love you" it really means: "I need you! Desperately! When we're together I feel whole. You fill all the empty spaces in my life. Before you came into my life I was nobody, if you leave I'll be nothing again. I'll do anything you want, in order to make you happy, just please don't ever leave me."

With a slightly different spin, the *codependent* lover says "I love you," but really means: "I need to rescue you. I need you to need me. When you're dependent on me, I feel OK about myself. Also, I feel secure knowing that because you need me so much, you won't ever leave me for someone else. Even if you remain addicted to alcohol or disabled from working, you can count on me to care for you. I'll enable you to use drugs, sex, alcohol, welfare or alleged pain to avoid responsibility. You won't have to go to work like others, won't have to earn money, won't have to punch a time clock, only promise you'll depend on me and never leave me, and I'll take care of you."

Ken and Natalie illustrate moderately dependent and codependent styles respectively. It is not unusual for such people to find each other. Codependents typically form side-by-side relationships with other dependent partners. Sometimes the partner's dependency is on alcohol or drugs to help soothe feelings of anxiety, or depression. Such individuals are sometimes referred to as substance abusers and their codependent partners seen as "enablers."

But this is not always the case. There are numerous people with *dependent styles* whose dependency is not on chemical substances, but on other *people.*

Ken, had no addiction to alcohol, didn't need rescuing from substance abuse but his dependency—his wanting to please Mamma—propelled him in Natalie's direction. She was dominant like his mom, but in a more caring way. She seemed compelled to rescue others rather than boss them. This, to Ken, felt like the best of all worlds, to be in the presence of a woman who seemed strong, but who took care of you instead of belittling you. Natalie found Ken attractive because her inner radar told her he would never abandon her and that she could take care of him. Neither partner was malevolent, both cared about others, both loved their children. There was a level at which they genuinely cared about each other.

Such is not always the case. Since for many dependent/codependent persons their relationships are dominated by intense needs to be liked, they typically make poor choices in friends or marriage partners and often wind up in relationships where they are exploited. It is difficult for them to distinguish between genuinely, *reciprocal* relationships and exploitive, *using* ones. Feeling devastated or helpless when relationships end, they are vulnerable to manipulation by others. They're too nice to say "No!" responding instantly with compliance if someone gets upset. Consequently a sexual partner or significant other can easily pull the dependent person's chain by having a temper tantrum, or threatening to leave if submission isn't forthcoming.

Dependent persons often go to great lengths to avoid being alone, such as volunteering to do unpleasant things, or putting up with demeaning behaviors in order to keep other people liking them. They take a lot of garbage from others—often uncomplainingly.

Ken related to his mother by constantly trying to please her, continually seeking her approval, being endlessly concerned about her evaluation of his performance on a variety of tasks. Since he incessantly heard his father being put down, he constantly sought to avoid angering his mother.

When he married Natalie he used the same tactics, but she soon found his sycophantish ways distressing and tried to encourage him to "Be a man." At the same time, however, she took over all family responsibilities except balancing the checkbook, servicing the cars, and mowing the lawn. Thus, although Ken wasn't a dictator, he came to expect Natalie's caretaking as a matter of course. She, accepted this as her lot in life and consistently, if grudgingly, took care of the family.

Natalie's *codependent style* manifested itself in the classic way: *taking responsibility for meeting others' needs to the exclusion of acknowledging one's own.* Like many codependent persons Natalie had great difficulty initiating projects or doing things on her own—especially if it involved doing something pleasurable for herself. And it was unthinkable that other family members should put themselves out for her. She saw this lack of appropriate entitlement as unselfishness or putting others first, but in fact it was a symptom of her low self esteem and her fear of abandonment.

Natalie's psychological style had been deeply etched one morning when she was only four years of age. At that time she and her two-year-old sister Lisa were taken to an "orphanage" (as group homes for children were called in those days). Although thirty-five years had passed, Natalie could still recall her mother kissing her goodbye and saying, "I'll see you tonight darling, take good care of Lisa." Mother never returned. Especially significant to Natalie were her mother's instructions "Take good care of your sister." This turned out to be a "life sentence," for Natalie, who spent the next three decades of her life caring not only her sister, but for everyone else as well. This alternated with searching for mother. She confided to me that each time she heard a small private plane fly overhead on a warm summer day, the thought would pass through her mind "Maybe that's Mommy, coming back to get me."

Mom never came back, and in spite of numerous searches in which Natalie enlisted the aid of librarians, genealogists, social workers, and distant relatives, she was never able to make contact with her mother. She clung desperately to the one bit of evidence that her mother cared—a letter written to her when she was five, stating that "Mommy loves you very much, and will come and get you and Lisa as soon as possible." Natalie is still waiting.

At the orphanage, Natalie, constantly worried about her little sister, and according to a nun who had worked at the home, they were "inseparable." Natalie always "looked out" for Lisa.

The original abandonment had a catastrophic effect on Natalie's young mind, but equally important were the subsequent events. After spending about a year at the orphanage, she was taken to live with her grandmother—a rather stern, emotionally-distant lady. These early experiences forcefully fashioned her childhood style into codependency. Even as a toddler, she learned to take responsibility for other's needs before her own, the essence of codependency.

Such a style fits lock-and-key with various exploitive styles such as sociopathy and narcissism. Every victim needs a rescuer and every invalid a caretaker. Natalie's role was that of perpetual rescuer and caretaker. Consequently she saw anyone in need—and this literally included stray animals along the highway—as her responsibility. She took seriously her Christian beliefs which also seemed to reinforce the notion that "anyone in need is my neighbor." Natalie became so overloaded with responsibilities of family, friends, church, and stray animals that she burned out and took the bus out of town.

Her decision to take the Greyhound to Las Vegas was one of the most important decisions in her life since it was the beginning of her rejection of codependency as a lifestyle. Her marriage improved only after she took the risk of losing it (she thought) by not overextending herself for everyone.

Mother Theresa syndrome is at the heart of the codependent's sexual experiences. Most codependents are not as unselfish or kind as Mother Theresa, but they often try to convince themselves that they are. The codependent's primary error is believing they are nicer than they really are. Trying to live like Mother Theresa when you're not generates enormous amounts of resentment, because deep inside you expect reciprocity when you're kind or helpful to someone—you expect a return on your investment, however small it might be. At the very least, you expect some recognition—a simple thank you at least. When this is not forthcoming, resentment builds and you end up feeling more like a martyr than the missionary you intended.

Codependents are *compulsively* compassionate instead of genuinely choosing to dispense charity. It isn't that codependents are phony when they're rescuing others, it's rather that such helpfulness is driven more by the urges of the helper than by the needs of the "helpee." This of course makes the codependent lover a prime target of exploitation because you're not likely to pass up a free ice cream cone if someone is urging it on you.

Similarly, if your lover insists on "doing you" in every way—meeting all of your specific preferences without regard to what they might like—you're not likely to argue about it. However this kind of non-mutual love-making doesn't work well over time. You begin to lose respect for someone who will do "anything" for you, and they begin to resent your lack of appreciation.

Furthermore, codependents need victims to rescue. They build self esteem around "saving" others. They typically save animals from the dog pound and bring them home for pets, much as they try to save drug addicts, sociopaths, single pregnant mothers, and crack cocaine babies.

I'm not saying that some of these rescue missions might not be worthwhile efforts, but they don't succeed very well in the case of codependents because such persons have very poor boundaries, becoming quickly enmeshed in the lives of the victims they're trying to save. The "victims" are often manipulative, over-entitled people who might appear helpless but who have made a career out of being saved and are adroit at exploiting their rescuers.

Dependent and codependent lovers often find themselves in abusive sexual relationships where their good intentions simply reinforce the sick behavior of the victims they intend to rescue. Volunteering a few hours a week at the Pacific Garden Mission to save the derelicts might be viable, but trying to save someone by marrying them or "loving them enough" is a prescription for disaster.

In more subtle forms this occurs when the dependent lover engages in sexual acts she dislikes in order to please her partner. This often begins as something moderate like performing fellatio on your partner even if you find it a bit distasteful. Soon, however, this is not enough and he ups the ante for what it takes to keep him happy. As the stakes rise, you feel trapped into journeying farther into offensive frontiers until finally you find yourself engaged in what is offensive and disgusting. He secretly despises you because he knows he's asking you to put up with more than any self-respecting woman ought to, so the cycle just goes on becoming more intolerable as time passes. Intolerable, that is, for a healthy person. A dependent or codependent partner seldom breaks up a relationship because they have such a fear of being alone they believe anything is better than loneliness.

Differences between dependent and codependent styles are really quite minimal. Both have at their core anxiety about abandonment and a compulsive need to be liked. The excessive dependence on others is an attempt to never "rock the boat" of interpersonal relationships. If you never make decisions without seeking reassurance, advice, and encouragement from others, you are less likely to offend them.

If there is a distinction, it is that codependents are a bit stronger psychologically, functioning more often as caretakers or rescuers than as invalids or victims. But this caretaking is a counterfeit of genuine nurturance, because it is a manifestation of the codependent's needs rather than an expression of inner strength. Such caring typically has strings attached. The price tag typically reads "I'll take care of you as long as you promise never to leave."

Codependent parents make it very difficult for adolescents to leave home or to marry. There is always some residual guilt about leaving and some worry about "how Mom will get along now that I'm gone." Parental overprotection, while it may feel good to the child, is really a disservice, because it strengthens dependency behavior and such children are at risk of using home as a shelter from the responsibilities of growing up and learning to stand on their own.

This also occurs in the case of children who have special physical needs or whose health problems are life threatening, even if their parents weren't originally inclined to be codependent. Children with chronic heart ailments, asthma, blindness, extreme reactions to bee stings, etc. are at high risk for dependency problems in adulthood because of parental overprotection when they are young.

In summary, I would emphasize the great similarity between the two styles (hardly necessitating a distinction) but add that the codependent has moved up a notch to *apparently* caring for others. This is only a veneer, for the codependent's own deep dependency needs, functioning as insurance that the cared-for person will never leave. The core motivation in both cases is *abandonment anxiety.* The dependent *clings,* to avoid being abandoned, the codependent *cares* to avoid being deserted.

Penny

Penny was a member of a therapy group for former drug addicts. She'd been married to Gunther for nearly twenty years, but had recently divorced him. It finally came down to her realizing that "I had to choose between drugs and threesomes."

Early in the marriage Gunther had talked with her about having an open marriage and trying some threesomes. Penny was distressed by the suggestion, thinking that marriage was about loyalty and intimacy. It was one thing to share a duplex with neighbors or to share a condo on vacation, but quite another to "share" your husband. He persisted, however, and in good codependent fashion she eventually submitted. Gunther owned and operated a German restaurant, and he suggested that Penny, who worked there part time as a cocktail waitress, get friendly with one of the regular male customers and invite him home for drinks, where the three of them could proceed to get intoxicated and "friendly."

Although she despised herself for participating, Penny nonetheless—in order to please Gunther—engaged in a succession of *menage a trois* encounters over the next fifteen years of their marriage. In order to deal with her guilt and revulsion Penny began overusing prescription diet pills. Soon she was addicted to uppers. She had to stay drugged in order to live with herself. It was only after completed an inpatient drug rehabilitation program that she had to courage to confront her addiction to please others. When she did, Gunther, who was no longer satisfied with "only" her, filed for divorce. Penny is presently married to a much healthier man and they are happily contented—without threesomes or drugs.

The beguiling thing about most dependent-exploitive relationships is that they appear pleasant at first and only begin to sour *gradually*. If, while dating Penny, Gunther had said to her, "Penny, I hope you enjoy threesomes, because that's what I have in mind for us a little way down the road." she would have immediately quit dating him. But it seldom works that way. The partner of the dependent lover usually senses the insecurity early, but only exploits it when the relationship is well enmeshed. This is why it is so important to recognize the dependent style in yourself or others *before* you are deeply into the relationship. Once the victim-rescue dance begins, it's almost impossible to get off the dance floor.

Typically such relationships end only when the nondependent partner tires of it, and goes out looking for greener pastures. By this time the dependent lover is both resentful and relieved. Resentful because of the tremendous unfairness they've experienced in the 90–10 give-receive ratio, and relieved that the relationship is finally over (They know they could never have broken it off themselves.).

Dependent/codependent people allow others to make important decisions such as where to work, live or what kind of house to buy. But unlike obsessive-compulsives who avoid decisions for fear of being wrong, dependent persons dislike deciding because they fear rejection. This may be euphemistically explained as "not wanting to be selfish," but in fact it is based on a lack of self confidence, a fear of rejection. Not only major decisions but simple choices are driven by the need to stay in the good graces of others. This is how choosing a restaurant with a codependent works:

Partner: "What would you like to do tonight?"

Codependent: "I don't know. Whatever *you* want to do will be fine."

Partner: "How about going out to eat?"

Codependent: "That sounds nice."

Partner: "Do you have a preference?"

Codependent: "Not really, you choose. Wherever you pick is OK."

In the above example we could have labeled the acquiescing partner as *either* dependent or codependent, but the flavor here is one of looking out for *your* needs, making sure *you* have a good time, in spite of how *I* feel. This moves beyond simple dependency to the next step—the "caring" step.

These kinds of interactions appear innocuous but are deeply destructive over the long run for both the codependent and his/her partner. *Everyone* has preferences about *almost everything!* If the dependent were going out alone to eat, she would have little difficulty making a choice. It is only because the dependent fears crossing the partner that he/she maintains the pretense of being flexible or going with the flow.

Dependent persons could well wear T-shirts with the following messages: "Like me, and I'll always agree with you." Or, "Promise you won't leave, and I'll do whatever you want." Codependents could wear messages reading "Since you need me so much, I'll take care of you." Or, "My friends think you're a jerk and I'm a fool for staying, but I'm the only one who *really* understands you."

As we noted earlier, most psychologically healthy people find this kind of echo-chamber relationship boring and do in fact leave. The kind of people most attracted to these living mirrors are those with overwhelming dependency needs themselves, those who desire to control others or those who seek gratification or uncritical admiration.

In future chapters we will examine in more detail how dependent/codependent individuals "mesh" with other complementary styles such as narcissistic, sociopathic, and avoidant styles. Here we will only briefly mention a few of the possible dysfunctional combinations.

Dependent/codependent parents and conduct disordered (pre-delin-

quent) children make a particularly unsuccessful team. When parents need a child's love too much, they work too hard at being good parents. Too often this translates into endlessly trying to win the child's cooperation or approval. This is problematic even in a relatively normal family, but if one of the children is prone to delinquency, or "acting out" as professionals call it, such parental behavior is disastrous because it reinforces the child's undesirable behaviors with concern and overattention.

Dependent/codependent teachers have an excessive need to be liked by students and typically have difficulty maintaining classroom discipline and integrity of grading. Grade "inflation" alongside lower SAT scores is sometimes more a symptom of codependent teachers than "lazy" students. It's my guess that students tend to work at the level expected by their instructors, who in turn reflect family and cultural values. I doubt that Japanese or other Asians are smarter than Caucasians, but they are the products of a much less codependent culture

Much the same can be said about numerous mental health workers. Many in the helping professions suffer from codependency, seeking to make a career out of rescuing others. If a particular professional has received personal analysis or therapy (as I think all should), such unconscious motivations can be understood and the effect on clients reduced. However in many cases, codependent therapists take far too much responsibility for their client's lives, becoming enmeshed in endless cycles of the three R's of codependency: relapse, rescue, recovery.

Codependency is seen on the national level in the symbiotic relationships that form between social workers and welfare recipients, probation workers and delinquents, police and prostitutes, politicians and lobbyists. In many such relationships, it turns out that over time they become more cozy than is in the ultimate best interest of either participant.

Dependent/codependent wives and sociopathic/narcissistic husbands— the selfless and the selfish. In future chapters we will discuss sociopathy and narcissism in greater detail, but here we merely point out that codependents and sociopaths/narcissists are a common combination because only a codependent would live with a sociopath for more than a few months. This allows the sociopathic male to have multiple affairs, be irresponsible with finances, "slap up the old lady" from time to time and generally behave in unsavory ways without paying the price. His wife—often to the chagrin of friends and relatives—repeatedly forgives him, giving him another chance. Of course the same kinds of interactions can occur with sexes reversed. Sociopathic women living with codependent men often act out in areas of sex, credit cards, alcoholism or drugs.

Luther and Jessica

Luther and Jessica were such a couple. At his bachelor's party, Luther had been "presented" with a stripteaser as a gag, but then managed to spend several additional hours with her. On their honeymoon, Luther spent as much time ogling at other women on the beach as he did looking at Jessica. And things never changed. Twice, while Jessica was pregnant with one of their four children, Luther had affairs—always expecting her to forgive him, since he had been honest in telling her. During a therapy session with both of them present, Luther—in classic sociopathic style—suggested that if Jessica would have been more creative in bed and had been willing to try more things, perhaps he wouldn't have been tempted by other women. And Jessica—in classic codependent style—sat quietly looking hurt and humiliated but didn't challenge his preposterous suggestion.

Luther's typical style was to maintained he wasn't cheating until the evidence was overwhelming. Jessie's friends told her she was naive to believe that when he took his secretary to lunch for the entire afternoon, nothing was going on, but Jessica chose always to believe Luther's version of such happenings, and after a while, her friends quit trying to tell her what was really going on, choosing to remain friends by not challenging her contrived view of reality.

Having experienced the divorce of her parents when she was seven, Jessica had coped with the loss of her father by harboring the fantasy that if she were a "good girl" and grew up to be "pretty" Daddy would come back and they would all be a happy family again.

When Jessica was an adolescent Mom remarried and when several months later her stepfather made sexual advances, Jessica found it both psychologically disgusting and biologically exciting. On Mom's bowling night, her stepfather would come into Jessica's room and insist on giving her a back rub to "relax" her. He would then apply baby oil and sensuously rub her back until she felt goose bumps all over.

The "back rubs" eventually expanded to include her breasts as well as her genitalia, but since her step father never actually engaged her in coitus, contenting himself with massaging her body and manually stimulating her clitoris, he was able to convince her that it was OK. Jessica was highly conflicted about these episodes, feeling like she was betraying her Mom, but her stepfather was able to assuage her guilt by reminding her that they weren't "going all the way," and that these "tender times" were just a special bonding between them.

One evening when Mom returned home early from bowling because she was feeling ill, she came upon a situation in her daughter's bedroom which caused her to throw up convulsively for the next several hours. Upon recovering sufficiently to speak, she screamed at her husband, calling him every foul name that she could muster and told Jessica she was to move out and never return, as she didn't want a "whore living in the house."

Jessica, who was thirteen at the time, spent the night at a friend's house. Her mother moved to another part of the country and never spoke to her again. Her bio-father threatened to murder her stepfather, and it was probably only the fact that her stepfather was taken into custody by police that the murder threat wasn't carried out.

That happened thirty years ago, but Jessica still lives with the guilt on a daily basis. Although most people would not hold a thirteen year old responsible—as indeed the courts did not—she could never absolve herself of the guilt. Her mother's refusal to talk with her has scarred Jessie deeply, but probably not as severely as her Mother's refusal to acknowledge that she has "four beautiful grandchildren."

Thus we see that Jessica's trying to make it work with Luther—against all odds—was primarily an attempt to absolve herself of her own chronic guilt by being forgiving, even as she wished her mother would have forgiven her. By keeping her current family together she avoids the guilt of breaking up yet another family. This tragic "logic" of the unconscious mind is highly resistant to change and codependent people seldom seek psychotherapy.

There are a lot of Luther-and-Jessica couples out there, obviously dysfunctional to all outside observers, yet resistant to change or dissolution. When one has the opportunity to become acquainted with such individuals from the inside, there emerges a certain "reasonableness" about the way they've tried to solve their problems. You or I might not choose to stay in such a relationship, but great portions of these people's lives have been shaped by situations over which they had little or no control.

I facetiously tell my students, "If you want excellent mental health, choose your parents *very* carefully." Most of our life "choices" regarding careers, spouses, and lifestyles flow from our earliest interactions with parents—interactions we obviously had little choice in creating.

RECOGNIZING Dependency/Codependency Sexual Styles

Self Quiz

1. When I see someone frowning, do I immediately wonder what I can do to help?

2. When someone loses their temper, will I do almost anything to restore the peace?

3. Do I automatically think, "You first?"

4. At smorgasbords, church picnics, or family gatherings, do I naturally avoid taking the biggest cookie on the dessert plate? Will I *insist* that someone else have the last piece of lemon meringue pie?

5. Has it been at least seven years since the family vacation was where *I* wanted to go?

6. Are these the kinds of Bible verses that especially appeal to me?

    "Blessed are the meek,
    for they shall inherit the earth.
    Blessed are he peacemakers,
    for they will be called the sons of God."

7. Do I worry incessantly about how my children are going to turn out?

8. Do I feel responsible for my children getting their homework done?

9. Do I often practice my children's music lessons with them—encouraging and participating with them?

10. Have I won any "Best-Den-Mother" awards or other such honors?

11. Do I receive at least one phone call a week after 9:00 p.m. from a friend or acquaintance who "just needs to talk?"

12. Have I volunteered to work on a suicide or runaway "hot line?"

13. Do I have (or wish I had) a car phone, so family or friends can reach me at all times?

14. Do I think answering "No" to any of the above items is a sign of selfishness?

15. Do friends ever drop off a sick child for me to baby-sit so they don't have to miss work? Do they drop off healthy kids for me to baby-sit?

16. Have I been called any of the following: "glutton for punishment," "masochist," "saint?"

17. Do my friends tell me I understand them better than anyone else, which is why they "count on me" to listen?

18. Do I regularly bring pets home from the Humane Society, or pick up strays from along the roadside?

If you've answered "Yes" to many of these, you probably possess a significant streak of dependency or codependency.

Social Impression. Dependent and codependent lovers make similar impressions. Both styles result in a kind of insecurity-based hovering or clinging that makes you feel uncomfortable. It's a little like entering a clothing store and having an eager salesperson jump you at the door with "May I help you?" You usually feel like trying another store immediately, but can sometimes buy a bit of breathing room with "Thank you, I'd like to look around a bit...I"ll let you know if I find something I like."

Dependent people are like that. You sense their hunger for relationship in their urgent attempts to please, and ironically it is the intensity of their efforts that puts you off. You feel like saying, "Give me some room! Let me breathe!" but of course you don't, because, after all, they're just being "nice."

Des and Kelsey

Desmond had been dating Kelsey for several months. His only complaint was that she was "too nice." She readily agreed to whatever *he* wanted to do. Kelsey was an intelligent, attractive, woman who ran a successful senior citizens center. They'd been dating for several months, but for Des there just wasn't any chemistry, he found her not really boring, but flat. He felt guilty, even thinking of breaking if off with her because she was always so happy when they were together. They dated for several months before he finally resolved to end the relationship. The decisive moment occurred during a movie. Des was engrossed in the movie when he noticed that Kelsey was watching *him:*

Des: "Why are you looking at me? Is something wrong?"

Kelsey: "No honey, I just like looking at you when you laugh. It makes me happy to see you enjoying yourself so much."

"I'd paid $6.50 for her to watch the *movie,* not *me!*" exclaimed Des. "I knew then that I could never marry this kind of person and I knew that to date her any longer would just be leading her on, so we broke up later that night."

Disappointing as such relationships are during dating, they often lead to lackluster marriages. Each partner evaluates the other as a good person, who will make a good spouse. Having been cautioned to "Use your head, and don't get carried away with the excitement of sex," they often feel this is the kind of solid, stable relationship upon which to establish a family.

But over the long run, dependency or codependency lead to an ever-increasing distance between partners, because of lack of balance in the relationship. It's a little like a suspension bridge that begins to oscillate out of control—only slightly at first, but with increasing intensity until it self destructs.

Marriage operates best as a reciprocal relationship; but if you go into it with a codependency bias, there is significant risk that you will ultimately be living alone. Those early marriage accommodations, "Of course I'm glad you play softball with the guys on Wednesday nights," soon require more expansive acquiescence to include basketball on Mondays, bowling on Tuesdays, poker on Fridays, and golf on Sundays, allowing hubby to "jock out" of the marriage.

Our culture tends to encourage exploiting husbands and compliant wives, but this is not always the case. The "henpecked" husband is a code-pendent who buys his wife's approval through compliance.

The Rescue Reflex is what characterizes codependent lovers. Empathy, discernment, and sensitivity are key components in optimal love relation-ships. Often dependent or codependent partners *appear* to have these traits, however, dependent or codependent lovers are *compulsively* driven to be "nice" no matter how they've been treated. They strive to be always benevolent, always considerate, even when anger or frustration would be a more appropriate feeling.

Living that way can be infuriating. But since anger or even annoyance isn't acceptable to the dependent/codependent, such feelings are repressed—put out of mind. But over time, resentment begins to build and finally overloads the unconscious, breaking out in occasional flashes of anger or turning inward and being experienced as depression or physical symptoms.

But under such circumstances most dependent/codependent persons try even harder to contain such feelings. Instead of solving the dilemma, however, such tactics invite further exploitation from others, and since the codependent never (apparently) gets angry, she continues to be taken exploited. Although this fuels the cycle with more fury, relatively few codependents take the bus to Vegas. Unlike Natalie, they stay in dysfunctional relationships, developing depression, incurring numerous physical problems, or suffering in other indirect ways.

REORGANIZING Your Expectations

Ordinary people, however, with mild streaks of dependency or codependency can often function reasonably well, gravitating to professions or work situations where their compliance is valued and their helping spirit appreciated. Nursing, teaching, social work, and similar professions attract codependents in greater numbers than do business, computing sciences, and the like. Among those working with chronically troubled populations-physically handicapped, poor, retarded, chronically ill, or the aged—one will find more than the usual number of codependents.

This is not to say that all persons working with chronic alcoholics, for example, are codependent. The key issue is whether one is able to assist clients without becoming enmeshed with them. Healthy professionals assist their clients without taking on primary responsibility for change. They recognize and resist the ubiquitous manipulations of the needy. Codependents are entrapped by them.

At the risk of sounding cavalier, I would suggest that healthy professionals *work* with alcoholics while codependents *marry* them—and worse—*stay* married to them!

Lifestyles of dependent/codependent persons are most often characterized by years of self-sacrifice, concern for others, and community service. But as we saw in Natalie's case such meritorious careers of putting others first are sometimes abruptly terminated. Her bus trip to Las Vegas was the first rung on the ladder she eventually climbed to better mental health. Others sometimes break out of codependency cycles by beginning an affair, renouncing church membership, resigning from the board of the local animal shelter or beginning career changes which require moving to other parts of the world. Sometimes beginning a massive projects (such as building one's own home) is a way of using up all their time and giving them a ready excuse to turn down taking care of others. It's all the better if such career changes can be construed as entering a "larger realm of service." Thus, the harried floor nurse, becomes a consultant to industry, or the third-grade teacher returns to the university to work on a doctorate.

If you now **R**ecognize that your lover has streaks of dependency or codependency, what can you do? Maybe you've dreamed of taking the bus out of town, but know you never would. Short of leaving, here are some suggestions that might help to rejuvenate your sexual relationship if you or your partner have slipped into a codependent or dependent relationship.

REVITALIZING Your Sexual Relationship

(1) Begin making daily decisions on your own, for yourself. The key phrase here is *for yourself.* If you're *dependent,* this will feel scary and you'll want to defer-as you have in the past to your partner, but don't! Only you, truly know what you like or prefer, and it's time you begin to feel you deserve having your own preferences met. This is equally true at the office or in the bedroom. Quit being a martyr or a saint. It doesn't work. She won't respect you anyway and you'll always be doing what someone else—not you—wants.

If you're *codependent,* making decisions *for yourself,* is still key. Instead of finding someone to rescue and then always thinking first of what's best for them, learn to look out for yourself. You don't have to be brash or aggressive about it, you don't have to become mean or hateful, just honest.

"But what happens," you wonder, "if we can't agree? What if he leaves me?"

Healthy compromise is based on a secure sense of self esteem and an appropriate sense of entitlement. It can be differentiated from codependent compliance by the presence of debate and discussion—even argument. There is lots of give-and-take. Plenty of compromise, but the compromise is mutual. The lopsided compliance of codependence is replaced by genuine dialogue, taking into account *both* partners' needs.

Instead of a reflexive rush to rescue by the codependent partner, both persons genuinely discuss their needs, and the couple reaches a compromise *after* such communication.

(2) Don't agree just to keep the peace or to make him happy. It won't work over the long run. Inwardly, you'll resent always having to give in and he won't respect you for being a pushover. In the long run he'll be more likely to leave you if you compulsively agree with him than if you have some backbone and stand up for your own needs. Ironically, your worst fear—abandonment—will be more likely to come true when you try too hard to be nice than when you look out for your own needs.

(3) Quit volunteering for every local charity, church, or club project. Don't allow yourself to be the lackey around home either. If there's work to be done, let others do their share. At home split it evenly between you and your partner. Include the children in messy chores as well.

Why should you always be the one to pull weeds while he operates the riding mower? Why should you prepare, serve and clean up after each meal while everyone else sits around watching TV? You hope to earn love this way, but by now you know it doesn't work. What really happens is that you *lose* respect, and without respect you're likely to lose love as well.

In your sexual interactions, don't always be the one giving the massages or back rubs, submitting to whatever new variations your partner suggests or volunteering to do "Whatever makes you happy." Don't lie about what you like or don't like. You think you'll win your partner's love by cheerfully trying to please, but it will never happen if you lose your own dignity in the process.

The key to successful sex is *mutuality*—that means approximately a 50–50 split of doing what each partner prefers. If you're prone to dependency or codependency, you're probably in a 70–30 relationship—maybe even 95–5. You must regain the balance or you'll never really be in love. No one feels good about having their needs genuinely met only 10% of the time.

(4) Don't worry constantly about what will happen if your relationship ends. Otherwise you find yourself in the same situation as parents who *need* their children to *like* them. Kids sense this and swiftly become little monsters demanding that their parents do all kinds of special things for them, and nearly causing family bankruptcy each Christmas.

Insecurity is exploited by children and sexual partners as well. Be clear in your own thinking. Spend some time figuring out precisely what really like best, and then be appropriately assertive in asking for what you desire. If your partner tries to blackmail you by threatening to leave, show him or her the door. With the world's population currently over five billion and growing rapidly, there must several thousand other persons on planet earth who would be willing to engage you in a *mutual* relationship. If your current partner will only remain connected at the expense of your self fulfillment, it might be time to look elsewhere.

(5) Don't be oversensitive to criticism. If your lover criticizes you, begin thinking of criticism as "feedback," "his opinion," or "her preference," not as an absolutely valid statement about what you've done *wrong*. Try thinking of all negative statements from your partner as *subjectively—based feedback,* not reality. And don't make matters worse by agreeing or even by putting yourself down. Besides, self deprecation never wins any points with the other person anyway, it only solidifies their own egoism. Docility, clinging helplessness and the search for reassurance only makes you less attractive to others. No one wants to be in love with a clinging vine.

(6) If you persistently find yourself getting the short end of the stick, it may be a signal that you're enmeshed in dependency and codependency relationships. Sometimes some outside help from a therapist, friend or support group can assist you in achieving more equilateral relationships.

Taking Out the Trash

Dependent and codependent lovers are prone to believe sexual myths that are consistent with their personality styles. Dependents believe relationships with others are so precarious that you have to put in a lot of effort in order for them to work, and codependents believe that "I am here to make others happy." This kind of thinking makes them particularly vulnerable to certain sexual myths.

MYTH # 1: You can never love too much. It is in giving that we receive, and the more we give the greater our chances of receiving the love we need.

TRUTH: Dependent/codependent people "love" too much. The greatest counterfeit for love is dependence/co-dependency. What "I love you," really means in far too many cases is "I love the way you need me, it makes me feel important." Or, "I love the way I can depend on you, it makes me feel so cared for."

Many a young person has become intoxicated with the exhilarating chemistry of romanticized *dependency* masquerading as love. Sadly, these relationships—like castles of sand—seldom weather the inevitable squalls of daily living, leaving their occupants adrift on an ocean of bitterness and disappointment. If such couples stay together, it is often at immeasurable cost to someone's personhood.

Over the long haul, dependent or codependent relationships—like other master-slave or host-parasite relationships—are ultimately demeaning to both participants.

MYTH # 2: In marriage or a close sexual relationship, I will find the love I never got from Mom or Dad. Such a relationship can fill my emptiness and heal my hurt.

TRUTH: Marriage is a poor substitute for psychotherapy. What appear as "needs" early in a relationship typically grow into demands and disappointments later. It is difficult for individuals "in love" to distinguish between healthy needs and neurosis, but if either of you "needs" the other to "make up" for deficits, you ought to seek counseling.

Dependent and codependent lovers frequently seek, in their adult relationships, to fulfill the childhood dreams and wishes that were never realized. Consequently the partner is seen through the eyes of a child as "Earth Mother" or "Fulfilling Father." Such dependency-dominated dreams are doomed to fail because the child's grandiose wishes are seldom fulfilled by parents, and even less so by another adult in later life.

If you're dating someone who's looking for a parent substitute, refer her to a competent therapist, *before* you marry her! If your lover is looking for economic security, refer him to a financial planner, don't find yourself in the front of a church saying "For richer for poorer" in a codependent attempt to keep him out of bankruptcy.

MYTH # 3: If I say "No!" or if I insist that he use a condom, he won't date me again.

TRUTH: What so many guys have known for years, but dependent and codependent women have not always understood is that saying "No" usually increases a woman's attractiveness. She shows herself to be a person of self-sufficiency, character and one who has the self esteem to set boundaries on her own terms. The woman who is too "easy" is in danger of becoming just another "notch in his belt."

Even if your relationship exceeds the shallow cat-and-mouse game I've just described, a dependent or codependent lover is seldom as attractive as someone with a healthy sense of entitlement. Some of the allure and enchantment found in romantic love has to do with winning the other's heart. If the race is won before you're out of the starting gate, why bother to run? If she finds you in all ways perfect, why try to "court" her affection?

Beyond romantic considerations, managing your dependency/codependency can save your life because dependent or codependent lovers are more likely to risk contracting a sexually transmitted disease, including the deadly AIDS virus. The same is true of acquaintance rape, though I would hasten to add I am not saying that women who are raped are responsible for this tragedy or that they subtly "asked for it."

It's probably the case, however, that if a woman's dependency or codependency pushes her to compulsively please her partner, she is more likely to engage in unprotected sexual acts or find herself unable to stop an intrusive male's sexual advances.

MYTH # 4: All sexually normal women love to perform fellatio.

TRUTH: In the most carefully conducted sex survey to date (Michael, Gagnon, Laumann, & Kolata, 1994, pp 146-147), it was found that about 57% of women ages 18–44, and 31% of women ages 45–59, reported that giving oral sex was appealing. The point is this: you have a right to enjoy whatever you find pleasant, and—most importantly—to dislike what you dislike! When you plant flowers, no one forces you to plant tulip bulbs if you prefer roses. It ought to be the same in your bedroom. You have a right to be honest about what you really prefer.

You might creatively explore a wide variety of sexual activities, but finally you must be honest about what you prefer, even if this differs from your partner's favorites. If these differences are significant, it does *not* mean you're inhibited, prudish, or "frigid," and you must not allow your partner to define you in negative terms. It only means that people have differences in sexual tastes.

Should that really be surprising? Is there *anything* on which all people show agreement, except perhaps a desire for lower taxes or a smaller waistline? Everywhere we see diversity. Some musicians play Bach and spurn Springsteen, others love both. Some athletes excel in ping pong while others master the shot put. Collectors compile everything from stamps to Ferraris.

Guess what! People have differing tastes in sex as well, and your preference is as legitimate as the next person's. This is an area where honest communication, caring, and gentle exploration of new ideas may facilitate growth in new directions, but it's not something you should ever feel forced into.

Summary

There are numerous situations in which dependency on a powerful "other" arouses erotic feelings. Thus the female student may be dependently attracted to her male professor—at least while she's in his class, sitting at his feet learning; the office nurse is frequently attracted to her physician "boss," and Henry Kissinger—not particularly a handsome man—frequently could be seen dating ravishing women at the height of his political career. "Power," he observed, "is the ultimate aphrodisiac."

Often, however, in such situations, when the power fades, the eroticism tags along with it. Thus, if the young co-ed marries her middle-aged professor, she may find that when she gets him home things will change. When she actually lives with him, when she no longer sits at his feet as he soars about the classroom plying students with questions and dispensing wisdom, much of the magic may vanish.

Eroticism fueled by power differentials and dependency tends to be short-lived. Dependency may get you into bed with him, but once you're there, you are likely to discover that power, position or wealth are poor substitutes for psychological intimacy and intellectual mutuality.

This concludes our discussion of the dependent and codependent styles. In the next chapter we will examine a somewhat opposite style. The smooth (psychopathic) lover characterized by *overentitlement*. As we move from the *selfless* to the *selfish*, we will probably find ourselves looking over our shoulder from time to time and reminiscing with a bit of nostalgia about those people who were "too nice."

Chapter 4
Slick/
Manipulative
(Antisocial)
Lovers

"What do you mean, impersonal sex? *I love you very much Karen!"*

SLICK/MANIPULATIVE (Antisocial) LOVERS

When Charm Becomes Poison
or
"Tough Break, but That's How the Cookie Crumbles."

The term *antisocial* lover is a bit misleading. This is a person who is typically quite skilled in social relationships, but who uses these skills to exploit others. An expert salesperson—even a "con" artist—this is the kind of smooth-talking person who can "sell ice to Eskimos."

Sometimes, if his irritability and impulsiveness are severe, he might drift toward criminal activity, but often such a person succeeds in sales, politics, religion, or other endeavors where smooth talking is an asset. They exploit others while privately ridiculing them as "naive" for having trusted anyone. They enter personal relationships with the intent of finding out "what's in it for me."

In this chapter I use the term *slick* or *manipulative* lover to describe what is a *milder version* of the antisocial style (also called the psychopathic personality or sociopathic personality).

In childhood, some of these persons were involved in lying, stealing, truancy, fighting, vandalism or running away from home. In more extreme cases there may have been fire setting, as well as physical cruelty to people and animals. As adults this is slightly refined and typically appears as failure to keep promises, sexual promiscuity, inconsistent work history, harassing others, stealing or engaging in illegal occupations.

Antisocial behaviors often intensify during adolescence, heightened by the hormonal changes and drive for independence which most adolescents experience. Although the flagrant promiscuity, drug abuse and violence of adolescence and early adulthood often "mellow" with time, the lying, irresponsibility and lack of remorse often persist throughout life, making manipulative lovers an extremely poor bet at any stage.

Of all the different kinds of lovers discussed in this book, slick/manipulative lovers are the most hazardous. Their most ominous characteristic is the their *lack of remorse* about how their behavior hurts others. It is this callous, ruthless quality which makes them so destructive and so unresponsive to treatment.

In the previous chapters we've suggested ways that you can **R**ecognize a particular style, **R**eorganize your expectations and **R**evitalize your sexual relationship with a partner of that particular style. By contrast, in this chapter, I want to help you **R**ecognize the slick/manipulative lover, but instead of **R**eorganizing your thinking and **R**evitalizing your relationship, I will encourage you to **R**eject such a partner. *Avoiding* involvement with, or *disentangling* yourself from such lovers is the only healthy alternative.

The reason I'm so cynical about manipulative lovers is because their impaired capacity to sustain close, warm and responsible relationships with friends, family, or sexual partners makes it impossible to relate to them in a trusting way without being exploited. Their facile social skills combined with impulsivity and lack of guilt means that whenever the going gets difficult at home, they have someone else waiting in the wings with whom to pursue a self-gratifying sexual relationship. "A gal in every port" is the *modus operandi* they proudly proclaim.

Actions speak louder than words is an aphorism worth remembering when dealing with slick lovers. Such lovers are often charming and gifted in words and promises, they can be captivating conversationalists, but their *behavior* which is traitorous over time nullifies their words. This is the lover who sends you a dozen long-stem roses while having sex with your best friend. He knows how to "I love you" with flowers, with words or with exquisite sexual techniques, but *not* with consistently loyal behavior.

Words from manipulative lovers are like the checks they write, which often come back marked "insufficient funds." When a smooth lover says "I love you" beware! This really means "Trust me, so that I can exploit you for my own pleasure or purposes." When the slick lover uses words like love, marriage or trust, they have an entirely different meaning from what you've come to expect. Like bad checks, they aren't backed with cash and can never be trusted. A characteristic common to all manipulative people— whether violent criminals or ordinary "jerks"—is their glib use of words.

For slick lovers, life is a giant Scrabble game or crossword puzzle where words are carefully arranged to win points or fill in blank spaces, but where they have no larger meaning, and where their use is decided only by the needs of the moment.

We've previously noted that obsessive compulsive lovers are in many ways the opposite of histrionic lovers. Similarly, we'll come to see slick/manipulative lovers as opposite of dependent or codependent lovers. Whereas dependent lovers use their social skills in a passive way to please and ingratiate others, manipulative lovers are *independent* in their attitudes and use social skills to accumulate power over others so that they don't have to worry about pleasing anyone. Whereas dependent lovers trust others for support, manipulative lovers have learned to trust only themselves.

If manipulative lovers are highly irritable and impulsive, as many are, they gravitate toward criminal behaviors and are known as antisocial, sociopathic or psychopathic personalities. But, as with all sexual styles, it is important to be aware that these core characteristics—impulsiveness, lack of remorse, glibness with words—vary across an entire range of people and not all manipulative people engage in criminal behavior. In fact, in many highly competitive careers such as business, sales, law, politics or the military, such propensities may prove valuable in getting to the top.

Manipulative lovers look at the world as a place permeated with frustration and danger. They view others with distrust, and follow the not-so-golden rule: "Do unto others, before they do to you!" Trusting only in themselves, they have few loyalties and little remorse. *"C'est la vie"* is as close as they come to saying "I'm sorry."

Kirk

"There! I hope you learn your lesson! Maybe from now on you'll remember to lock up your pets when I tell you to!"

The harsh words hung heavy in the morning air and as eight-year-old Kirk watched Dad disappear into the house, the significance of what his father had done began to infiltrate his mind, inciting a riot of thoughts:

"What if Roy tells other kids at school?"

The thought of his brother telling others sickened him, because he knew Roy *would* tell. He never lost an opportunity to make himself look good by putting others down.

"What if Jimmy comes over to play ball?"

It was Sunday and although the appearance of his best friend usually filled him with excitement, today would be different—*awfully* different. He anticipated Jimmy's arrival with a sense of dread and excruciating shame.

"What if my cousins come over?" he wondered.

Jimmy's arrival was certain. It was Sunday, and they hadn't missed playing ball in months. He already knew what he'd say to Jimmy. The thought of his best friend seeing him like this was bad enough, but the possibility that his favorite uncle and family might see his humiliation was more than he could bear, and he began to cry.

It wasn't just the many thoughts reeling about his brain that made him nauseous, the sun was warm that July morning and the dead puppy hanging around his neck was beginning to smell.

"I'm sorry Pal!" he sobbed "I didn't mean to leave the gate open! I just forgot, Pal. I didn't mean to do it!"

The sight, smell, and feel of that dead animal so close to his body intensified his grief at losing his beloved pet, but his shame was so excruciating that it seemed to numb his feelings of remorse.

It was one of the last times Kirk remembers feeling strong emotions. Feelings of remorse, shame, and affection were gradually replaced with sadistic humor, callous bravado, and hypersexuality. Something happened to him that Sunday that changed him forever.

He'd been so proud of his new puppy. He'd already tried teaching Pal tricks, but all the excited young Cocker Spaniel would do was lick Kirk's face. Dad had said Kirk was too young to take care of a pet, but Mom had insisted. When Dad went out to collect his Sunday paper, he found Pal had been run over by a passing car. He checked the dog pen and found the gate open. Kirk had violated "rule number one" which was to always put the puppy back in the pen and latch the gate after playing with him.

The punishment of tying the puppy around Kirk's neck and making him wear it for a day was Dad's idea of how to "teach him a lesson he won't forget."

And remember he did! Years later, when we were in high school together, Kirk remembered that day as the worst in his life and viewed his father as a "loony tune." "I hate the bastard!" Kirk told me, "he taught me never to trust anyone. Pretty good lesson eh?"

Kirk saw that Sunday as a turning-point in his life. He even referred to his life in terms of BP and AP (Before Puppy, After Puppy) stating "My old man really fucked up my mind that day. I was never the same after that."

But it didn't really begin (or end) with the puppy incident. What is more important than understanding a single traumatic incident in a child's life is understanding the *daily* context in which such incidents take place.

Imagine the *chronic* trauma, the day-by-day experiences of living with the kind of father who would "teach you a lesson" by tying a dead pet around your neck. This had a far greater effect on Kirk's life than the puppy incident. The way his father related to him when his puppy died, was the tip of the iceberg.

Kirk's father was an alcoholic who was out of work more often than he was employed. When he did work, he typically stopped at the bar after punching out, and several hours later arrived home drunk. Whenever Kirk and Roy saw their drunken father staggering up the driveway, they would get out of his sight as quickly as possible, either retreating to their rooms or playing with neighbors. Both boys were frequently (and *unpredictably* beaten). The violence itself would have been traumatic enough, but it was unrelated to their behavior in any logical fashion. Rather, it was related to how much their father had been drinking.

In such an unpredictable but emotionally intense environment, Kirk began to resort to violence as a way of getting rid of his own inner turmoil. This in turn created an "aura" which accompanied him everywhere. Kirk became known as a "fighter." For example, when playing ball, if he were tagged out on a close play sliding into home, he would typically come up with his fists swinging.

His positive feelings were limited to impulsive actions of self gratification, rather than genuine emotions of caring for others. By the time he was twelve, he was sexually active, seeking to "score" at every opportunity and bragging about his exploits to other boys.

I was well acquainted with Kirk because he grew up in our community and we attended the same schools—until he dropped out that is. The local law enforcement officials were also well acquainted with Kirk and his family. His father had served time for repeated drunk driving offenses, theft, drunk and disorderly conduct and—of course—domestic violence. He was more of a community nuisance however, than a serious criminal. On several occasions neighbors summoned police to quell domestic violence at Kevin's home and although his father often abused his wife when intoxicated, she never pressed charges or even called the police, fearing it would just "make things worse."

By adolescence, Kirk seldom went into a store without shoplifting. He bragged about all the things he owned thanks to his "five-finger-discount." But although his father drank excessively, Kirk wasn't ever in dire financial straits because his mom worked two jobs and used her earnings for food and basic family necessities. Thus, when Kirk shoplifted even minor items—candy, gum, or a water pistol—it seemed he did it more for excitement than out of necessity.

He lacked conscience, stealing bills and change from the local Catholic church's poor box as well as rummaging through the Salvation Army clothes drop for anything that might catch his fancy. Even more remarkable than his stealing, was the aplomb with which he carried it out.

Kirk was always "cool" and on several occasions when caught "red handed" was able to concoct such a convincing story about his "Mother's illness," that the store manager allowed him to go free without prosecuting him—on one occasion even "donating" the stolen items to his "hungry" mother. This of course delighted Kirk beyond imagining, because he had really "fooled" the manager. There wasn't even a tinge of guilt for his own behavior or appreciation for the manager's kindness.

When a tornado devastated a well-to-do neighborhood in a nearby town, Kirk went at night to see what he could find. He reasoned that if he were the first to find some bodies in the ruins, he might be able to remove their wallets, jewelry or other valuables. He returned early the next morning with his "loot"—several items of jewelry and some cash—bragging about how he'd found these bodies and struck it rich. We later found out that no one had been killed, though damage to homes had been severe. Kirk had actually looted several homes under cover of darkness but had exaggerated his story for our benefit.

We'd grown to expect this however because Kirk almost never told the truth. Even when it would not have caused him any discomfort or inconvenience to have been honest, he delighted in exaggerating. Not surprisingly, it was usually in the service of enhancing his image. Of course if he were "in a pinch," he prided himself on being able to lie his way out. He boasted about how many traffic tickets he'd been able to talk his way out of.

After junior high, Kirk began failing most of his subjects in school because he goofed off instead of studying. He was truant much of the time. He contended that "school is only necessary if you're not smart to start with," and he practiced what he preached. He was handsome, charming and gifted with words, and he used his verbal abilities and quick wit to con the people he interacted with.

Once for example, while employed at a local gas station, he decided he wanted the week end off, even though he was scheduled to work. At the time, he was engaged to a local girl who was very fond of him and planning their summer wedding. Kirk wanted the time off in order to travel North to consort with one of his many girlfriends "on the side." He always had "extra" girls because, as he put it, "You can't put all your eggs (or sperm) in one basket!"

On this particular occasion, he told his shift manager that his mother had suddenly been hospitalized with a heart attack and that he needed to visit her in the hospital. Her condition, he said, was very serious. He told his boss that the doctors had phoned saying they didn't know if she was going to pull through. Of course his boss let him take the week end off.

Kirk laughingly told me that he worked for a "stupid boss," that "even a retard could outfox him!" That's what seemed to drive Kirk's life, the desire to outwit or outsmart others. For him all relationships were a contest to make certain that you were always in a position to take advantage of others and not vice versa. The "golden rule" of his life was "Do unto others, before they do to you."

A corollary to this rule was "Do it *now*, tomorrow may never come." "A bird in the hand is worth two in the bush." Since his fiance didn't believe in "putting out" unless you were married and Kirk had no intentions of denying himself sexual gratification, he simply lied to his boss and had a "hot weekend" with one of his "babes up north."

It's not difficult to see how Kirk's impulse—ridden pessimism grew out of his chaotic childhood. With his father's cruel and capricious punishments, it became impossible to live with the emotions these experiences generated. This was most obvious in the puppy incident—how does an eight-year-old deal with intense feelings of grief, shame, and anger, while being banished from his family?…much like Kirk did, by turning off feelings, building up bravado and not counting on emotional support from anyone. The puppy incident was only an extreme version of what occurred routinely. Almost daily there was some kind of emotionally-intense conflict involving his father. Either he witnessed his father and mother quarreling, heard Roy being beaten, or received physical or verbal abuse himself.

During his adolescence Kirk was involved with authorities almost on a daily basis. Lying, stealing, truancy, vandalism and fighting characterized his experiences at school and in the community, bringing him almost constant contact with police, principals and other officials. After the puppy incident, he engaged in cruelty to animals on several occasions. Usually these were just minor incidents such as chasing or teasing neighbor's pets, but once he set a neighbor's cat on fire. The irate owners pressed charges and Kirk had to spend a weekend in the county jail, but as was typical for him, he made himself a kind of celebrity among the neighborhood boys who disliked cats and the effect of the "punishment" was only to draw attention to his exploits.

Kirk's psychopathic style began to escalate during the high school years. His stealing became more serious with drug trafficking and car theft replacing shoplifting. Still a great "talker," Kirk was *initially* able to convince almost anyone of almost anything. But now the more serious nature of his crimes began to catch up with him. For example he date raped a fifteen-year-old, who reported him. When police arrested him for the alleged rape, he was driving a stolen automobile.

He spent three years in the state prison, in what turned out to be a kind of criminal "apprenticeship." When he got out he was much more "savvy" and determined not to do any more time. He married Sandy, a girl he'd met while in prison and as a "unique wedding gift" he had "Kirk and Sandy" tattooed on his buttocks. He was proud of the way the tattooist had evenly divided the words between the two sides of his buttocks.

The tattoo was obsolete almost before it had dried, because his marriage to Sandy lasted only a few months (since she was *not* codependent). Upon returning from their honeymoon, he bragged to his buddies that he'd "scored" with some "hot broads" he'd met in the Caribbean. He went on at length about the white sandy beaches, easily available drugs, tax-free liquor and the like, never even mentioning Sandy or how he felt about being married. He seemed intent only on impressing us with how slick he'd been...how he'd "banged this native broad" in the motel room across the hall after he'd satisfied Sandy and she'd fallen asleep. The idea of taking his marriage vows seriously seemed utterly foreign to Kirk.

It wasn't that he didn't know that one wasn't supposed to sleep around, it was rather that he seemed always drawn to excitement and affairs provided him more of the "forbidden fruit" stimulation than sex within a committed relationship. His pattern was to vigorously pursue sexual affairs with either young teenagers or wives of prominent community professionals— both of which provided "danger" and excitement but no real prospects for marriage.

He loved to brag that he was "screwing the police chief's wife," etc. We could never be certain how much was his usual exaggeration and how much was truth, but he apparently got seriously enough involved with several married women that he had to leave the state to avoid bodily harm at the hands of an enraged spouse. After things cooled off however, Kirk always returned to continue the same pattern.

I never saw Kirk professionally. Like most antisocial people he felt no need for treatment, and the only therapy he ever received was while incarcerated. In prison he was required to participate in group therapy sessions, which he sarcastically dubbed "bullshitting time."

Clinicians use the following guidelines to decide whether children or adolescents are at risk for becoming manipulative adults. Have a history of at least *three* of the following:

1. was often truant
2. ran away from home overnight at least twice while living in parental or parental surrogate home
3. often initiated physical fights
4. used a weapon in more than one fight
5. forced someone into sexual activity with him or her
6. was physically cruel to animals
7. was physically cruel to other people
8. deliberately destroyed others' property
9. deliberately set fires
10. often lied
11. has stolen without confronting a victim on more than one occasion (e.g., shoplifting, forgery, etc.)
12. has stolen with confronting a victim (e.g., purse snatching, mugging, armed robbery)

In adult life, the following guidelines are used to diagnose antisocial personalities. At least *four* of the following:

(1) unable to sustain consistent work as indicated by (a) repeated absences from work unexplained by illness in self or family, (b) abandonment of several jobs without realistic plans for others, (c) unemployment for six months or more within five years when work was available.

(2) fails to conform to social norms of lawful behavior by e.g., destroying

property, stealing, harassing others, or pursuing an illegal occupation (whether arrested or not)

(3) is irritable and aggressive as indicated by repeated fights or assaults, including spouse or child abuse

(4) repeatedly fails to honor financial obligations as indicated by defaulting on loans, child support, etc.

(5) fails to plan ahead or is impulsive as indicated by (a) traveling from place to place without a prearranged job or clear goal, (b) lack of a fixed address

(6) shows no regard for truth as indicated by repeated lying, use of aliases, or "conning" others for personal profit or pleasure

(7) reckless in matters of safety as indicated by numerous speeding tickets, driving while drunk, etc.

(8) fails to function adequately as a parent or guardian as indicated by one or more of the following:

(a) malnutrition of child

(b) child's illness resulting from lack of hygiene

(c) failure to obtain adequate medical care for a seriously ill child

(d) child depends on neighbors or nonresident relatives for food or shelter

(e) failure to arrange for caretaker for a young child while parent is away from home

(f) repeated squandering money required for household necessities

(9) has never sustained a totally monogamous relationship for more than a year

(10) lacks remorse, even feels justified for having hurt, mistreated or stolen from another person.

Such list of problem *behaviors* looks like a probation officer's check list, but it is more important that you keep in mind the core *personality style* of the slick lover. Such lovers can be violently cruel, often cunning, usually contemptuous of authority, they're almost always impulsive, restless, and remorseless

Needless to say, such people are not good partners in any kind of long-term relationship whether it involves business, recreation, education, or sex. Since they seek only immediate, short-term gain and consequently, although they might seem initially charming, they soon wear out the patience of any who try to maintain long-term ties with them.

Living in a ten-minute time frame is how the smooth lover exists. Envision living your life in a ten minute window of time. What happens to your world? Suddenly, you have no future goals—nothing beyond getting out of the store with this stolen merchandise, hitting on that chick who's waiting tables, or using this stolen credit card without getting caught. Long-term goals such as graduating from college, rearing a family, writing a novel, or developing a successful business, are simply not high on your agenda, because they take too long to accomplish.

Living in the "now" becomes your dominant mode of functioning, transforming your reality into a moment-by-moment milieu where all events are treated as separate and unrelated and primary emphasis is on the immediate. "Don't cry over spilled milk," portrays your view of history, while "A bird in the hand is worth two in the bush," embodies your vision of how to plan for the future. This is why a slick lover's behavior is typically disjointed and destructive *over the long run,* but appears highly competent and efficient in the *immediate* sense.

If someone looks good, why not try to hit on her *now?* The question of how this might affect my marriage is irrelevant because it takes me too far into the future. If I want to buy something I can use plastic, and if my credit cards are at their limit, I can use someone else's or write a check. If it bounces (as I know it will) I'll deal with that *later*—in the distant future.

Living this way generates chaos for long-term relationships such as marriage, work, or education. Nonetheless, if you only had only ten minutes to live, this lifestyle might make sense. Grab it *now* because it won't be there later.

First Impressions. For slick lovers, the *initial impression is paramount.* It in their first impression that slick/manipulative lovers look best. They know how to play the dating game and will shower you with perfume, flowers, and other attentions that will make you feel like a very loved woman. Far from appearing maladjusted, they seem just the opposite. Manipulative lovers can be downright impressive *initially.*

Slick lovers may not wear well over time, but their first impression is often superb because they typically experience *little anxiety,* and thus appear poised and confident. Hysterics are highly emotional, often "losing it," and making a "dizzy" impression; obsessive-compulsives' rigid efforts to control anxiety through uncompromising orderliness or rigid rituals make them appear stiff; and dependent or codependent persons try so hard to be "nice" that they appear insecure. Manipulative lovers, however appear calm, relaxed, and well adjusted.

Cleckly, a leading authority on antisocial persons, has described them in the following words:

"We find extraordinary poise rather than jitteriness or worry, a smooth sense of physical well-being instead of uneasy preoccupations with bodily functions. Even under concrete circumstances that would for the ordinary person cause embarrassment, confusion, acute insecurity or visible agitation, his relative serenity is likely to be noteworthy (1976, p. 340).

Cultural factors. In many respects our culture is fascinated with manipulation—when it is successful. We admire individuals who get to the top, sometimes with little thought for whom they stepped on to get there. "Rags-to-riches" stories inspire us and we are sometimes not very critical regarding how the riches were earned. Donald Trump made it, and so what if he cut a few corners along the way? Business is business. Politicians rely on multiple special interest groups in order to get elected, and reelected, so it's axiomatic that they talk out of "both sides of their mouths," on many occasions. The ability to lie glibly, keep one's cool in an argument, and never admit error, characterizes politicians as well as sociopaths. Presidents Nixon and Reagan conveniently "forgot details" when it has suited their purposes, and Clinton smoked an occasional joint but didn't inhale—sure.

The kinds of movies that achieve popularity at the box office are an indicator of the kinds of lives people identify with. We tend to be fascinated with the private lives of those with whom we aspire to identify. Movies about street people, like *Ironweed,* never become blockbusters, in spite of excellent acting by such actors as Meryl Streep and Jack Nicholson. On the other hand, movies of the *Godfather* genre, which glamorize *successful antisocial persons,* even when they are violent, do very well.

The quick-draw, keep-your-cool, gunslinging hero of the TV western fascinated viewers for decades, and I hardly think it was because moral goodness was being portrayed. With some significant exceptions, such as *Little House,* most westerns gave a lot of screen time to antisocial cowboys.

We identify with success, and are not always discerning of how our heroes/heroines advance to the top. Whether they are religious (e.g., Jimmy Swaggert, or the Bakkers), business moguls (e.g., Donald Trump,

Ivan Boskey), or successful politicians (almost anyone who spends more than a million dollars to get elected), we tend to be very forgiving of white-collar, professional smoothies. We are less forgiving, but nonetheless fascinated with "successful" serial murderers as well. Ted Bundy, for example, was a media sensation.

In summary, there seem to be many in our culture who admire those who believe "All's fair in love and war," "Business is business," "Finders keepers losers weepers," or "It's just politics,"—just so long as the person being guided by such smooth proverbs is *successful!* We *expect* our politicians to lie, our movie stars to be involved in numerous superficial sexual relationships, and business persons to live by the "bottom line." They seldom disappoint us.

Words and emotions are loosely coupled for the slick lover. "So what's the problem?" you might ask, "What's wrong with not getting flustered?" There's nothing wrong with serenity, calmness, or poise, of course; but in the case of the manipulative lover it is a *symptom* that all is not well. It results from the lack of a normal connection between feelings and words. For the slick lover the relationship between words and emotions is peculiar. For them words are like chess pieces in the game of life. They know how words affect others and use them to manipulate emotions in others. In their own experience however, the normal *close coupling* between *words* and *emotions* is absent. Thus, the antisocial lover *intellectually knows* that telling someone "I love you very much," is an emotionally-potent communication and he will use it when it suits his purposes, much as he might use a queen on a chess board. But for him, the words do not express an emotional reality, they are *only words!*

Lack of sufficient feelings characterizes the antisocial lover. He *says words* much like he *writes checks;* and like his checks, which often bounce because of lack of sufficient funds, his words are equally empty because of lack of sufficient feelings. This allows him to manipulate others, almost at will, because the ordinary person *assumes* a connection between words and emotions and is not likely to worry that the words will "bounce" for lack of emotions.

In recent years most businesses that accept credit cards instantly check your line of credit before accepting your card in payment. If this were possible in the world of emotions, antisocial persons would not be nearly as successful in conning others, because nearly always their "Emotional Visa" would be rejected as having exceeded their "line of credit."

These inner "principles"—glib use of words and emphasis on the instantaneous—are at the core of much that we call the slick/manipulative style. Emotions are connected with thoughts are only loosely, if at all. Hence, there is very little "balance of power," and emotions tend to be primitively experienced and only crudely contained. Antisocial thinking is insufficiently nuanced by forethought or consideration of consequences; nor is it appreciably influenced by anxiety, shame, or punishment. Consequently it functions primarily in the service of obtaining immediate gratification. Childhood experience has taught the antisocial lover not to count on tomorrow.

Using others is how the antisocial lover relates. Since he lives in the "now," seeking instant gratification, it should not be surprising that his relationships with other people also serve the same purpose. People, like paper plates or plastic cups, are disposable; to be used and discarded. Words are used to shape the other person for the function you need, and once they've "served their purpose," you're on to someone else. As Jack put it, after breaking up with his girlfriend:

"I was really down when she left. I thought I couldn't go on living. The next day, you wouldn't believe it. I met Rachel and, well, that was it. My life was complete again (Wishnie, 1976, p. 54)."

For smooth lovers, people are like car parts—interchangeable. Once an oil filter has done its job, you simply pull it off, put on another, unused one, and you're ready to go. You don't shed tears over the loss of the old, or spend time admiring the new. An oil filter is an oil filter. There may be some slight variations, but in general one's as good as the next, and your auto parts person can tell you which ones are interchangeable. People, for the smooth lover, are like oil filters—pretty much interchangeable.

Tin Men. This view of others permeates antisocial persons of all varieties. In milder, antisocial persons, it often takes the form of seeing other individuals as a "potential sale." This was entertainingly, but accurately portrayed in the movie *Tin Men,* in which Richard Dreyfus and Danny DeVito portrayed two men who sold aluminum siding by whatever means they could concoct to whomever they could sucker into buying. One of my favorite scenes in the movie is where Richard Dreyfus negotiates to buy a car. Here, eyeball to eyeball we see two con artists at work, each using all the skills at his disposal to outmaneuver the other:

Dreyfus: "Hey, let's skip all the bullshit and just talk straight—no games, OK?"

Salesman: "Sure, how much do you want to pay for a car?"

Dreyfus: "See, there, you're doing it! What do you mean? 'How much do I want to pay for a car?'"

Salesman: "Yeah, just tell me what you want to pay for a car."

Dreyfus: "OK, I'll tell you how much I want to pay for a car, I want to pay two dollars! Yeah, two dollars, that's how much I want to pay!"

I'm certain that many salesman, politicians, and even preachers have wide streaks of the manipulative style in their makeup. Anyone who is engaged in a business that requires him to present a questionable product in a favorable light, or an over-priced product as a bargain, assumes an antisocial posture *vis a vis* others. In such interactions the target person becomes for the antisocial person a "life insurance policy," a "convert," a "vote," or the like. And in each case the smooth salesman makes use of his talent with words to say whatever the potential customer wants to hear.

In violent or criminal cases, although the target person experiences consequences much more serious than simply buying overpriced aluminum siding or unwanted life insurance, the *depersonalization* of the victim by the perpetrator is similar to what we've seen in milder cases.

Bruce described a random shooting of strangers:

"I was standing there in the woods shooting at cans when this truck drove by, with a group of men in the back. I thought, wow, I wonder if I can hit one. I just picked up the rifle and *blewee,* that guy jumped. I read in the paper that he had been shot in the shoulder (Wishnie, 1977, p. 54)."

When questioned how he felt about it, Bruce failed to comprehend that the "it" the psychiatrist was interested in was the other *person,* not the gun.

"Well, you know, that gun really felt great, you know, against my shoulder. It had great balance, it had this special walnut stock—"

"No, No! What about that man? What about his being shot?"

"Oh, that, nothing special."

This distancing from the victim occurs along the entire spectrum of the manipulative style from the used car salesman who knowingly sells the customer a car with a bad transmission to the most violent forms of criminal behavior.

"Contemptuous delight" is how one writer describes the antisocial's sense of pride in "putting one over" on someone else. Recall how proud Kirk was upon returning with his loot from the tornado-devastated town. A similar dynamic operates in petty crimes such as shoplifting, or even in the glib exaggerations and inconsequential lying of the milder antisocial persons. The boy who lies about how many home runs he hit during the ball game after school is bolstering his sagging self esteem (for having struck out each time at bat) by exaggerating his prowess and simultaneously deceiving the listener. This same attempt to restore pride in oneself, to bolster the grandiose self, is present in the most violent antisocial persons as well.

Albert DeSalvo, the Boston strangler, recounted a family New Year's Eve party in the following words:

"Well, I find out one of my sisters is taking judo to protect herself—against the Strangler! She and her friends, they all get together and they're taking lessons at a gym. I says, 'Sure you can handle the Strangler if you get him?' She says, 'Oh, I'm pretty well prepared; for him,' I says, 'What would you do if he got you in this hold?' And before she knew it I had her in that hold. She could do nothing. She says, 'Well, I'm learning.'"

He looked up with his boyish grin, "Her husband has eleven sisters, all beautiful—fabulous! I tried to make all eleven of them (Frank, 1966, p. 296)."

In addition to his concealing his identity as a criminal, DeSalvo's bragging that he tried to make it with all eleven of his brother-in-law's "fabulous" sisters is reminiscent of how Kirk used to exult to us of his sexual exploits, and of his braggadocio upon returning with his "tornado loot." Both Kirk and the strangler were bolstering a grandiose sense of self which upon closer scrutiny would be seen to be extremely fragile.

"Son of Sam" showed the same kind of "I'm-putting-one-over-on-you!" attitude as reported in Abrahamsen's (1985) account of David Berkowitz, the serial killer:

He never aroused any suspicion. At the Post Office, for instance, where his co-workers often discussed Son of Sam and whether or not he was insane, Berkowitz never told them Son of Sam was insane. "I was only a casual listener. Sometimes I asked, 'What do you think of this guy? Is he crazy or what?'" With a triumphant voice he added, "Nobody really figured out that I was Son of Sam."

He played his double role with incredible coolness: "I would walk into work at the Post Office one day after a shooting. I would see the faces of confusion and fear. Then I would say 'What happened? Gee, that's too bad. I hope they catch the bastard (p. 189)."

"Don't Blame Me!" is commonly heard from the mouths of antisocial persons of all varieties. They pass blame on to others with as little thought as normal people pass bread and butter at the supper table. Again, this serves to protect the fragile yet grandiose self, by alleging that *all* faults lie outside oneself. Recall that the obsessive-compulsives avoid being wrong by not making decisions, hysterics by rapidly changing their minds if necessary, and dependents by relying on others to decide; however the antisocial person avoids being wrong by blaming others—quickly, easily. This is pervasive among antisocial persons, but is most repugnant to ordinary persons when it involves violence:

"One patient explained his theft of a tape recorder as being the owner's fault because the owner did not have it securely bolted to the cabinet. Another man explained his shooting of a robbery victim as the victim's fault: 'He made it happen. It was his fault. He saw I had a gun. He shouldn't have come at me (Wishnie, 1977, p 119).'"

Reducing the pain. Such outrageous behavior as the shooting of strangers is repulsive to most of us, but it is only an more extreme version of the antisocial process we saw earlier in Kirk. The smooth style develops in response to experiences which are too painful to endure without the assistance of a soothing parent. The resultant turning off emotions, functions to protect the fragile self with an exterior shell of "I don't give a damn!" This originates to protect the self, but results in a lifelong lack of empathy.

Aggression without empathy is what makes antisocial rage so frightening. It may seem strange to speak of anger and empathy in the same breath, but for normal people, even anger is empathically anchored. Most of us become angry—we call it "righteous indignation"—if we witness the physical or emotional abuse of another. We also become angry when we have been shamed or embarrassed, especially if we perceive it to have been intentionally induced. In all such instances, however, our anger is closely linked to emotions. Not so with the antisocial person. Since they lack empathy (the ability to identify with the plight of another) they are not "moved" by witnessing the abuse of others. And of course this is why they are able to inflict abuse in a calm, cold, predatory fashion.

The difference between psychopathic aggression and normal anger is like the difference between a cat calmly, quietly stalking a bird and two tomcats engaged in a fight. The first instance is a predatory aggression, the second is emotionally triggered. The aggression seen in antisocial person is generally of the first variety. They sometimes "lose their cool," but for the most part they are distinguished by their predatory aggression and their complete lack of empathy for their victims:

"Two youths robbed a woman of ten dollars near her apartment. She put up no resistance, and, almost as an afterthought, one of the young men had her kneel down and shot her in the back of the head with his .22 caliber 'Saturday night special.' When arrested and questioned, he freely admitted his act, saying only that he 'felt like it. It was no big deal (Meloy, 1988, pp. 233,234).'"

It is such "callous" detachment which makes antisocial crimes particularly heinous to normal persons. The total lack of regard for the victim reaches its zenith with antisocial personalities.

Antisocial style probably begins during the earliest hours of neonatal life, because of the unavailability of consistently nurturant, soothing parents. We've stated several times the antisocially-bound young child "turns off" emotions because they are too painful to bear. Although this is indeed part of the developmental process, it probably begins during neonatal life as a failure to attach to parents or parent surrogates.

Antisocial style is a failure of internalization. Missing in the psyche is the deep, unconscious, *identification* with the primary parents. Subsequently, the sense of identity and *empathy* with other persons *fails to develop from the earliest moments of life.*

At the heart of antisocial style and related disorders of diminished feelings for others, is the *lack of empathy.* Empathy is the bedrock upon which all genuine psychological concern rests. It is the basis for ethics, justice, social concern and other such social concerns which form the very fabric of civilization as we know it. The "Golden Rule" enjoining us to "Do unto others, as you would have them do unto you" assumes an *empathic capacity* on the part of the "doer" to identify with and understand "others." If this vital component of emotional life is diminished or missing, we see the parody of personhood known as the psychopath. Virtually all of the psychopath's problems derive from this lack of capacity to genuinely feel another's emotions.

Although Kirk traced his problems to the "puppy incident," I suspect they began during the earliest hours of his life. He was born on a Tuesday and his mother returned to work the following Monday, leaving his thirteen-year-old sister in charge of his care. It was impossible for Kirk to *identify* with his abusive, alcoholic father and his mother worked such long hours, that when she was home, she was too exhausted to be emotionally available. Kirk grew up in the care of his teen-aged sister who resented him, wishing instead she could have been with her friends. Consequently, at multiple levels, Kirk got the message: "Don't attach to me, I don't have time for you."

Likewise, Mark, a smooth janitor/gigolo, also experienced violent parenting. His father would slap him and throw him on the floor or against the wall if he cried too much as a toddler. He was often hit in the head, choked or locked in a tiny, dark closet for punishment throughout the early school years. Such experiences obviously do not foster the development of empathy.

The making of a Boston Strangler is not much different, except that the beatings may have been more severe and the environment was also permeated with sexuality:

"'My father,' DeSalvo spoke dully. 'We used to have to stand in front of him, my brother Frank and me, every night and be beaten with this belt. I can still to this very moment tell you the color of the belt and just how long it was—two inches by 36—a belt with a big buckle on it. We used to stand in front of him every night and get beaten with that damn thing—every night, whether we did anything wrong or not. We were only in the fourth or fifth grade...

My father used to go around with prostitutes in front of us (Frank, 1966, pp. 316,317).'"

Life Style. It hardly needs stating that of all the styles discussed in this book, the antisocial style leaves the widest swath of destruction. This is not only the case in crimes where victims are murdered, having been profoundly violated before, during and after the killing, but in lesser cases as well. Antisocial lovers of even the mildest sort violate trust, family boundaries, decency, and truth; and thus contribute to society's downward slide.

They do this in numerous ways but probably the most significant is in contributing to the dissolution of family structures, and ultimately society.

Most of the people you know are not such severe cases of antisocial style as Kirk and they're certainly not Boston stranglers or Son of Sam serial killers. Yet, you'll find some of the same characteristics in a much milder form in some of your ordinary co workers or friends. The slick impulsiveness, a failure to learn from experience, repeated affairs, lack of remorse, the manipulative use of words without the intention to follow through, and the callous disregard for the feelings of others, are all too common in today's society. The manipulative style is much more common in males, but the basic characteristics are also found in females such as Roberta.

Roberta

"Bobbie" had been named after her father, but she was unappreciated by him from the day of her birth because she was "the wrong sex." Her parents had always wanted a boy-and-girl family, so when Bobbie was born she was a disappointment to them both, but especially to her father. Having grown up with three sisters—"surrounded by women" was how he put it—he intensely desired a son and was extremely disappointed when Bobbie was born female.

She must have sensed this and tried to win his approval by being "Daddy's helper." She faithfully followed him about the yard and assisted him when he did such "man's work" as tuning engines or rebuilding transmissions. Dad was a mechanic by trade and part-owner of a local garage. Additionally he took on a lot of side jobs. Their driveway always looked like an elongated used car lot. Thus while her sister was learning to bake bread, sew, and "look pretty," Bobbie was watching Dad overhaul engines and learning to rebuild lawn mowers.

What young Bobbie didn't realize was that Daddy's "garage" was really a chop shop where stolen cars were disassembled and their parts sold to black market dealers in other states. When she was seven, he began a prison sentence and was never heard from again. From that time on, their family life drifted downward. They moved to a small apartment and Bobbie's mother began to engage in prostitution in order to support the family, frequently bringing her customers home to the apartment.

As she sat in my office telling me of her past, Bobbie's pain was palpable as tears mixed with childhood memories:

"Most nights I remember crying and covering my head with a pillow in order to muffle the sound of men with my mother. I wanted to go in there and make them stop hurting my mother, but we had been strictly forbidden to go near her room when she was 'occupied.' Sometimes they actually beat her, because I remember seeing bruises on her body, but I know now that what I heard most of the time, was the sound of sex penetrating the thin walls of the bedroom.

I didn't know what to do with my feelings. It was terribly confusing, because I thought they were hurting my Mom, but I knew from a very early age that these 'nice men,' as Mom referred to them, were paying the rent and putting food on our table."

By ten, Bobbie was stealing to supply her own needs and to supplement the family's income. At thirteen she started doing and dealing drugs. Soon thereafter she began following her mother's example by using sex to provide some of the things she wanted. She didn't formally engage in prostitution, but promised boys she'd sleep with them in exchange for various gifts, which might include boom boxes, jewelry, TVs, and other substantial items.

When one considers the pain-filled nights Bobbie endured, as a young child and again during her own adolescent prostitution, it is little wonder that she dropped out of school and became increasingly involved with drugs.

Children who experience such turmoil, unassisted by a soothing parent, seldom develop the capacity for tolerating or enduring unpleasant emotions. Understandably they are at risk for seeking "chemically-assisted" (alcohol, drugs) solutions which bring about predictable, and immediate mood alterations.

In more intact families, one or both of the parents are emotionally available—from the first weeks of life—to soothe, comfort and explain during times of emotional arousal. Such interactions become "internalized" as the person's own, enabling them to manage their moods without chemistry and significantly reducing the risk of either drug abuse or psychopathic turning off emotions. Bobbie, however, wasn't so fortunate.

When she first came to my office, she was taking so many Tylenol with codeine (up to 50/day), that her blood was not clotting properly. When she would bump herself, she would have huge black and blue spots where internal bleeding had occurred which would linger for weeks. Not only was she addicted to codeine, she was in the midst of her sixth divorce.

She didn't come for help with her addiction, nor to save her marriage, but because her lawyer thought it would go better in court if she put in a few marriage counseling sessions. I sensed in her a deep emptiness, an absence of genuine feelings. In spite of the appalling circumstances of her childhood (or, more correctly, *because* of them) she seemed devoid of any real internal "pain." What little remained, she diluted with codeine.

Usually it is psychological pain that motivates people to seek help, to enter and to remain in psychotherapy for the extended period of time it takes to work through such problems. Bobbie, however, was essentially free of anxiety, reported seldom feeling depressed, and communicated a kind of "street savvy" about "doing what you gotta do."

Although she spoke surprisingly well during her sessions, her words weren't accompanied by appropriate feelings. They didn't "ring true." She *talked* about feeling sad, but her face didn't reflect her stated sorrow. Although she *spoke* of anger, remorse, sadness, or even love, her facial expressions changed little. Her emotional life was exceedingly sparse and her words, for the most part, just words. Consequently, it came as no surprise when after three sessions she failed to keep any further appointments.

RECOGNIZING Manipulative/Slick Styles in Ordinary People

Kevin and Roberta may seem like extreme cases, but one often sees echoes of them in the lives of more ordinary people. Even mildly antisocial people cause emotional pain, while seeming oblivious to the suffering they bring about in others. They experience little or no remorse and appear callous to the distress of others. However we've seen in both Kevin and Roberta, that their emotional numbness was rooted in the unbearable feelings they had experienced in childhood.

What we see in ordinary smooth lovers, is not complete numbness or compulsive lying, but a milder version of that tendency. They may not lie outright, but will put a "spin" on the truth. They may hold a legal job, and be in a long term marriage, but this is only because their spouse is moderately codependent and has forgiven them for several "minor" affairs. But like the more severe smoothies, they still impress you as "slick." They exaggerate the truth to aggrandize themselves and are constantly concerned with manipulating others, even if this is in a legal business. Thus, the mild smoothie is likely to be in the five-million-dollar club for his insurance or real estate company. He may have "fast talked" his more gullible clients into insurance coverage they didn't really need, but he is proud of his sales ability. He doesn't really consider how this affects the clients' family finances, only his own. His interest in others is propelled by sales goals, not by a genuine concern for what the buyer needs.

Slick/Manipulative Sexual Styles in Ordinary People

Mark and Amy

Mark and Amy were an ordinary couple, the kind that could easily live just down the street from you or next door. They weren't having severe marriage problems, but Amy stated that their marriage was "going nowhere."

"We have a two-year-old," she told me, "and I want him to have a better childhood than I did." What I remember most about their first visit was Mark's mellow baritone voice and the velvet-smooth way in which he ended nearly every other sentence with a respectful "Doctor."

"I've told you all I can think of that might be of help *doctor,* but if there's anything I need to work on, *doctor,* I hope you'll point it out to me, because I really do love Amy, (putting his arm around her) and I think we both want this to work out."

And, near the end of the session:

"*Doctor* Berecz, I want you to know how much we appreciate your help. Now do you want us to pay you today, or do you bill monthly *doctor?*"

I didn't mind the title or the respect, but it was a bit much. It reminded me of the way telemarketing salespersons try to use your name in each sentence:

"*Mr. Berecz,* I'm sure you'll want to resubscribe to *Time* magazine at our new special rates. May I call you *John?*...Have you heard, *John,* that we have a special discount for professional waiting rooms? Now, would you prefer the special three-year rate, *John,* or do you want to re-order for a year? Think about it *John,* this is one opportunity you won't want to miss!"

Salespersons, trained that "The sweetest sound in the English language is the sound of the customer's own name," tend to overdo it. Mark was like that. *Too* respectful, *too* personal, *too* nice. It was subtle, but I felt I was being conned from the moment he walked into my office and his work history confirmed my suspicions.

After completing a semester of a two-year business curriculum he dropped out because of poor grades and started a janitorial service. He told me that at first he worked cleaning residences, but soon discovered there was more money to be made in commercial contracts. Amy later confided that the real reason he switched was that he'd gotten in trouble working in homes because he'd provided "services" other than janitorial. He was a handsome man and found he could get substantial "tips" by spending extra time in the bedrooms of wealthy, but lonely housewives.

His janitorial/gigolo business thrived until the day a business executive, returning home unexpectedly from the office, found Mark "working" (on his wife) in the bedroom. He nearly killed Mark with a nearby sponge mop. This ended Mark's "janitorial" business and he began installing alarm systems. As usual, his smooth manner and apparent competence won him numerous clients and his business *initially* grew rapidly.

However, as is typical of antisocial persons, he simply couldn't resist the opportunity to take advantage of a situation. After he installed an alarm system in a medical building, a large supply of narcotic drugs was missing. Since he had been given a key to the building during the time he was installing the alarm system, he was a prime suspect. He later confided to me that he "was no dummy" and had worn gloves in order to avoid leaving fingerprints. He was able to keep his "cool" during a lie detector test, so the authorities were never able prove he had taken the drugs. However since he was extensively investigated by both local and federal officials and the incident got a lot of local media coverage, this was not the kind of publicity that his "Secure Systems" needed, and he eventually went into bankruptcy.

Soon, however, he started another operation, selling vitamins, beauty aids, health care products, and a weight-loss system through chiropractors and other "professionals." This was a pyramid sales organization where he made a percentage off the sales of others he'd enlisted. Most physicians and dentists wouldn't have anything to do with his line, seeing it as a scam rather than a service to patients, but this didn't discourage Mark, who vigorously recruited everyone from real estate agents and motel proprietors to attorneys and bankers. When I last saw Mark, he tried to recruit me, telling me that his yearly net income exceeded two hundred fifty thousand dollars a year. Of course with smooth antisocial persons, one has to take into account the "liar factor," but even at that, he *appeared* to be doing well. He drove a top-of-the-line Mercedes, dressed in nine-hundred-dollar suits, and had all the trappings of success.

Amy had her own streaks of antisocial style which were manifest mainly in her assorted sexual relationships. She was a highly intelligent woman, who in spite of possessing a four-year college degree in the humanities, worked as a recreational director in the local school system. She'd begun working with children's athletic programs while a student, and her organizational skills, love for children, and willingness to sleep with the boss won her rapid promotions. Even before she completed college, she was in charge of summer athletic programming for all the elementary schools in the county. This she accomplished without formal training in physical education, and at an age when most people would have been at entry level positions.

Amy and Mark's two-year-old Elliott was the shining star of grandparents on both sides of the family. Being the first grandson, he was showered with adoration, attention, and gifts befitting a prince. Since Mark and Amy were too busy most of the time to be bothered with a child, Elliott was emotionally closer to his grandmother than he was to Amy. She had mixed feelings about how much attention her parents showered on Elliott, "They never did anything like that for me," she complained, "I'm the one who took care of them!"

During her childhood and early adolescence, Amy's father had been completing his engineering degree while her mother taught school in order to keep the family financially solvent. This left Amy, the oldest girl, with the bulk of household chores, including meal preparation, laundry, and many other tasks disdainfully identified as "women's work" by her father or brothers. She bitterly told me of the many evenings her brothers would go outside to play softball or shoot baskets with friends, while she was left to clean up supper dishes, do laundry, and tidy up the house.

Her mother spent many evenings at her school, where she was assistant principal, and when she was home, she spent most of her time grading papers and preparing the next day's lesson plans.

Consequently, Amy never played as a child and she was making up for it during adulthood. In addition to organizing the athletics program for the school system, she coached a girls soccer team, and officiated at women's track meets. Thus, Amy's evenings were taken up with athletics while Mark claimed his best times to contact business clients was in the evening. This meant that for the most part Elliott was being cared for by one of the grandmothers.

Amy felt absolutely no guilt about this, nor did she wish to take a more active role in parenting. As she told me:

"My Mom never took care of me when I was growing up, so I figure she owes me something. Besides, she really loves Elliott, and is more patient with him than I am."

Amy's sexual promiscuity had an unconsciously rebellious quality to it. Her father taught engineering in a small Catholic college, and Amy's upbringing had been strictly along traditional church lines. She'd attended Catholic schools from kindergarten through college, and her parents were by-the-book faithful—which is one of the reasons Amy had six younger siblings. Although her father was a devout churchgoer, he was not happy, nor was he kind.

He frequently became enraged over relatively minor infractions of "rules." Tragically, he failed to understand the natural playfulness of children and often punished them severely—to a point barely short of brutality—for minor incidents which were a result of mischievousness rather than a challenge to his authority.

Amy despised her father and spent many therapy hours unleashing her bitterness. She recalled with great detail his near-sadistic punishments of her and the younger siblings. As angry as she was regarding his violence toward her, she became infuriated when recalling how he punished her little sisters.

"I was so 'crazy' with anger that I *know* if there had been a gun in the house, I would have killed him with it.!"

She hated him, and this hatred carried over to most of the other members of the male species. "Men!" she would snarl, ""they always try to use their power over you!" It became clear that her role as "little mother" was never appreciated by any of the males in the family, who simply took it for granted with seldom a word of appreciation. Her younger sisters did try to help her from time to time, but were too much younger to be of much help during the most difficult years.

Subsequently, she used promiscuity both as a way of punishing her father and exerting control over men. From the time Amy was fourteen, she began going out with the kinds of boys that drove her father "up the wall." These were other Catholic boys—her parents wouldn't have heard of her dating Protestants or Jews—but they were never the "nice" boys her Mom and Dad wished her to date. They were always outside the mainstream: native Americans, blacks, Asians, truck drivers, "bouncers," jazz musicians living on the street, etc.

Amy wasn't discretionary with her "love," stating to her father that *she* could *accept* other people whatever their differences. She gleefully pointed out that *she* wasn't prejudiced, arrogant, or pompous, like many people. Furthermore, she inveighed, whatever else she might be (Her father stopped short of calling her a whore, said she at least had the appearance of being "fast.") she wasn't a *hypocrite,* going to church and talking about loving our neighbors while practicing racial or social discrimination in daily life.

In her sexual interactions, Amy called the shots regarding time, place, and even positions. Indeed, she chose men who were by most societal standards regarded as "second class citizens," which further enhanced her dominant position and angered her father who referred to her friends as "mostly scumbags."

She was sexually active from an early age, but used birth control to prevent pregnancy—a double defiance of her parents' values. After numerous promiscuous relationships, she finally married Mark, a Christian Scientist whose father was Japanese and whose mother was Native American. Dad couldn't have been more displeased, which of course, delighted Amy. The fact that Mark was a college drop out, was like the maraschino cherry atop a hot fudge sundae.

Dad refused to give away the bride, which was fine with Amy, and it wasn't until he appeared at the door of the Unitarian church with Mom, that anyone was certain he would attend his oldest daughter's wedding. Since she was marrying outside the faith, the wedding wasn't held in the Catholic church, nor were the ceremonies performed by a priest. Score another point for Amy!

Antisocial parents are often negligent in providing adequate nutrition, medical care, and educational opportunities for their children. This was not obvious in Elliott's case, because his grandparents supplied his psychological needs, and his parents weren't grossly negligent with him. However, they did tell me one week of how they had both gone to work, each thinking the other would take Elliott to the baby-sitter. Sometime about mid-morning, the baby-sitter called Amy at work to find out if Elliott was sick.

Mark and Amy had each driven off to work thinking the other parent would take Elliott to the baby-sitter.

Amy panicked, rushed home, and found her toddler safe but forlornly crying in his bed. She subsequently became enraged at Mark, whom she blamed for being so careless. Mark, of course, returned the blame. In the argument that followed, both were more concerned about placing the blame elsewhere than about Elliott's condition.

I saw them separately in therapy, and found theirs to be a "balanced" marriage, with each cheating on the other. I suspect that each sensed what the other was doing, but because they "respected" each other's privacy, they never pushed too far in asking: for example, "Where were you last night from ten until two in the morning?" Surely Amy didn't believe that Mark was selling health products at one o'clock in the morning, nor could Mark have believed she was coaching soccer until midnight.

Each of them had many individual issues to work through before their marriage could become viable. In therapy Ann focused on issues with her Father and with other men, while Mark used his time regale me with tales of his sales exploits. He quickly tired of therapy, stating that he was going to be working with a Scientology "auditor" for awhile, and that he was going move to the west coast to explore new sales markets.

Amy continued in therapy for several months. As she expressed her bitterness against her father, which had been held inside for so many years, her promiscuity subsided. She was making good progress, I thought, when, without warning, she abruptly announced, "Tonight will have to be my last session." She informed me that Mark was moving his operations west, that she had found a job opportunity in Los Angeles. They moved two weeks later.

She sent me a Christmas card recently telling me about her job, and stating that business was booming for Mark. She said that Elliott was enjoying kindergarten, but missed his grandparents terribly. Although she told me they still have an "open" marriage where each "respects" the other's "privacy," she confided in her letter that she'd only gone out twice on Mark in the past year. I know she felt that for her this was quite a significant accomplishment.

This is the kind of couple where one is tempted to feel they "deserved" each other. Each had moderate antisocial tendencies and both stayed in the marriage because the rules allowed them plenty of freedom for outside relationships. However the duplicity typical of antisocial persons permeated their relationship and sabotaged any chance for real intimacy.

RECOGNIZING the Slick/Manipulative Sexual Style

Now that you've had a chance to learn about manipulative styles covering the entire range from antisocial criminals to ordinary smooth/slick lovers, take a few moments to see if you have some streaks of slickness in your own personality.

Self Quiz

1. Do I find myself usually "feeling nothing" when others around me are crying, as in a "sad" movie?
2. Do I privately think the Humane Society people are a bunch of "kooks?"
3. Have I ever engaged in shoplifting or other petty crimes?
4. Am I good at talking my way out of traffic tickets? Do I have numerous occasions to do so?
5. Do I find it easy to "pick up" a date at a shopping mall, bar, or most anywhere?
6. As a child did I often play "hooky" from school?
7. Do I often take my friends for granted?
8. Did either of my parents punish me severely on a regular basis?
9. Do I "exaggerate" or embellish facts on a regular basis?
10. Do I always know how to make a "good deal?"
11. Am I known as a "party animal?"
12. Have I always been "oversexed?"
13. Do I find it hard to keep promises when they interfere with my plans?
14. Did I grow up believing "Finders keepers, losers weepers?"
15. Have I ever shot stray animals?
16. Do I own a handgun?
17. Have I ever owned a switchblade?
18. Do I enjoy movies like the Godfather series? Do I usually identify with the "bad guys" hoping they'll outsmart the cops?

19. Was I sexually active before age fourteen?

20. Have I had sex with more than a dozen persons in my life?

21. Do I believe most cops are jerks—or worse?

22. When a friendship or love relationship breaks up, does the other person usually hurt a lot more than I?

23. Does it make me smile when I hear of Ivan Boskey or someone like him beating the stock market stiffs at their own game?

24. Have I fantasized about pulling off a successful Brinks truck robbery?

25. Do I have a reputation for keeping my "cool" in all kinds of tense situations?

26. Have I seriously thought about being a CIA operative?

27. Do I find myself frequently saying, "That's how the cookie crumbles?"

28. Have I ever forged someone's signature?

29. Do I like showing up at a parties with a "new number" on a regular basis? Do I especially like to be seen with "knockouts" or "hunks?"

30. Have I been called a "ladies' man" or a "flirt?"

31. Do I have the "gift of gab?" Can I make people believe almost anything—and sometimes do, just for the fun of it?

35. Do I find myself wondering why everyone else is so broken up at funerals and I don't feel much?

36. Do I sometimes take silverware from a restaurant? Towels from a motel?

If you answered "Yes" to a few of these questions, you may be a bit slick or manipulative in your style. It's something you can probably change if you try. But if you notice that *many* of these statements describe you or your lover, it should turn on a caution light-if not a stop light. Let's briefly consider how you can relate to a slick partner.

REORGANIZING Your Expectations

Let's suppose you've just discovered that your partner is moderately manipulative. Until now, you always thought he was just forgetful of special days such as your birthday, or that he got so busy he didn't have time to shop for your anniversary. Those affairs that he seemed to "slip" into were really not his fault, those flirtatious women at work were more than any man could resist for very long. Now you know that these various slips represent a pattern. Worse you know the pattern is at least slick, and you strongly suspect he might even be antisocial. What can you do?

(1) Give up your romantic notions that she is going to change. It's probably a streak of codependency in you that keeps you forgiving her, affair after affair. Face it, she's not likely to change. Oh, I know, her *words* say she will change, but if you plug your ears and look at her *behavior* you'll be forced to be more realistic. Bottom line: Base all decisions regarding your lover—whether to break up or to stay together—on *behavior,* not words. As you've learned, his/her words cannot be relied upon. They are only used to manipulate others, and cannot be counted on as describing your partner's inner reality. When she says "I'm sorry," it likely translates: "I'm sorry I got caught." or "I'm sorry you're angry." When he says "It'll never happen again," you'd better add…"at least not for a couple weeks."

Don't feel bad about not trusting your partner, because if past *behavior* has been indicative of the manipulative or antisocial pattern, it's naive to trust. To put it more bluntly, it's senseless to trust time after time if you've not seen consistent *behavior* to go along with the words of commitment.

(2) *Time is on your side.* Since slick lovers are typically impatient, impulsive lovers, you won't have to wait long for her to show her "true colors." In the life of an antisocial lover a week is a long time, a month is like a decade for others, and a year is *forever!* If you've just started dating this person and after finishing this chapter, you suspect he might be a slick lover by all means *wait!* You've got everything to gain and little to lose by playing the waiting game with this kind of person. If she can't be true to you for six months, how do you expect your relationship to weather the adversities of a lifetime? If he has another affair within the year, is there really much hope that the following year—and the ones after that—will be any different?

So whatever you do, do it deliberately. Rome wasn't built in a day, and neither are worthwhile relationships. You can talk, play and work together, but don't wed! Feel free to ask him to go bowling, shopping, to the movies, to concerts, to baseball games, but don't ask him to move in. Basic rule of thumb: On any really important decision such as marriage or living together make yourself wait at least six months if you have even the slightest suspicion he might be antisocial.

And during those six months, don't allow romance to blinker your eyes. Don't let your body chemistry—which he'll probably be expert in igniting—cloud your vision. Try to be objective, but if you err, let it be on the side of suspicion and cynicism—I can't believe I'm saying this! But yes, the slick lover requires an entirely different kind of readjustment than any other kind of person. It requires you to become almost skeptical in your scrutiny and computer-like in your evaluation. And remember, *behavior* is the key to understanding such persons.

(3) "Don't judge a book by its cover," is excellent advice when evaluating a slick lover. These people have developed first impressions to an art form. They take particular pride in sweeping people off their feet and are very good at it. But remember first impressions are like appetizers, designed to whet the appetite, but hardly adequate for genuine nourishment. You can't build an intimate relationship on the foundation of a ten-minute encounter.

(4) All relationships weren't meant to be. Some people are hopeless when it comes to being friends. These are difficult ideas for most of us to accept because we've grown up with a perennial optimism about other people's motives. If you have a streak of codependency such cynicism comes even harder, but it is essential when you're dealing with a manipulative lover.

You have to come to a new reality. You have to readjust your thinking otherwise you'll be a sitting duck for slick lovers' maneuvers. You don't have to go out of your way to be unkind, just try to stay unattached. Try not to get involved with the slick lover. Your encounter is not likely to be with a professional pimp or a serial killer or some other severe antisocial individual. Instead, you'll have to deal with much milder manifestations, such as the person at the office who always looks for opportunities to butter up the boss and get another promotion.

Slick lovers gravitate towards codependent and other caring people who believe that you always have to be "nice." In the presence of the manipulative lover, this means that you'll always be enmeshed, attached, involved. The inner belief that you must help everyone is like a Venus fly trap when you're around slick partners. It dooms you to being stuck in this person's system until they consume you. Don't let it happen. With over five billion people on this planet, you can't become socially involved with everyone anyway. Why not choose to be involved with people who don't have antisocial or manipulative tendencies?

To recap, if your partner is definitely antisocial, get disentangled. Give up and get out! Leave, or have them leave. Continued involvement only means unending exploitation. However, after reading this chapter, you are convinced that your partner has just a few mild tendencies in that direction, you may want to try some of the suggestions in this chapter, and give the relationship *time*.

If you notice positive changes in your partner as a result of your own newly emerging assertiveness and confidence—i.e., if he or she respects you without exploiting you—there is a scanty possibility that things will permanently improve. You might cautiously continue in the relationship for a while, but only if you see *sustained* commitment, with no "slips" over at least a two-year period of time. This doesn't mean errorless living on the part of your partner but it does mean absolutely no affairs—none. Zero.

REVITALIZING Your Sexual Relationship

Recognizing the antisocial lover is essential if you're not going to spend your life being exploited. As we've just said, reorganizing your expectations must be in the direction of taking care of yourself and developing a healthy cynicism about any promises or verbal commitments. Slick lovers secure your loyalty with fluent promises and articulate vows. However if the going gets difficult they escape through linguistic loopholes, much as people escape burning buildings down fire escapes, leaving you angry and smoldering with resentment in the ashes of their betrayal. There is little on which to build a relationship with a manipulative lover.

If, however, such tendencies in your partner seem very mild, you might risk trying to be in the relationship *for a short time*. If you do, please keep in the mind the suggestions already given about taking care of yourself, and be prepared to deal realistically with the sexual myths a slick lover is likely to bring into the relationship.

Taking Out the Trash

MYTH # 1: Sex with no strings attached is best. You don't have to worry about whining, bitchiness, moodiness, periods, etc. You just have good sex and get out.

TRUTH: "No strings attached" really means sex without intimacy, and as I've insisted throughout this book, sex without intimacy is not satisfying. Only antisocial or manipulative lover find impersonal sex, casual copulation satisfying, and then it's primarily because they've "scored" another victory, not because they find pleasure in genuine closeness.

MYTH # 2: So, I've got a STD—doesn't everybody? No big deal.

TRUTH: Not everyone suffers from a STD and "Yes!" it *is* a big deal. The antisocial lover thinks:

"It's not my responsibility to worry about protecting everybody. I got it from somebody, so if somebody gets it from me, it just keeps things even. If you're chicken about getting something you shouldn't be fooling around."

The notion that infecting your current sexual partner with a STD gets "even" for someone having infected you is antisocial thinking at its worst. It's also the reason why Herpes is rampant and AIDS has become the nightmare of the nineties.

MYTH # 3: *Real* men don't wear condoms.

TRUTH: The manipulative lover's thinking goes as follows:

"What? Me wear a condom? You've got to be kidding! Have you ever tried taking a shower in a raincoat? If you expect me to deprive myself of pleasure just because of your squeamishness, you'd better think again. Besides…you're lucky to have the chance to make it with someone so experienced, so don't get prissy on me."

This outlook reveals the antisocial lover's lack of mutuality in sexual encounters. There is here no real concern for the other person. Instead there is an attitude of entitlement with little concern for consequences.

MYTH # 4: Great lovers are experienced lovers. The more different partners you've been with, the better lover you'll be. Experience counts.

TRUTH: Psychological sensitivity, not sexual technique is what makes a great lover. Often those people who've had the largest number of sexual encounters are superficial, manipulative, or egotistical.

They lack depth, as indicated by the large number of past encounters. Worse still, their past typically gives evidence of lack of commitment and flippant abandonment of a relationship when the going gets difficult. I would much rather bet on the sexually inexperienced but considerate person. Sexual technique is relatively easy to learn, kindness is cultivated over a lifetime.

MYTH # 5: Partner swapping can enhance your marriage. If you've only slept with one person in your life, you can't possibly know what your missing.

TRUTH: This again goes to the core difference between manipulative/slick lovers and more authentic partners. Multiple affairs, partner swapping, and all such behaviors designed to expand one's sexual experience are based on the faulty notion that more is better. Quality, not quantity is what you desire in sexual relations and excessive quantities are usually an indicator of pathology. Like compulsive eaters who become obese in the search for comfort through food, people who frantically search for sexual satisfaction with numerous different partners are often deeply insecure and use sex as a way of reassuring themselves they are attractive or that they are able to triumph over others.

MYTH # 6: "A bird in the hand is worth two in the bush." Or, in sexually explicit terms, "A bush in the hand is worth two on the street." Sex *now* is the only thing worth pursuing, because you can never count on tomorrow.

TRUTH: The best sex is based on intimacy and won't disappear if you don't access it immediately. Truth is, it takes time to develop an authentic relationship—a friendship where the sexual encounter is like the "frosting" on the relational "cake." One-night stands (lays) are a caricature of good sex and don't typically endure the test of time.

MYTH # 7: "If a woman doesn't have an orgasm with me, it's her problem. She's frigid." Or, "If he can't get it up, it's not my fault. He's impotent."

TRUTH: We've suggested earlier that responsibility for orgasm ought to be shared, since orgasm is a relational product. Antisocial lovers have so much ego invested in being the "best" that they are threatened by any implied failure of their lovemaking abilities. Consequently if they fail to arouse the partner, it's blown off as if it doesn't matter:

"Other women I've been with (and I've been with a lot) never complained. If you didn't have an orgasm, you'd better fake it, because I *know* I'm a great lover, and I like my women to respond."

Again we see the tendency of the manipulative/slick lover to place personal gratification at the top of his/her shopping list and to discount all failures as someone else's fault.

This concludes our analysis of the antisocial or manipulative sexual style. This is the most destructive style I discuss in this book. Although I've presented cases illustrating a variety of styles from severely antisocial to mildly manipulative, lovers of this style—severe or mild—tend to be exploitive and difficult to change.

What is so disconcerting is that the millions of antisocial persons, alcoholics, criminals, etc. continue to recreate the kinds of environments which spawned them. And our prisons, overcrowded as they are with antisocial persons and the like, provide fertile soil for apprentices and journeymen to become master criminals.

What the depletion of the ozone layer, pollution of the oceans, destruction of tropical rain forests, and global warming are doing to our planet; alcoholism, drug abuse, crime, and the resultant dissolution of the family unit are doing to society. Families suffused with physical, sexual or verbal abuse cannot provide the foundation of mental health so badly needed by so many at this time.

It is particularly frustrating that so few antisocial persons voluntarily enter treatment. Typically it is the spouses and children of antisocial persons that I see in my clinical practice. This isn't surprising, however because anxiety, depression, or other forms of psychological pain impel people to seek treatment. The antisocial person's lack of anxiety and emphasis on being "cool" prevents him from feeling the need for treatment. Only when a spouse threatens divorce, or otherwise upsets the system, does a clinician see the manipulative lover seeking treatment, and then often superficially.

I dislike ending a chapter on such a pessimistic note, however I find it difficult to be optimistic about the overall picture. Nonetheless, my hope is that in clearly understanding the severe consequences children suffer from abuse—even in the milder forms which include verbal abuse, shaming, or lack of empathic mirroring—we will be inspired to practice empathic parenting, and to build, rather than destroy family boundaries.

It is sometimes said that this nation's greatest resource is its children; however it would be more accurate to suggest that this nation's children provide the raw materials, but *empathic* parents are the most important resource. Without empathic parents, children are at high risk for developing antisocial personalities and other maladaptive styles of functioning. The hand that rocks (or fails to rock) the cradle *does* rule the nation.

It is also my hope that helping you *recognize* the lover with manipulative or antisocial tendencies will lessen the likelihood that you will marry or form a long-term relationships with a destructive lover.

In the next chapter we will consider the "first cousin" of the slick lover, the narcissist. Narcissistic persons suffer from a lack of internally soothing parental images and memories. However narcissists are less "reptilian" in their anger, less predatory in their manipulativeness, and more socially concerned. Their social skills, like the smooth lover's, are usually employed for the purpose of self aggrandizement, but they are not usually destructive or dangerous in an antisocial way.

They are capable of rage when their fragile sense of self-esteem is challenged or damaged ("narcissistic injury"), but they don't exhibit the predatory coolness of the antisocial person; their anger, although self-centered, usually has some empathic components as well.

As we've suggested earlier, all persons exhibit *blends* of the various styles, and many of the narcissistic traits will seem like muted versions of what we've seen in the current chapter. The differences between mild antisocial style and narcissism are sometimes difficult to discern—like the differences between late twilight and darkness. Subtle though they might be, there are important differences, and this will be the topic of our next chapter.

Chapter 5:
Narcissistic
Lovers

"Nice place. I take it you like mirrors."

NARCISSISTIC LOVERS

When He Calls Out His Own Name During Orgasm—You're In Trouble

"Mirror mirror on the wall, don't you think I'm the loveliest of them all?"

Before beginning, a comment about the term *narcissism* is in order. Our English word, usually defined as "love or sexual desire for one's own body," has its source in Greek mythology. Narcissus, the offspring of a river and a water nymph, grew to be so strikingly beautiful that he attracted many would-be lovers of both sexes. However he spurned the attentions of them all, and catching sight of his own reflection in a pool on Mount Halcion, became so entranced with his own beauty that he could not tear himself away. Held in the grip of passion for himself he lay beside the pool day after day until he wasted away and expired. Narcissus thus became the quintessential model of self-absorbed love.

Today mental health professionals use the term broadly to include not only self-absorbed people, but those who constantly crave the admiration of others. Nonetheless, the image of a narcissistic person preening in front of a mirror for hours at a time still has meaning that directly derives from Greek mythology.

Narcissistic lovers want, above all else, to be *admired.* Like histrionics, they seek attention, and are sexually seductive and overly concerned with physical attractiveness. But they seek more than mere attention. They want to capture your admiration. Narcissistic lovers have a grandiose sense of self importance, tending to exaggerate their accomplishments and talents in order to be noticed as "special." They expect admiration even without appropriate achievement. When adequately stroked or flattered, they respond with charm and effervescence—almost purring—but they react to criticism with feelings of rage or shame.

Narcissistic lovers share much in common with two other sexual styles we've examined. Like histrionics they are emotionally intense, yet shallow. They love the limelight and crave adoration, but expect to be admired even if their accomplishments are ordinary. Thus, like antisocial or manipulative lovers we've just studied, they have an unrealistic sense of *entitlement,* viewing themselves as special, elite, a cut above the common folks who have to earn praise by achievement.

Sometimes they become preoccupied—as much of our culture seems to be—with the rich and the famous, attempting to improve their status by "hanging out" (even if in fantasy) with celebrities. They sometimes develop elaborate fantasy relationships with other "special" people such as movie stars or important political figures.

Envy and *disdain* are the poles of the narcissistic lover's world. Other people are either put on a pedestal and admired (as the narcissist wishes to be admired) or disdained as "below" the threshold of social worthiness. Narcissists live suspended between movies stars and street people, between Hollywood and hobos. They try to come off as stars, but secretly fear they're bums. The narcissist's air of superiority and haughty disdain for "lower types" is really a social facade—a thin veneer of pretended confidence covering a fragile sense of self.

Clarissa

"Sissy," as she'd always been known, sat on the edge of the long leather couch nearest my chair. She looked like she was fresh off the California beach near her home, but since we were in the Midwest, and it was March, I guessed she'd been "bagging rays" at the local tanning salon. Wide set eyes, full lips, streaked hair and flawlessly smooth facial skin gave her the appearance of a goddess, but her dilated pupils and breathy voice made her seem more like a frightened little girl.

"I have trouble swallowing. I've felt anxious a lot lately, and when I do, I feel nauseated, get cramps in my stomach, and feel like I'm going to choke, like I won't be able to swallow!"

Her face, now slightly moistened with traces of perspiration, grew increasingly bewildered. Simultaneously her eyes began to brim with tears, but like mist droplets on the tips of leaves, they formed slowly and clung stubbornly, yielding only an intermittent drop at a time. There was no flood of tears or convulsion of sobs; instead, confusion seemed to stifle the free flow of feelings, much as anxiety stifled her swallowing.

"Randy had to take me to the emergency room last night. I had trouble swallowing, then I got scared and began to hyperventilate. They gave me Valium and told me that I needed to see a psychologist or psychiatrist, so that's when I called you."

As she spoke, Sissy became engulfed in the memories of the previous evening. Her rib cage beginning to expand and contract rhythmically as her breathing became more rapid. Consciously summoning as much soothing into my voice as I could, I began:

"It sounds like it was pretty frightening…but that was last night…You're here now…and everything is going to be alright…It's safe in here. Why don't you try lying on the couch and just relaxing?…There, you're probably feeling a bit better already…."

I strung my words together slowly, hypnotically. She responded immediately, and her breathing soon returned to normal, but her facial expression remained one of apprehension.

Much of Sissy's psychological life was permeated with concerns about swallowing. It became apparent, as therapy proceeded that numerous incidents in her childhood had formed a constellation around issues of swallowing.

Swallowing food is something that occurs without effort or conscious thought in a relaxed family, but for Sissy it was entwined with painful memories:

"My father slapped me when I was still in a high chair because I wouldn't swallow my vegetables. He kept forcing strained peas into my mouth. I've always hated peas—still do. When I wouldn't swallow them he got madder and madder. Mom says I just kept spitting them back out until he got so mad he slapped me several times."

Mom and Dad divorced when Sissy was four or five. The reasons were never very clear, remaining shrouded in mystery to this day.

"Your father had unnatural affections for you," Sissy's mom had once told her; but beyond this no amount of probing would yield more details. Such a clear reference to her father's sexual inappropriateness left Sissy convinced that her confusing nightmares and occasional daytime flashbacks must have had a basis in reality.

She recalled sensations of gagging just before going to sleep:

"I'm feeling something soft and hard at the same time in my mouth…a feeling like I'm gagging, choking."

She remembered how she always worried—still did—about biting the end off a thermometer while her temperature was being taken. Afraid she would swallow the mercury and become poisoned by it.

She remembered as a teenager, swimming in the pool with her stepfather, how he tried to fondle her breasts. She became so frightened she swam to the bottom of the pool and swallowed quite a bit of water before coming up—hoping he would be gone when she surfaced.

At the time she began treatment, Sissy was suffering recurrent nightmares, from which she awakened with a choking sensation, feeling sweaty, nauseous, and sweaty.

"I dream that I go to visit my father. I go to his house, and sometimes he's there with his new wife, and sometimes it's with my mother. Anyway, I feel like I'm little, but in the dream I'm grown up. He says that if I'd been nicer, maybe we could have had a relationship when I was little, but that it's never too late. We go into his bedroom—I lead him in there and tell him it's alright. I lie there on my back and he's kissing me and touching me. I'm responding. Holding him, cooperating. He's telling me how good it is and how glad he is I'm finally cooperating. He penetrates me and it's all over. He tells me not to tell mother and we can have a good relationship. I'm mixed up, but happy. I feel like I can finally have the love I always wanted. Then I wake up. Sometimes my vagina is quite moist."

It wasn't until much later in therapy that we completely uncovered the dynamic source of this dream. It wasn't only her father who had molested her, though he was likely the first, her older brother had sexualized her as well. Although it's impossible to know with certainty what took place during the first four years of her life while her parents were still together, her memories of sex with her brother became increasingly explicit as treatment progressed.

Early in treatment, I had asked her if she remembered any incidents of family sexuality, she recalled none. However once she felt safe and her defenses lessened, she began to explore her past, and a multitude of memories surfaced:

"I remember it started when I was in junior high. One night I was lying there in bed nearly asleep. My mom and step dad were gone for the week, but that was no problem because my brother Todd was home from college for the summer, and I felt perfectly safe with him in the house. We got along great, so I kind of enjoyed it when just the two of us were home alone.

I'd been kind of dozing. I think it was maybe 10:30 or 11:00, I'm not sure. Anyway, I'm lying there and I hear the door open and I'm scared, because I don't know who it is. Then I see it's just Todd, so I'm not scared anymore, but I pretend to be sleeping, 'cause I wonder what he's doing in my room. Well, he's just got his shorts on and I notice this big erection poking out and I'm kind of scared but also fascinated.

'Hey Sis!' he whispers kind of loud, 'you awake?' I keep pretending to be asleep. Then he sits down on the side of the bed and starts stroking my back, real gently. It's summer so I'm wearing a nightie with no bottom. Pretty soon he's touching my bottom, and I've got goose bumps all over.

I'm scared, but excited too. Next thing I know he's got his shorts off and asking me to touch his erection. By now I'm breathing hard—like I've been running fast—but I'm kind of scared too. I can't tell him no. He's my big brother, I've always looked up to him. I touch it and it's hard and soft at the same time. He's acting real weird, moaning and stuff and before I know what's happening, he's squirting this gooey stuff all over.

After that, Todd came into my room every night for the rest of the week, and we did all kinds of things. We really got close that week…I mean, not just sexually…I felt like I had really made him happy and that he really cared. He made me promise I wouldn't tell Mom—as if I had planned to!

From then on, whenever he was home from college, if Mom and Dad were gone, we'd have sex. Mostly oral sex, because once when he tried to penetrate me, it really hurt.

"Come to think of it, that's about the time I really started having trouble swallowing. Well, except for when I was really little and my real father would slap me for not swallowing my food. After junior high, whenever I got really nervous or excited, I could feel a knot in my throat. I've heard people talk about having a "knot" in their stomach—well I always would get one in my throat."

Overstimulation of the False Self

Sissy's life had been one of overstimulation beginning soon after birth. She recalled her mother telling her:

"It used to relax me so to have your little body against mine. When you were just a tiny baby, I used to lie there in bed and put you between my breasts. It would relax me so I could go to sleep. You were better than Valium!"

It should be clearly understood that closeness in early life does not *necessarily* produce narcissistic personalities in adult life. The intimacy of the mother with her newborn is,in fact, one of the pillars of mental health.

What was pathological about the interaction between Sissy and her Mom was the *intensity* of Mother's *need* for the infant. "You were better than Valium," indicates that Mom was *using* the newborn to deal with her own anxieties. If her mother lacked appropriate boundaries that early in Sissy's life, it's safe to assume that in thousands of other ways throughout her daughter's development, she *needed* Sissy to be a certain way.

Sissy experienced erotic stimulation by her father—what mother described as his "unnatural affection" for her. During adolescence her brother continued this line of overstimulation with his sexual advances, again involving primarily oral stimulation. After that, she became sexually involved with numerous men. What all these interactions share in common is a disregard for what Sissy needed.

They were all "conditional" relationships: ""I will love you *on the condition that* you _____." Here the blank might be filled in with various requirements ranging from "lie quietly on my tummy, and be my little Valium," "eat your food like a big girl," "play the piano nicely;" to the more destructive and intensely erotic "perform oral sex" or "allow me to penetrate you," etc.

All these "conditions" served to develop in Sissy a false self. Conditional messages communicate to a child: "Please don't be who you *are,* I need you to be a certain way." This is the core foundation for the narcissistic style. The parent has an "agenda" for what the child must become in order to be acceptable—in order to meet the parent's needs. Such parents relate to the child not as a unique human being, but as an extension of themselves. They subconsciously nudge the child to fulfill *their* parental dreams and wishes instead of encouraging their child's own unique development.

Narcissistic parents foster a *false self* in their child because they unconsciously need their child to provide *for them* the nurturance they missed as children, or the beauty they lacked, or the importance they never felt.

Such agendas lay the groundwork for the narcissistic style by fostering a *false self* or phony identity, which is a major flaw of the narcissistic style. This contrived self may become so automatic as to seem real to both the child and parent, but it is false at core, because it is based on the *parents'* needs, *not* on the child's realities.

Sissy was such a child—used by her mother, father, stepfather, brother, and many other persons outside her immediate family. She became adept at being like others wanted her to be.

Although she was used sexually, this is not always the case for narcissistic persons, nor was it the only way Sissy was used. Any expectation which pushes a child to be a certain way in order to please a parent carries the risk of promoting a *false self*. This results in what is sometimes called an *adapted child,* one whose personality is formed by *adapting* to everyone else's expectations instead of her own.

The essence of the narcissistic style is the *development of a false self instead of expression of the real self.* Therapy with the narcissist involves a search for and enlivening of the *real* self, which is often buried under layers of conformity, glitz-and-glitter grandiosity, entitlement, manipulativeness, hypersexuality and an insatiable seeking for admiration. Such admiration is sought, however not for the intrinsic joy it might bring, but rather to *reassure* the narcissist of his worth and to bolster the false (and fragile) self.

Bereft of inner experience, the narcissistic child creates a false (pleasing) self to meet the needs of others, but gradually mistakes this false self for who she really is. Narcissism is just one of the possible styles shaped by needy or emotionally ill parents. As we've seen previously, children may also become obsessive-compulsive—trying to be perfect, codependent—learning to take care of their parents, or antisocial or manipulative—learning to look out only for themselves.

What characterizes narcissistic lovers is *inner emptiness.* This results in shallow sexuality which lacks psychological intimacy or genuine caring. Although narcissists often in high levels of sexual activity, seeming to have an insatiable sex drive and portraying the image of being a "stud" or "nymph," this is really a pseudosexuality. They appear flashy on the outside, but are bereft of inner experience.

Growing children need to experience *empathy* in order to learn how to appropriately relate to others, and in order to receive nurture for their *real* selves. This is where narcissistic parents fail most notably—they are incapable of *empathy.* Children who receive consistent acceptance and empathic responding to a variety of emotional experiences, learn how to nurture themselves and others, but failing to experience empathy from parents, developing children are at risk for becoming like chameleons—changing color to suit their surroundings—pleasing whomever is nearest.

And that's how Sissy's infancy and early childhood were most seriously flawed. From the very beginning she learned to be what *others* needed her to be—not only sexually, but in myriad other ways as well. As she grew older, the conditions for acceptance continued to demand that she *adapt* to the needs of others and she got a lot of strokes for being musical, sexual, or whatever someone else needed from her.

For example, Sissy's mother was a frustrated and unfulfilled musician. As a little girl she'd become quite accomplished on both the piano and violin, but when in high school she "went wild," abandoned her family values and married Sissy's father, music was one of the casualties. Not surprisingly, Sissy incorporated musical performance as one of *her* goals, spending hours toiling at the keyboard, in spite of mediocre talent.

During a more optimal childhood, a sorting-out process occurs wherein children gravitate toward activities in which they excel and consequently enjoy. Since "nothing succeeds like success," a positive loop is formed in which enjoyment spurs further effort, which in turn creates more pleasure, and so forth. However, in the case of narcissistic parents the child is acting out the parent's desires, so there is likely to be a misfit, as there was with Sissy's musical "talent." Since the child is attempting to succeed in a area for which she may be ill-equipped, success often eludes her. When failure occurs in the face of such high expectations, it brings disappointment not only to the performer, but also to others who had so much invested in the enterprise. Such failure can be a particularly painful blow to the attempting-to-be-splendid self, and is referred to by clinicians as *narcissistic injury.*

Sissy's years of piano lessons and recitals were an effort to please mother more than a genuine interest of her own. Mom was so uptight during Sissy's eighth-grade graduation piano performance that the fingernails of her clenched fists left deep marks on her perspiring palms.

"We made it!" she exulted to Sissy during intermission, "and without any mistakes!"

But when Sissy entered a high school music competition "we" didn't make it, and the injury to her fragile but grandiose self was enormous. After that she refused to enter any more competitions and seldom played even for her mother's enjoyment. Since she had never especially wanted to play piano anyway, she glibly termed it "no great loss." This, despite the fact that she'd practiced and performed for over ten years.

So we see that Sissy was narcissistically injured in multiple ways: (1) Soon after birth she was used by her mother as a "tranquilizer" and later to fulfill her Mom's frustrated musical ambitions. (2) She was sexualized by her father, then abandoned (through divorce). (3) Her brother "replaced" father as a sexual partner. (4) Sissy was not considered pretty by other children during elementary school. She wore "coke bottle" glasses, and suffered from acne. Her breasts were her only social asset, getting her much attention from the boys.

Although Sissy appeared in my office as a poised, competent, beautiful woman, in fact this was a false self, precariously produced by years of eroticized relationships and sustained by her physical attractiveness and continued sexual acting out.

Now, although contact lenses replaced her "coke bottles," and her face was free of acne, she remained a frightened little girl whose real self had never been nurtured or allowed to develop.

Not surprisingly, she tried to use therapy as she did other relationships, to seek closeness through sex, to aggrandize her false (sexual) self by seducing her therapist, or by being special in other ways.

"I must be special to you!" is the message narcissists send to others. In therapy this means manipulating for extra time, special appointments, and a unique relationship in numerous ways. It was hardly surprising that one of the ways in which Sissy sought specialness was by seeking to be erotically close to me.

She'd been subtly seductive from the first appointment, but as the dreary gray of March gave way to the generative greens of April and the floral explosions of May and June, Sissy's "dress code" became more intimate. She sometimes showed up in silky jump suits that looked more like lingerie than casual clothing.

As the hot sultry days of August settled in, she frequently showed up wearing G-string shorts which all but vanished between her shapely legs and skimpy halter tops which barely contained her breasts. She discussed her frequent sexual encounters in vivid terms, frequently leaning forward and punctuating her animated descriptions with sensuous body language and gestures.

Undoubtedly, I was one of the few men she'd encountered who didn't responded by sexualizing the relationship. This troubled her, although she wasn't consciously aware of it, and she became more and more agitated. She began starting her sessions by asking "Well, do you like my outfit today?" I would reply that it "looked nice," and begin the hour as usual, asking her about her thoughts.

This kind of casual indifference to her obvious sexuality was an important part of her therapy. Narcissists typically test out their false self in the treatment situation to see if the therapist will respond as they expect.

The inexperienced therapist who even subtly reinforces the false self (In Sissy's case the "erotic self") pays a high price over the long run. This replicates the climate of earlier interactions, thereby *affirming* the validity of the false self. By refusing to "dance" with the narcissistic patient, the therapist often incurs anger and runs some risk of having the patient terminate treatment prematurely. Typically there are angry accusations of "You don't care!" or "You don't understand!"

In Sissy's case, her unconscious formula seemed to be "If we don't have sex, how can we ever be close?"

During this phase of her therapy, she wrote several long letters. The first few were permeated with sensuality:

Dear Dr. Berecz,

After today's session I felt all warm inside—like I'd swallowed a sunrise. I don't know what to do with it. I can't hold it in any longer. I feel as if I'm exploding with ecstasy. I wish I could tell you in person how I feel. Maybe next session I'll be able to. Maybe I'll even be able to say the forbidden words "I love you." It feels so good inside to think I could be strong enough to face you with those words. But not just the words alone, but also the feelings and the eye contact. I love you, I love you so much it makes me cry to think about it. No man ever cared for me like this before. I love you more because I realize now that you're not some kind of god, but a man, as I am a woman, with just as much love burning inside of you as I.

I'm too sensual. Everything I do has that quality. I want to hold, and hug, and kiss—that's the only way I know to let it out. I even kiss old people—people who haven't been kissed in years. They usually cry.

I wish everything didn't always turn into sex. I hate sex—men frighten me. I sometimes fantasize about eunuchs. Eunuchs care, they don't just want to push a penis into you.

But you, you're different. Not really a eunuch but not threatening me with your penis. Please show me how to love you. I'm not suggesting we do everything...but if you can't touch me a little and hold me once in awhile, and I you, then I'll have to deny my feelings and love for you. And that's been one of the most beautiful things about therapy, is learning to be honest with my feelings. I'm trying to be honest with you. Please help me!

Love, Sissy

The seasoned professional can usually manage this difficult phase of the treatment, and the long-term dividends make it worthwhile. At the deepest level, such patients do *not* want yet another interaction based on the false self. Sissy did *not* really want to have sex with yet another man. It is precisely this kind of unconscious pull that sometimes leads therapists to forsake training and ethics to blur the boundaries of the professional relationship with sexuality.

After several sultry sessions of intense eroticizing of our relationship, Sissy became angry at what she felt was my rejection of her, and precipitously switched from seductiveness to rage. She became intensely confrontational and berating both in her sessions and in her letters:

John,

Frankly, I don't think you deserve to be called "doctor!" I'm hating you with every ounce of strength I can muster at the moment. I never knew how much capacity I had to hate before! I think your "therapy" stinks! For all I've cared about you, I sure didn't get much in the other direction. You got me into this thing. You and your deceitful, trifling with my brain. Damn you! You just can't treat people like that. I know you'll say you're not withdrawing, but I can tell. I can see it in your eyes, your looks, and even the way you gesture with your hands.

What's wrong great doctor? Did things get too hot for you? Are you afraid of me now? I know you are, so don't try to deny it. If you're so smart with your Ph.D., why did you let me love you the way that I did. Does that give you a big ego trip? To sit there and say you "care" but we can't touch? You S.O.B. I hate you. All this time, I thought your caring was at the same level as mine, but I was obviously wrong.

Therapy stinks!—except for shrinks! How's that for poetry? You bastards sit around in your plush offices and think up this G.D. system that works best for you and if it causes your patients to go through hell, so what? You'll never admit you're wrong, and that you've caused me unnecessary pain and grief. But you were afraid of it all. I know you'll never admit that, but I know it's the truth.

I would never have cared or become emotionally involved with you, but you pulled me into your world...so gently. I came into your world to love you and to care about you, but just because I didn't know how to do it without giving myself sexually, you got scared and ran away. You wimp! And you tried to say it was me—that I was "acting out" my feelings. Bullshit! Keep your psychology mumbo jumbo. I was just trying to show you I cared, and you couldn't handle it. Admit it, great white doctor! You're not so perfect yourself. Just because you could have had me—twice a day anytime you wanted me doesn't make me a slut.

You've damaged me. I'll have scar tissue forever Dr. Berecz! I cared and loved even though it was so hard for me, and you just stick your foot out, watch me trip, and fall flat on my face. And you call that therapy!

You are a joke! You remind me of one of those lawyer jokes, but I think it applies better to shrinks: These two shrinks are walking down the beach together. One of them steps in a pile of dog shit and says "Oh, no!" His friend looks down and says "Don! You're melting!" That's what I think of all you high and mighty "helpers," I think you're mostly dog shit!

Sissy

As these letters illustrate, the middle months of therapy were emotionally tumultuous for Sissy and difficult for me as well. However after she had engulfed me with her seductiveness and assailed me with her rage, it apparently satisfied her unconscious need to test the limits, and in the months that followed, Sissy made genuine progress.

She became less seductive and more open in a real way. Less of her time was devoted to obvious seductive talk and gestures and she began to explore aspects of her real self. This was most evident in her art work. She renewed her interest water colors and began painting sailing vessels and lobster boats. She had always loved the ocean and had begun painting seascapes as a teenager, but her mother thought it was taking to much time away from piano practice, so she gave it up.

Now, her considerable natural talent in this area began to flourish and she soon had more orders from local art galleries than she could fill. Toward the end of her last year in therapy, just before Christmas, she presented me one of her paintings with the following note:

"For Dr. Berecz: If you won't have my body I at least want you to have something to remember me by."

This comment, though somewhat tongue-in-cheek, illustrates the level of insight she'd achieved.

A sleek schooner now sails a choppy, moonlit sea, just above the fireplace in my den—a product of Sissy's *real* self, produced as much for her own pleasure as to please me. An unconscious symbol of how we survived the treacherous shoals of psychoanalysis together.

Kathryn

In her recently published memoir "The Kiss" Kathryn Harrison describes how, as a little girl, she struggled to learn French in order to please her mother. With stunning clarity, she describes her narcissistic mother's agenda and her own desperate attempts to shape herself into the child her mother wanted.

Her mother and grandmother spoke French flawlessly. Even Parisians would comment upon it. "Not possible," they would say, "You must have lived in France as a child."

But though she began French lessons at the age of two, Kathryn made no progress beyond *la table, le crayon,* words that sounded similar in English. Intelligence tests confirmed her mother's suspicion that her daughter's failure was due to reluctance rather than a lack of aptitude. Perceptively, Kathryn writes that her reluctance was because she did not want to be "ushered into this language of conflict, the one in which my mother and grandmother fight, and which when allied they use to secretly eviscerate their foes."

Kathryn's mother quizzed her with flash cards, but nothing worked. She would drop helplessly inside herself to a place from which she could not respond. Silence only further angered her mother, and she once threw the flash cards down and slapped Kathryn's face.

By the second grade, following five years of failure, Kathryn decides to "prepare" for a French test in a different way--by cheating: "We have been told to memorize the colors. Red = *Rouge.* Yellow = *Jaune.* Green = *Vert.* I write all the equivalents on a slip of paper and hide it in my sleeve. The test is a mimeographed picture of a clown holding a bunch of balloons, and on each balloon is the French word for one of the colors. With our crayons we are to color them in appropriately.

"My mother's excitement over my perfect score is devastating. She hugs me, she kisses me, she buys me gifts; and even at the age of seven I understand how damning is my success-that my mother's love for me (like her mother's for her) depends on my capitulation. She will accept, acknowledge, *see* me only in as much as I will make myself the child who pleases her.

"'I knew you could! I knew you could, if only you tried!' she says. I pull out of her arms, sobbing.

"'I can't!' I cry. 'I did it with this!' I shove the grubby crib note at her.

Her mother was so upset that she couldn't speak in any language.

The next day Kathryn's mother made her confess. In anger she drove Kathryn to her grandparents' and dropped her off.

That night she came down with an illness no one could define or cure. It began like the stomach flu but didn't stop. It went on for several weeks, until the day she overheard a pediatrician tell her grandmother that she was becoming so dehydrated she would have to be hospitalized, and then it stopped, just as suddenly as it began.

She returned to school a different child -- thinner, paler, and with hair cut very short.

"Why this isn't the same child!" said everyone who saw her.

Kathryn did finally learn French, but never with facility, and never with pleasure. She learned it well enough to read novels in French, and she writes, "Very occasionally, I dream in French, and on those mornings I wake up ill: I vomit. (1997, pps. 18-21)

As an adolescent, grappling with how to both please and defy her parent, Kathryn Harrison discovers the power of thinness. Anorexia becomes her psychological scalpel: trimming away body fat, cutting mother out of her life, sculpting her own desperate third-generation image of narcissistic preoccupation with self.

She writes graphically of her struggle to free herself of her mother's narcissistic web through the use of food.

Discovering that through food, she could defy her mother while at the same time fulfilling her own narcissistic compulsions, she became thinner and thinner. She writes about "The dizzy rapture of starving. The power of needing nothing. By force of will I make myself the impossible sprite who lives on air, on water, on purity."(1997, pps. 39-41)

Now that we've looked closely at Sissy, a clinical case, and briefly at Kathryn a successful novelist, we'll turn to more ordinary people. We'll see many of the following traits.

RECOGNIZING the Narcissistic Style

Now that you've looked over my shoulder in the treatment of Sissy, and gotten the flavor of Kathryn Harrison's struggles with her narcissistic mother, you'll better understand the following features of clinical narcissism. These include a pervasive pattern of grandiosity and seeking attention, hypersensitivity to criticism, and a lack of empathy indicated by at least *five* of the following:

(1) reacts to criticism with feelings of rage or shame (even if this isn't expressed)

(2) is socially exploitive, taking advantage of others to achieve his/her own ends

(3) has a grandiose sense of self importance which leads to exaggerating achievements and expecting to be noticed as "special" even without appropriate achievements

(4) believes herself/himself to be unique and can be understood only by other special people

(5) often preoccupied with fantasies of power, success, brilliance, or romantic love

(6) has a sense of entitlement—expectations of special favors and treatment—doesn't feel she has to wait in line when others must do so

(7) demands constant attention and admiration, often fishing for compliments

(8) lack of empathy, an inability to recognize and experience how others feel, e.g., annoyance or surprise when a sick friend cancels a date

(9) is preoccupied with feelings of envy, rivalry, and jealousy.

Narcissistic people usually do not wear well. Their compulsive insistence on admiration usually produces the opposite. Their "subtle" attempts to impress others through name dropping, knowing everything or refusing to apologize soon become transparent to everyone but themselves, resulting in the opposite of admiration. In spite of, or because of, their constant concern with image and public posture, they frequently elicit from others aversion rather than the admiration they so desperately seek.

RECOGNIZING Narcissism in Ordinary People

"GQ"

Kevin was an ordinary kind of guy; well, as ordinary as narcissistic persons are able to be. The first impression you would get seeing Kevin was "Wow! what a dresser!" He was a clothes horse of the first order. Throughout his childhood, Kevin's father, a successful attorney, had incessantly emphasized the important of appearance. Young Kevin had hooked into this concept with brittle conformity, since it was obviously of such importance to his father.

Whenever the family went out in public he and his sister were often dressed in complementary attire, even though they were not twins. If Kristen wore a navy dress, Kevin wore the obligatory sailor suit; if she wore a seersucker sun dress, he wore a complementary outfit. Their picture Christmas cards looked like clothing store brochures with Father wearing a luxurious wool sweater that Bill Cosby would have envied, Mother opulently attired in velvet and brocade, and Kristen and Kevin in complementary outfits.

Kevin regarded Hart Shafner & Marx suits and Florshiem shoes with the same mixture of condescension and contempt that most people accord K-Mart "blue-light specials." Kevin was more than a clothing connoisseur, the way he dressed was one of the many ways in which he defined himself to be "special," someone above the crowd, someone significant.

I met Kevin when we were both interns at Children's Hospital. Prior to this I had thought of myself as reasonably well dressed. I didn't wear white socks with dress shoes, I wore narrow ties when they were in, and wide ties when they took over. But being around Kevin invariably made me feel like some sort of Neanderthal, barely walking erect, wrapped in a few crude animal skins. And it wasn't just me. After the first week of our training, Kevin was dubbed "GQ" by the rest of the interns and if someone called for Kevin, even the secretaries would ask if anyone had "seen GQ."

For GQ there were no casual occasions—times when you forget how you look and simply hang loose. I recall vividly his matching shirt, suspenders, trousers, socks and shoes at the departmental picnic. From his "casual" dress shirt with the venerated polo label on the pocket, to his matching suspenders, trousers and argyle socks, GQ was prepared to picnic in style. Here was no ordinary shorts-and-tanktop kind of guy wearing Aqua Velva, this was Kevin.

Naturally, he didn't participate in most picnic activities, preferring to walk about and flirt with the women. It was probably a good thing because Tug-of-War, egg-throwing contests, and water fights clash with Christian Dior and Calvin Klein. You'd think twice before throwing a water balloon or a raw egg at someone like GQ, because if he were to sue for damages, it could cost you upwards of $1500 to replace his "casual" picnic attire.

I never recall seeing the same clothing on him twice. He probably did wear things more than once, but you couldn't have proved it by me. And most of his silk ties were striking enough that you would have recalled seeing them before. But if his neckties were a visual buzz, the rest of his behavior was not, and as our internship year wore on, Kevin wore thin.

From the first, his impeccable fashion-magazine-appearance made him seem too good to be true. When you were with him you felt clumsy and awkward felt like you'd won a "Star for a Day" contest and were in Hollywood interacting on a movie set with a star. Each time you talked with Kevin it felt like the cameras were rolling—like the interaction was another "take"—and you were definitely the supporting actor. Although he could cover any body blemishes with exquisite clothing, his narcissistic personality style wasn't as easy to remedy. He soon turned off most of the interns and staff with his patronizing pretentiousness, which was merely a veneer covering his desperate need to be admired. This became apparent in numerous ways that fashionable clothing could not mitigate.

"Carl and I"

A couple of years previously Kevin had apparently attended a week-end workshop conducted by the renowned psychologist Carl Rogers. Subsequently, it seemed that "casual" references to Carl were scattered throughout Kevin's discussions of treatment cases. "Carl and I discussed a similar case..." he would begin, and we would inwardly cringe. To hear Kevin talk, you would have thought he and "Carl" were from the same town or had developed a significant relationship in graduate school. When, under questioning, he conceded that he'd only attended a weekend workshop, we were flabbergasted. All this time we'd assumed that Rogers had been a professor at his university, or directed his dissertation research.

Kevin never really bragged, narcissists usually don't. To brag is too obvious. It might appear that you were *needing* admiration and this is unacceptable to the narcissist who tries to maintain a stance of needless superiority or aloof self-sufficiency. Instead, narcissists attempt to elicit admiration indirectly.

A non-narcissistic person might say, "It was so exciting to attend a work shop conducted by someone as famous as Carl Rogers!" The narcissistic person would "casually" allude to "lunch with Carl." Notice how differently these affect you. The first invites you to join in the experience—to ask questions about the man and to share in the pleasure of interacting with someone who has met someone famous. The latter induces a sense of inferiority, and any pleasure you might derive form knowing someone who has "met Rogers," is sabotaged by a sense of inferiority and insignificance you feel in the presence of the narcissist.

"I'm Sorry"

Kevin could never apologize and it caused him suffering to utter the words "Thank you." This was because like other narcissists, Kevin tried to protect his fragile but grandiose self. This, "God complex" as it's sometimes called, results from the narcissist's desperate attempt to maintain the illusion of self sufficiency. The narcissist attempts to bolster the fragile (but false) self by living an illusion—the illusion of needlessness. In their interactions they attempt to be needless and sinless, i.e., self-sufficient and perfect—obviating the necessity to say "Thank you" or "I'm sorry."

As we've seen, Kevin desperately craved admiration but tried to live as if he could amply provide for himself. Thus, he couldn't say "I'm sorry," because that would admit to a *need* for pardon and simultaneously concede that he wasn't perfect. Similarly, he couldn't say "Thank you" because that also acknowledged that some else had provided something he needed.

"I'm sorry...but..."

When the narcissistic person says "I'm sorry," it may at first sound like a genuine apology. But it soon becomes apparent that what is really occurring is not an attempt at repairing a breached relationship; rather, the narcissist is really seeking to restore his own *illusion of perfection.*

This is what psychoanalysts refer to as *undoing.* For example, the wife who has hurt her husband, may prepare him a special dinner, or signal her availability for sexual intercourse. The husband who has injured his wife may bring her flowers *instead* of genuinely apologizing. The narcissistic parent who insensitively hurts her child's feelings may offer a "treat" instead of apologizing. Such attempts to undo damage *without apologizing,* results in a poorer relationship, because the injured person is made to feel guilty for not being more forgiving to the partner who is now "sorry," and the narcissistic person feel resentful that the undoing "gifts" were not more appreciated.

Another way that narcissistic persons avoid genuinely apologizing is by appealing to their *good intentions*. They are often adept at making apparent apologies, which really amount to self justification. The notion that genuine apology includes *empathy* for the injured person's pain, regardless of whether it was intentionally or accidentally inflicted, seems to escape the narcissistic lover. Narcissists' expressions of sympathy are designed to first emphasize their own faultlessness, and secondly, their concern for the other.

When the narcissist says, "I'm sorry I was late, but I got caught in a traffic jam," to someone who has anxiously been worrying, he often communicates resentment that the other person was worried, not remorse or empathy. Non-narcissistic people would explain why they were late, while remaining empathically attuned to the other person's distress and feeling genuine remorse for having caused it.

It is just another way in which narcissistic persons are driven more by their insatiable needs for approval than by the real needs of a relationship with another human.

For example, Kevin failed to send a wedding present to a very close friend. Later, when this friend admitted how disappointed he had been, Kevin replied, "Gee, I'm sorry, I really was *planning* to get you a gift, but you just have no idea how busy I've been! I'm barely getting any sleep, much less going shopping."

Explaining is another way the narcissists artfully avoid apologizing. To the unsuspecting, the difference between apology and explanation may not at first be apparent, but it is a style frequently used by narcissists because it protects the grandiose self by avoiding asking for something (pardon) while shifting responsibility elsewhere. Typical explanations *sans apology* take the form of "I must have forgotten your birthday because my mother was in the hospital." Or, "I wanted to stop by and see you, but things at the office kept me there until late into the evening." Such "apologies" seem designed to elicit sympathy for the narcissist rather than to express genuine regret over hurt they might have caused.

Sophisticated as he was in psychological matters, Kevin was able to couch his "apologies" in psychological jargon. I heard him say to the unit secretary "Gee, I must have been feeling unconsciously irritated with you when I blew up, because you reminded me of my aunt, who was always on my case when I was growing up. Sorry about that."

A woman I know is married to a narcissistic partner who labels her a "masochist." Whenever she brings up a problem in their marriage, he tells to her work on her "martyr complex." This is a common ploy for narcissists. They typically label the other person as having the problem, accusing the partner of being "oversensitive," or as "overreacting," instead of assuming any blame.

"Thank you"

These two words are as difficult for the narcissist to utter as "I'm sorry,"— maybe even more difficult. This doesn't spring so much from ingratitude (sometimes they *do* appreciate what you've done) but rather from their attempts to appear self sufficient. Expressing appreciation or gratitude feels dangerous to narcissistic lovers because it acknowledges dependency on another. To express thanks is to admit to our having been helped or having needed something in the first place.

Narcissists bypass saying "Thank you" in a number of subconscious but clever ways. One is by *bestowing approval*. This allows the narcissist to maintain the grandiose self by cleverly converting the opportunity to express gratitude into a paternalistic pat on the head. The narcissistic parent of the hyperactive child who says to the teacher, "Jimmy's done very well in your room!" Instead of "Thank you for your patience with Jimmy this year," is subtly but surely avoiding saying "Thank you."

Narcissistic Lovers

Narcissistic lovers are notoriously difficult to please. This grows out of the narcissistic fantasy of a love relationship so perfect that the lover ought to be able to "sense" the needs of the narcissist without his asking. This combines the narcissist's intense need for approval with the avoidance of saying "Thank you" in such a way that others are expected to omnisciently "know" each need without being told. The wife of such a narcissistic man can run herself ragged trying to anticipate his every need. He, for example, may be moping around the kitchen occasionally rummaging through the refrigerator just waiting for his wife to ask: "Are you hungry? Would you like to eat early?" Instead of saying, "Thanks, I really am." He might reply, "OK, if that's what you want to do." This style of narcissistically-protected admission of need characterizes persons who attempt to maintain the posture of self sufficiency.

The narcissistic lover expects perfect anticipation and fulfillment of *his* needs, while remaining insensitive to the reciprocal needs of his lover.

If you make love with this kind of person you'd better be aware of how important it is to acknowledge that they are "the best!" They've read all the technique manuals and know all the "moves," but it's conspicuously apparent that at this is not primarily for your pleasure, but rather to elicit your admiration.

Omniscience

Kevin's narcissism went even further. Not only did he never say he was sorry and have difficulty expressing thanks, he couldn't admit that he'd *learned* anything new. Long before the year was complete most of the other interns had stopped discussing ideas with Kevin, because they just couldn't abide his "I-knew-that" attitude which, in one form or another, was his response to anything someone else might suggest as a new idea. He just couldn't admit, without great pain, that someone else had come up with an idea that he hadn't already considered.

Next to "Carl and I" Kevin's most frequent phrase was "I knew that," or "I could have told you that," or "I predicted that." He simply couldn't admit to being anything less than a fully-knowledgeable or fully-competent person. In elementary school he might have been taunted as a "Mr. know-it-all" and shunned by his peers, but since we were all "grown ups" Kevin wasn't chased off the playground, but I must admit he wouldn't have won any popularity contests either.

You will recall that we previously alluded to the obsessive-compulsive's need for omniscience. Although omniscience is important to both the obsessive compulsive and the narcissist, it has a different quality in each.

The obsessive seeks to know everything in order to maintain his tenuous sense of *control,* whereas the narcissist seeks omniscience in order to be *admired* by others. While the obsessive seeks shelter from anxiety through control (knowing everything means you can control everything), the narcissist seeks safety in admiration (being surrounded by admiring people means you're safe).

In both instances, however the strategy usually intensifies rather than reduces anxiety. Instead of facing his own infallibility, the obsessive strives ever harder to know everything. However as the impossibility of omniscience threatens to seep into consciousness, even more strenuous efforts are called for in order to stave off anxieties about helplessness. Consequently the obsessive rituals intensify. Likewise as the narcissist compulsively maneuvers to establish her omniscience among peers, these very attempts generate distance instead of the compulsively-sought admiration, leading to a redoubling of efforts to elicit admiration.

"I'm the Greatest!"

Once in awhile Kevin could be light hearted, almost humorous, about his own grandiosity. I recall one of his interactions with a patient when we were both working on the adolescent service. Burt was an extremely narcissistic adolescent, who rivaled Kevin in his need for aggrandizement. I overheard the following conversation one day in the hallway:

Burt: (To Kevin, with a grin) "Kevin do you know why you're such a great therapist?"

Kevin: "No, what makes me such a great therapist?" (I noted that Kevin took particular pleasure in repeating *verbatim* the words "such a great therapist.")

Burt: "I do, Kevin. You're great because of me! You're a great therapist because I'm such a great patient!"

Kevin: "Burt, I was great before I ever met you."

Both of them carried on this repartee with adroitness and wit, but it was nonetheless telling in its truthfulness, for each really believed what he was saying. Kevin didn't make great progress in treating Burt because the notion that "it takes one to treat one," doesn't work particularly well with two narcissists. Each is more concerned with *receiving* admiration than in giving it.

Nonetheless, a narcissistic sexual partner can be interesting and fun to be around so long as you are comfortable with flattering or at least over-praising them some of the time. They respond extremely well to compliments and acclaim of any kind, and if their need for praise isn't too tiring it's possible to live with them in peace.

Playing Doctor—All About Beepers, Stethoscopes, and Car Phones. Narcissism is frequently seen in the professions, because the social prestige and power implicit in many professions attracts narcissistic people. The psychotherapists position of being "in the know" while a patient struggles to make sense of her life, or the physician's ability to understand physical illness while the patient is puzzled, carries enormous narcissistic value for the professional. Helping professionals repeatedly experience themselves at the center of their patients' lives, in such a way that their narcissistic tendencies can be strongly reinforced.

Narcissistic doctors, for example believe that their own time is valuable, but the time of others is a commodity to be used. This is reinforced many times each day in any large medical office, where several dozen patients wait for long periods of time to spend a few precious moments with the doctor. The practice of overbooking and allowing patients to wait for long periods is intrinsically narcissistic, because it is based on the premise that it's OK for patients to wait for the doctor, but not vice versa.

Our society participates in reinforcing the narcissism of physicians, politicians, entertainment "stars," and professional athletes. Patients, political supporters, and movie or sports fans sycophantishly reinforce the "God complex" in persons who may have sought such professions for narcissistic reasons in the first place.

Have you ever noticed when meeting a large group of new persons, at a party for example, how quickly you find out who the "important" people are? Physicians form little clusters animatedly exchanging stories about their work, throwing in just enough medical jargon to keep the nonmedical party-goers at a respectful but admiring distance. Attorneys throw around their "legalese" with equal abandon, while real estate moguls talk "property." As if these verbal ploys aren't enough to make such persons clearly stand out, they invariably wear beepers. I suspect that beepers significantly outnumber emergencies, but it is exceptionally satisfying to a narcissist to be paged in the presence of other important people.

Have you ever noticed how many persons in a hospital have stethoscopes around their necks? Or beepers on their belts? Or phones in their cars? The frequency with which one encounters such "I'm-a-doctor" symbols among a variety of hospital workers from candy stripers to lab technicians suggests that "playing doctor" is not easily outgrown. I've seldom met a PA (physician's assistant) or a nurse practitioner who couldn't do everything a "real" doctor can. PAs routinely regale you with stories of babies delivered, lives saved, and surgeries performed—all this and more with a year or two of training beyond college.

Telephones sometimes give insights about their users. Sexually maladjusted persons use phones to make obscene calls or to avail themselves of

Diala-Porn services, telemarketers use phones to hawk their wares, swindlers phone to convince the naive of "investment opportunities."

Narcissists use the phone—no surprise here—to enhance their grandiose selves. The car phone is to the narcissist what the beeper or stethoscope is to the candy striper. This is why there has been a market for fake car phones and antennas. Narcissists feel left out or unimportant if when rush hour traffic is at a near standstill they aren't huddled over a car phone intently talking, or taking "emergency" calls.

"Call Waiting" is another made-for-narcissists phone option. Although it is a legitimate service, often used by others as well, it frequently provides the first clue that one is dealing with a narcissist. Being put on hold while the narcissist takes another "important" call lets you know immediately where you are in the pecking order.

Another, phone related snub—my personal *non*-favorite—occurs when your phone rings, you answer, and a sweet feminine voice says "Please hold for Dr. Jones." This communicates to me even before any conversation begins that my time is less important than my caller's.

Social Impression. For the narcissist the social impression is paramount. With many other lovers, the social impression is a *by-product* of the individual's personal style. For example, the most important thing to an obsessive compulsive is control, and this creates the first impression that he's authoritarian or rigid, but he doesn't consciously try to make such an impression. Even the psychopath creates an impression for a purpose—so he can con you. By contrast, the narcissist's primary concern centers around the social impression. Since a narcissist needs admiration like the average person needs oxygen, the social impression *is* the *raison d'etre.*

Thus, as we've seen, the way a narcissist lover dresses, talks and behaves is all calculated to elicit admiration from others. From the first moment you're in the presence of a narcissist you feel a subconscious tug for your admiration. Like fishing in a rapidly-moving trout stream where the current surrounds you and keeps trying to drag you downstream, in the presence of a narcissistic person you always feel the pull to admire them, to affirm their "specialness."

Parenting to Prevent Narcissism

Parenting to prevent narcissism requires a brief comment. In ordinary people narcissistic tendencies are left behind along with baby blankets, playpens, pacifiers, and tricycles. We observe a "healthy exhibitionism" during infancy and early childhood. When this is appropriately *recognized* and *empathically responded* to by parents and other caretakers, it provides the basis for healthy self-esteem in later life. Usually the *obnoxious* narcissism one sometimes observes in adult life is an indicator that such needs were *not* adequately met early in life.

This has important implications for child rearing, because if you think the toddler's narcissism is the beginning of selfishness, or the first indication of a "spoiled" child, you will not respond positively to your toddler's "showing off." This would be a mistake, because the narcissism of your toddler leads to healthy creativity and self esteem later in life.

Creativity and joyful self-appreciation in the adult is a natural result of the security that comes from growing up with parents who empathically respond to your childhood narcissism with appropriate admiration. You will never admire (or even like) yourself if, during early development, significant others didn't admire you. Healthy *self* esteem results from the internalization of *other* esteem.

Like so many other paradoxes of parenting, it is *lack* of admiration and praise that "spoils" children, not *too* much of it. The adolescent or adult who *compulsively craves* admiration does so because of an inner emptiness which was never adequately met in childhood. Thus, narcissistic style in adults is a product of *too little,* not *too much* attention during infancy and toddlerhood.

Creativity in adults is *refined* narcissism. Artists, writers, scientists, virtually all thought leaders, are adults whose childish attempts at building, devising, or creating were probably met with interest and encouragement.

In fact, as I sit here writing, I can hear my Mama's loving voice echo through the years with a "That's so good, Johnny!" Bottom line—don't hesitate to praise your children's accomplishments, it won't make narcissists of them! It is only when they must create a *false* self to meet *your* needs or when you selectively attend to things *you* think they ought to do, that difficulties arise.

Sexually, the affirmation of a child's emerging "boyness" or "girlness" is very important. Here we're not talking about perverted or incestuous sexual encroachments like we saw in Sissy's case, but appropriate affirmation of the adolescent's transition from childhood to adult maturity.

The father who appropriately affirms his daughter's emerging sexuality with comments like "My don't you look stunning!" as she's about to depart for the prom is lessening the likelihood that she will have to reassure herself about her attractiveness through promiscuous sexual activity. The man who refers to his wife and daughters as his "favorite girls," affirms the developing sexuality of his children without violating important boundaries of privacy.

The mother who proudly refers to her husband and sons as "my men" sends an important message of affirmation to the opposite-sexed child. These kinds of consistent affirmations of a child's psychosexual development promote non-narcissistic sexual development. Now take a few moments to ascertain if there is a significant streak of narcissism in your or your lover.

RECOGNIZING Narcissism in Yourself or Your Lover

1. Do I often daydream of being a movie star or sports hero? A famous politician?
2. Does it almost kill me to say "I'm sorry?"
3. Is it difficult for me to say "Thank you?"
4. Do I feel hollow or empty inside—unless someone is saying I'm great?
5. Was I a "show off" in high school?
6. Do I react intensely to criticism—with rage or humiliation?
7. Do I daydream about being rich, famous, beautiful, powerful, or at the top of my profession?
8. Do I typically feel either envy or disdain for other people?
9. Do I need constant attention or admiration? Do I fish for compliments?
10. Does it annoy me a lot when someone cancels a date, even if they're sick?
11. Is it hard for me to sympathize with others?
12. Do I date a series of partners, often for brief periods?
13. Do I like to "make an entrance" with a "show-stopping" date at parties?
14. Do I drive a late-model sports (or luxury) car? Do I trade it in at least every two years in order to have the latest model?
15. Are my clothes *always* the "sharpest?"

16. Have I seriously considered a "nose job," breast enlargements or reductions, liposuction, or other cosmetic surgery?

17. Do I have few long-term friends?

18. Do I regularly purchase lottery tickets and spend significant time day-dreaming about the many things I'll buy, places I'll visit, and people I'll impress with my winnings?

If you've answered "Yes" to many of these questions or if you feel your lover would answer yes, your relationship has significant narcissistic streaks.

Narcissistic Lovers

By now you'll be able to recognize the narcissistic lover. He or she will—in a thousand little ways—be more interested in eliciting admiration from you than in *giving* love. As we observed earlier, this won't usually take the form of outright bragging, but will masquerade in less obvious ways—difficulties in apologizing, indifference to the needs of others, excessive concern with appearance, and a compulsive need for admiration. When he buys you a new dress, you'll later find out it "goes perfectly" with his suit, and you uneasily wonder whether he bought it for you or for himself. When she primps and preens for what seems like hours before she's finally ready to make an appearance at the party, you find yourself questioning her protestations that it's "for you" she wants to look nice.

It's not much different in the bedroom. She wants you to make her feel special, but seems unaware of your needs. If, after a particularly tiresome day, you're not able to obtain or maintain an erection, she feels personally insulted, ruefully remarking "You *used* to think I was attractive!"

The narcissistic male lover assumes that your *raison d'etre* as a woman—besides rearing children—is to provide him pleasure. This is not so much sexist or "redneck" as it is narcissistic. He genuinely believe that making love *with him* is so exceptionally exciting that it ought to suffice as a reason for living. Any woman, he's convinced, would be happy to be a partner with him, and the orgasmic climaxes he provides are only slightly shy of paradise.

The cardinal characteristic of all narcissistic lovers—male or female, young or old—is that they *must* be admired. This seriously interferes with their ability to *empathically* relate to another person in an intimate encounter. Since their own needs are primary, they often fail to accurately understand their partner's desires. Furthermore since they are driven by an insatiable need for admiration of what may be a *false* self, they find themselves genuinely puzzled as to why their intimate relationships never seem to last.

Christopher and Angela

As they sit in my office for the first time, I know this couple is in deep trouble. Christopher's sad eyes portray guilt, and his face and body language register remorse. Angela, on the other hand, oozes anger from every pore of her body. Her rage is palpable. Sensing her fury, and not wanting to begin the session with shouting, I turned quietly to Christopher and attempt to start things on a "positive note."

"I suppose you're both here because of some problems between you, and we'll get to that soon enough, but before we do, I'm wondering, Chris, could you tell me a bit about what originally attracted you to Angela?"

Chris answers almost immediately:

"She's sensitive to peoples' feelings. Ever since I've known Angie she's been super aware of what other people think and how they feel. Me, give me a spread sheet or a tax form and I'm in my element, but when it comes to people's feelings, I'm not very expert."

"Well! maybe you think I'm an expert," Angie burst in, "but I sure had *you* figured wrong! You sure surprised the hell out of me!"

"Honey, I…"

"Don't 'Honey' me, you promiscuous panderer!"

Oh good, I think to myself, *we're less than five minutes into the session, and this relationship has more strain than an overtightened violin string—threatening to break at any minute.*

"How can you sit there and even pretend to care?" Angie's voice is shrill, her eyes accusatory.

Then, turning to me, her voice softens slightly, decibels dwindling, until she's quietly sobbing.

"As far as I'm concerned our marriage is over. There's nothing to talk about. I don't even know why I'm here, except that my friend Jim said I ought to try counseling before leaving Chris. But what does Jim know? Of course he'd take Christopher's side—he's a man isn't he? For all I know he may have a stash of girlie magazines himself!"

"Jim" was the mayor of Hudsonville, the suburb in which Chris and Angie lived. Angie—of course—was on a first-name basis with Jim.

As the session sputters and backfires, stumbles and lurches—like a car with spark plug and timing problems—I surmise that Angela likes to surround herself with important people. She knows several prominent people in local government and goes out of her way to speak of them on a first-name basis with a contrived casualness that is designed to impress me that these are her buddies.

She takes special delight, Chris mentions, in greeting the mayor as "Jim" whenever she encounters him on the street, even though others address him as "Mr. Mayor" or "Mr. Hotensted."

"Jim," I muse, *just like GQ and "Carl."*

Angie frequently fantasizes about relationships with movie stars like Robert Duvall and Harrison Ford. Although Angie is now in her late thirties, she writes fan letters to various stars, much like an enthralled teenager, and she is particularly proud of a handwritten note she received from Robert Duvall after she'd written him, going on at some length about his performance in Lonesome Dove.

When I ask her to tell me a bit about her favorite celebrities, she forgets her anger temporarily, and regales me with an accounting of the items in her "trophy case."

"Harrison Ford sent me an autographed picture. You should see it! 'Dear Angela,...Best Wishes, Harrison.' Can you believe it? Harrison Ford actually answered my letter! I should have brought his note to show you!"

"It's OK, I believe you."

Angela's attempts to feel important by associating with big names don't seem to bother Chris, who seems mildly amused by his wife's teenie bopper tendencies.

"She's always written to movie stars," Chris reports.

"Well at least all I did was *write!*" Angie glowers at Chris.

With further probing I find out that their marriage had apparently been going OK until that fateful night, a couple of weeks earlier, when Angie caught Chris at the office "having sex with other women."

It turns out, she didn't literally catch him with other women—at least that's not how most people would have seen it—but that's how *she* saw it, and this view point led her to file for divorce.

The night Angela "caught" Christopher, she experienced a severe *narcissistic injury*—not the kind of injury that sent her to the ER, but the kind that put them in the middle of divorce proceedings.

No, she hadn't caught Chris "in the act" with his secretary, but she experienced it as even *worse,* because as she angrily explained to me, "It's just like he made love with *dozens* of different women."

The calamity occurred late one night when Angie unexpectedly stopped by Chris's office with some packages for the morning UPS pick up. Entering quietly, she startled Christopher who had been engrossed the most recent edition of Playboy magazine. A quick search of his desk turned up additional magazines, and Angie was outraged:

"So this is what you do when you work late, is it? All this time I thought you were working extra hours for the family! I thought you were just staying late because it's tax season! How could you do this *to me?* How could you deceive me like this? And to think all this time I trusted you! You sonofabitch! You always said you'd never go out on me! Well what do you call this if it's not having an affair?"

Angie's tirade lasted for hours, and when it was finally finished so was their marriage. Chris admitted to Angie that he sometimes masturbated while reading the magazines—thinking this honest confession might placate her—but for Angela that was the final blow, the ultimate humiliation. She felt that by masturbating he had violated their marriage vows—not once, but numerous times.

For Angela it was a cruel betrayal. Christopher had double-crossed her in a most heartless manner, and no amount of therapeutic analysis on my part could convince her otherwise.

Magazines aren't people, I think, *my goodness, it's not like he was involved in an office Christmas party that turned into an orgy, but Angie isn't going to see it that way, she's too narcissistic—too insecure.*

"But *magazines,* they're not the same as people..." I begin.

"You've got that right!" Angie angrily interrupts, "they're easier to seduce, and he could have as many as he wanted, any time he wanted, like having an office harem! Bastard!"

I can see I'm getting nowhere, so I try changing tactics. Delicately I suggest that Angie has her own fantasy involvements with movie stars:

"You know Angie, you sometimes enjoy a bit of a fantasy life yourself—Harrison Ford, Robert Duvall. I'm not saying these are exactly sexual fantasies, but still, you think about being involved with them in some romantic way don't you?"

This only enrages Angie more:

"Of course you would take his side! You're a man! Men are all the same. They think with their penises! As far as I'm concerned adultery is adultery, and your calling Christopher's escapades "solo sex" or trying to accuse me of unfaithfulness doesn't change anything!

It's no use, I decide, *from her narcissistic perspective, Angie feels discarded, cast aside, abandoned for more beautiful women—so as a matter of pride she won't continue in a relationship with a "promiscuous panderer" as she puts it.*

Angie refused to return for another session, rejected the idea of delaying the divorce for a couple of months, and angrily walked out of the session after she thought I was accusing her of sexual fantasies with Harrison Ford. That was it. End of session. End of marriage. *Finis!*

I perceived almost from the moment they had begun arguing that Christopher's "magazine sex" had dealt a lethal blow to Angie's shaky image of herself as a beautiful woman—she was quite average in appearance. She never totally recovered, and though it meant dissolving their family, which included two young children, and though Angie knew it would mean a significant drop in monthly income, she divorced Chris even while he continued to apologize and reassure her of his love. I was helpless to change the course of events.

Except for her narcissism—her need for admiration, her fragile sense of self—Angie seemed otherwise pretty normal, and Chris was an OK sort of guy. Yet I knew their marriage wouldn't survive because Angie would never again feel admired enough. After that fateful night, it was as if the bottom dropped out of her personality, and for Chris there would be no second chances. One strike and you're out.

REORGANIZING Your Expectations

Living with a narcissistic lover is not easy. If you take them seriously, their arrogance, pomposity, and conceit can turn you off. The egomania and self-centeredness can really bother you if you don't see the *hollowness* of it all. When you do, they appear more pathetic than repulsive. You're able to look into the egotistical adult and see a neglected child, hungry for parental attention which never materializes—or compulsively demanding blue ribbon accolades for mediocre performance.

If you can keep your perspective and your sense of humor it's possible to live with a narcissistic partner, and even enjoy it at times. If their narcissism isn't too severe, there may be other qualities that compensate for it.

It's possible your partner might be narcissistic *and* humorous, intelligent, playful, and even affectionate at times. True, these positive qualities can quickly disappear if she feels criticized or unappreciated, but in a safe long-term relationship some narcissists can trust enough to be more real and not quite as concerned about their entitlement to special status.

The following suggestions may help ease the difficulties of living with a narcissist.

(1) If your partner gets enraged it's a temptation to become angry in return—tit for tat. However if she's narcissistic, you will be better off trying to *understand* the feeling of rage, and chances are it will be the result of a perceived "hurt" or "narcissistic injury." Such people are excessively sensitive to criticism—even when appropriate—and immediately feel hurt if you don't almost constantly admire them.

In real life it's hard to be constantly admiring, because no matter how perfect your partner may be, they are going to make mistakes, or irritate you from time to time. I'm not saying that you have to always tiptoe around as if on egg shells or constantly don the "kid gloves" when dealing with a narcissistic lover, but try to lavish with praise and be careful with criticism. Although you might offer some constructive feedback in a perfectly appropriate way, nine times out of ten it will be received as an insult, affront, or ridicule. This is the nature of the narcissist and you've simply got to let her rage run off your back, realizing it's really about her insecurity.

(2) Your narcissistic partner is likely to exaggerate his/her accomplishments in order to evoke "special" treatment from others. It never helps to correct his story. Avoid saying things like "But darling, I thought the fish you brought home was about a foot long, was it really four feet?" or "Was that *really* a sixteen-point buck you shot last year? I thought it was a doe." If she's going on about her education, it's not helpful in any way to chime in with "But honey, I didn't know you'd graduated from Harvard School of Business, I thought it was a two-year community college."

Your partner isn't interested in giving the correct facts; it's far more important to be admired, and if you sabotage the story, you're likely to be the target of rage on the way home from the party, and it won't really change your lover's personality anyway. So learn to think of his stories not as *factual* narratives, but rather as *myths* designed to entertain and evoke admiration. You may as well expect that there will always be a large "bullshit factor" in all stories, and don't feel it is your responsibility to make certain that "the truth, the whole truth, and nothing but the truth" is being told. You're not a prosecuting attorney and most of the listeners will factor out the exaggeration if they're familiar with your partner's narcissism.

(3) Your lover believes himself to be unique and quite special. He may indulge in a rich fantasy life about success, brilliance, or romance just around the corner. Such fantasies often occur alongside mediocre success on the job or other places in the real world. Since these fantasies serve to compensate for his lack of *real* achievement, it won't work to directly confront him with the ordinariness of his accomplishments.

Each time you try to bring him back to reality, he will simply invent another scheme that will *in the future* bring him fame or fortune. Such a scheme might be something as simple as buying an extra lottery ticket. Better to understand and accept his need for feeling important and stroke him with a bit of flattery if you're feeling up to it. You don't exactly have to lie, but you can make a big deal out of something commonplace. For example if he's "Employee of the Month" at the local Pizza Hut, and you know there are more months than employees, don't mention the obvious fact that sooner or later *everyone* who works there gets their name on the plaque. Don't laugh or ridicule him for his "achievement." Instead, take him out to celebrate or make a big deal of it with the kids. This will help him feel special and actually *lessen* his need to exaggerate his accomplishments or demand adoration from others.

If at home, you can treat her as special, she won't have to be as intense in seeking affirmation at the office and other places. It's not that you can eliminate the narcissist's deep need for admiration, but if you don't fight it—if you don't undermine it, it'll be easier to live with this "special" person. You can be one of the few people who really understands this person. In the long run, this will be deeply appreciated.

(4) We've already noted that narcissistic lovers have a sense of entitlement. They expect special favors and treatment. This is usually unrelated to their actual accomplishments. This may remind you of the antisocial/manipulative lovers we've analyzed, but there is a major differ-

ence. Narcissistic lovers feel primarily entitled to *admiration*. They feel you ought to *admire* them even if their achievements seem ordinary to others.

Antisocial persons are much more broadly entitled and feel you ought to admire them no matter what. Even if they've been involved in something illegal such as an armed robbery where a person was killed, the antisocial person feels entitled to admiration for daring or fearlessness. The narcissist's entitlement is usually more harmless. Just so long as you admire them, they're fine. They won't act in antisocial ways or harm you. It's only when you don't treat them with admiration that they can become enraged. If you understand this, you can work around some difficult problems.

For example, narcissists don't feel they ought to have to wait in line, like other ordinary people. They feel deserving of entering the restaurant's private entrance and being treated in a special manner by the *maitre de*. They resent the fact that the CEO and treasurer of the company have specially marked parking spots but they don't. They even resent handicapped parking, often complaining that "Half those people who get special licenses aren't handicapped, they just are too lazy to walk."

Again, this may become tiring to you at times, but if you understand what is really motivating his/her constant seeking for special treatment, it may be easier to live with it.

(5) Your narcissistic lover's need to be "special" may become tiring at times, but what is more difficult, over the long haul, is the lack of empathy you feel from your partner. This insensitivity to your needs tends to wear you down after awhile. In the old days this was simply known as *selfishness*. There were no fancy terms like narcissism and you weren't expected to tolerate it in others.

I'm not asking you to fulfill all of your partners demands for special treatment, or to ignore his lack of sensitivity towards you or the children, but I'm pointing out that it may be easier if you understand what's really at stake here.

All of this seeking admiration is really a fragile veneer for the deep insecurity within the narcissist's self. There is very little "inside" upon which to draw for self assurance or self esteem, so efforts to secure this must always be directed outward in the form of fishing for compliments, exaggerating, overdressing in the latest fashions, etc. When you understand that the narcissist's often obnoxious behavior is similar to the toddler's tugging on

Mamma's dress and saying "Look at me!" "See what I can do!" it may become a little easier to tolerate.

(6) Finally, many narcissists are preoccupied with feelings of jealousy and rivalry, which also becomes tiring to live with. Often your circle of friends becomes narrow, because sooner or later your narcissistic partner sees most potential friends as selfish, insensitive, unappreciative, ungrateful, etc. All qualities which the narcissist himself harbors but which are projected onto others.

If you're living with a narcissistic lover you have to make your peace with the idea that few people are "good enough" to associate with. You may have to be content with a few intimate friends whom your partner may ridicule or despise as inferiors, but with whom you yourself can form good caring relationships.

REVITALIZING Your Sexual Relationship

As we've noted, living with a narcissist isn't easy; having a good sexual relationship with a narcissistic partner may, at times, be quite demanding. Nonetheless, you may choose to stay in a long-term sexual relationship with a narcissist, and if you do, you'll find yourself contending with many of their mistaken notions about sex. As with other sexual styles, the key to a revitalized relationships is understanding your partner's sexual style and altering your expectations accordingly. It also helps to know what kinds of myths they believe so you can relate more realistically to them. The following myths are often espoused by narcissists, but are by no means limited to them.

Taking Out the Trash

MYTH # 1: Women with large breasts have greater sex drive, are better mothers, and are generally more feminine.

TRUTH: The desirability of large breasts varies from culture to culture and from era to era. Breast size and shape have *nothing* to do with sexuality, except psychologically—if people believe this myth. Breast development is mostly a matter of heredity, and exercise, hormones, exercise, or application of creams are generally useless in altering nature's design. Since silicone implants have been shown to be risky, and surgery is expensive, it seems wise to realize that breast augmentation is unnecessary. What is needed, is a change in *attitude* not a change in size!

Extremely large breasts can be surgically reduced in size, but again, unless size is extraordinarily large, a properly fitting bra, good posture, and good hygiene and eating habits contribute much to maintaining an attractive figure. Narcissistic lovers tend to be overly concerned with physical appearance anyway, so the answer is in re-thinking one's mental attitudes, not in re-making one's breasts.

MYTH # 2: A large penis is of great importance to a woman's sexual satisfaction.

TRUTH: Penis size is not of significance when it comes to sexually satisfying a woman. This myth of the large penis is propagated by pornographic materials, romance novels, and other sexually explicit materials which often emphasize penis size. The usual encounter has a male with a huge penis pleasuring a female with Dolly Parton-like breasts while both scream with pleasure. Such scenarios sell books, but are entirely misleading.

Some males become concerned about whether the size of their penis size because they compare themselves to other males in group showers or the in gymnasium locker rooms. Under such circumstances, two factors conspire to make many males feel inadequate. The first is that the visual angle of looking down on one's own penis when comparing size with another man, exaggerates differences in the direction of making one's own penis appear shorter. Secondly, differences in penis size are exaggerated when the penis is in a *flaccid* state. During erection, small penises grow bigger by a larger factor than larger penises. Consequently differences in size among erect penises are not nearly as great as one might expect from flaccid comparisons.

Finally, nature has provided an important *equalization* factor to assure that a female can accommodate penises across a very broad range of sizes. During sexual arousal the inner two-thirds of the vagina expands and the inner lips enlarge in diameter. This means that even a small penis will fit snugly. However, there is also significant elasticity in this area of the body, and abundant lubrication usually occurs during sexual arousal as well. Consequently a large penis can also be accommodated without discomfort.

Bottom line: Mother Nature intended that when a man and woman make love, they will be snugly compatible, no matter what their sizes.

MYTH # 3: *Real* men don't have vasectomies.

TRUTH: Numerous men opt for vasectomy because it is a simple and safe form of surgical contraception. Although a few men report decreased sexual pleasure after a vasectomy, most find sex more spontaneous and fun after a vasectomy—many reporting an increase in intercourse frequency.

MYTH # 4: Large muscular men have the largest penises and therefore make the best lovers.

TRUTH: We've already seen there is little relationship between the size of a flaccid and erect penis. Similarly there is less relationship between penis size and general body size than exists between the body and other organs. As we've already noted, nature tends to equalize differences in size so that penis size can vary from two inches in one man to ten in another, with neither being more capable of sexual performance than the other.

Much like histrionics, narcissistic lovers tend to overdo things when it comes to ideas about sexual attractiveness. They think in shallow dimensions—in terms of body build, physical attractiveness, and other cultural stereotypes—and are prone to be body builders and aerobics instructors, not so much for health reasons, but in order to be admired.

MYTH # 6: *Real* lovers use vaginal-penile intercourse as the primary method. Oral-genital sex is a sign of inadequacy. Bringing your partner to climax with your mouth, fingers or a vibrator, shows you're not a *real* lover.

TRUTH: Like we've just noted, narcissists find their center of gravity in the external sources—in the admiration of others. Whatever gains the adoration of others becomes a motivating force. Consequently narcissists are excessively influenced by movies, novels, and other media productions which emphasize penis-in-vagina sex as the "best" way to ignite the passions of your sexual partner and subsequently win adoration.

Alternatives often seem, to the narcissistic lover, as indications of inadequacy. Even many non-narcissistic lovers feel that alternatives to "missionary position coitus" are less than best. In truth, there are many excellent means to produce and enjoy orgasms and restricting oneself to what seems a "macho" way or the "perfect" way, is unwise.

MYTH # 7: Women should be virgins at the time of marriage, but men need to be experienced so they can "lead" their partners in lovemaking.

TRUTH: The narcissistic male is prone to believe this myth, because he is flattered by the notion that he must "shop around" so he can become an outstanding lover, while searching for the perfect "undefiled" virgin. Of course there's no reason why virginity is more important for women than for men, and this myth merely perpetuates the notion that women are helpless sex objects who ought to be willing to sacrifice their integrity for the passing male lover.

MYTH # 8: Circumcision makes a man more (or less) attractive and is an important factor in a good sex relationship.

TRUTH: Circumcision is not importantly related to sexual performance, sex drive, or any other aspect of sexuality. Again, the narcissist's overconcern with appearance might lead him to undergo surgery as an adult if he felt circumcision would make him more attractive to the opposite sex.

The only important issues regarding circumcision are related to health and hygiene, *not* sex. Just under the head of the penis are a couple of small glands which secrete oil. These secretions can coalesce with cells from the penis and form a cheese-like substance known as *smegma*. In the uncircumcised male smegma is more likely to collect and can emit a foul odor as well as provide a breeding ground for bacteria.

Another health concern is that some studies suggest uncircumcised males have higher rates of penile cancer and their spouses experience higher rates of cervical cancer. However, it is not certain that circumcision is the causative factor, since these were broad studies, comparing Jews (who are always circumcised as part of their religious rituals) and uncircumcised Protestant and Catholic males.

In summary, evidence is equivocal regarding the role of circumcision in preventing cancer, and uncircumcised men who practice good hygiene are unlikely to accumulate smegma or otherwise be more susceptible to infections.

Summary

This completes our discussion of the narcissistic style, and we conclude with a few final observations. Narcissistic lovers share with dependent personalities a "center of gravity" that is outside themselves. Their sense of worthwhileness is dependent not on satisfactions or qualities that they perceive to be within themselves, but rather on the *admiration* of others.

Unlike dependent or codependent lovers who often work very hard to "earn" the praise of others, narcissists frequently exhibit a sense of entitlement. They feel others *owe them* admiration. Narcissists believe that their own presumption of superiority constitutes proof. They "know" they are more savvy, attractive, and charismatic than others—in spite of their low

G.P.A. or lack of friends. This is reminiscent of the antisocial lover's gargantuan sense of entitlement, but it is not usually as destructive, because narcissists focus mostly on procuring other people's *admiration,* not their material possessions.

You've learned in this chapter that narcissism isn't too much love of self, it is rather the result of a *false* self. What appears as *too much* self love is not really self love at all. It is a *deficiency* of self-esteem that fuels narcissism.

The renowned psychoanalyst Heinz Kohut wrote extensively on the topic of narcissism, explaining how *healthy* narcissism in the infant and toddler is the foundation for later creativity. Kohut believed that a mother's joyful responding to her infant or toddler's early narcissism was one of the pillars of mental health. Kohut called it *mirroring* and believed that all children seek to be mirrored by their parents. He saw the toddler's "showing off" as a healthy developmental stage which would gradually recede if it were adequately recognized and appreciated (mirrored). He put it in the following words:

I do not believe that many cases of harmful maternal spoiling through overempathy or an excess of "mothering" do in fact exist…The fixation…was therefore essentially not the result of over-gratification, but of a specific traumatic absence of maternal empathy for the healthy grandiosity and the healthy exhibitionism of his forming independent self. (Kohut, 1977, pp. 78-79

So you see, it isn't too much attention to the *child's* self that causes later narcissistic fixations, it is too little! Narcissistic parents err not in giving their children too much attention, but in paying too much attention to a *false* self which they would like to see the child develop. Recall Sissy taking piano lessons and Kathryn learning French, not because they wanted to, but in order to please Mother.

In the bedroom, male narcissists typically over value their sexual organs, their sexual prowess, and all those external trappings of sexuality with which they believe they are endowed. Women narcissists find it hard to generate even the tenuous self-esteem of their male counterparts, choosing more often than not to wear clothing and cosmetics that are chosen to conceal their "blemishes." They attempt to "appeal" more than "demand" admiration. When male narcissists "strut their stuff" it often literally includes the penis, pectorals, or a hard derriere. Females are more likely to compensate with clothing or cosmetics.

But whether male or female—whether strutting body parts or clothing—narcissistic lovers *over do* it. Their desperate attempts to make certain that admiration always flows in their direction leaves their friends and lovers feeling empty.

In bed, the male narcissist doesn't even entertain the question "Am I not the best you've ever had?" Instead he frequently cops a narcissistic attitude: "Lucky you, so many women wish they could be in your place!" The female narcissist gives little thought to her partner's pleasure, focusing instead on what *she* desires and on how satisfied *she* is at the end of their lovemaking. In either case, the non-narcisstic lover is often left feeling emotionally isolated, alone—as if the time had been spent in masturbating instead of making love.

Remember, though, we've been looking at the more extreme narcissistic lovers. Like most of the other styles in this book (except, perhaps the sociopathic style) *mild* narcissism can be sexually quite attractive. We like people who dress well, keep themselves smelling good, and when the narcissism includes a good dose of *true* self-esteem, we often find such people attractive.

Chapter 6:
Shy/Shameful
Lovers

"Shy about sex?...Who, me?"

SHY/SHAMEFUL LOVERS

When Your Lover Feels Embarrassed Rather Than Erotic

Shyness and Shame in Handicapped Children

Cass

Six-year-old Cassandra's brown eyes flashed with anger as she slammed her backpack onto the freshly-waxed kitchen floor. "I...I...I'm *never* going back!" she wailed. "I *hate* school!" With that, her anguished emotions abruptly shifted, anger giving way to grief, tears tumbling down her freckled cheeks while great sobs shook her little frame.

These after-school outbursts, accompanied as they inevitably were by resolutions never to attend again, were becoming alarmingly regular. And if the pain to Cass seemed unbearable, Mom found it excruciating, because she, better than Cass, understood the lifelong implications.

By some cruel fate Cassandra had suffered a blood clot that blocked her cerebral artery, leaving her in a coma for three days. Although she recovered to a remarkable extent, there had been some irreversible brain damage. It was "very rare," doctors said, for five-year-olds to suffer strokes, but this brought little comfort to her parents, and the long hospitalization devastatingly disrupted Cassandra's early life.

Prior to the stroke, Cass had excelled in school, easily surpassing her peers. After six weeks in kindergarten, she'd been placed in the gifted track and was soon reading and doing arithmetic normally reserved for children in the third and fourth grades.

Now, as she limped off the bus to her waiting Mom, it was some of the very same children she'd academically "blown away" who jeered "See ya tomorrow brace leg!"

How little Cass hated those words! "Brace leg," "fake leg," "wood leg," "peg leg"—those cruel nicknames found their way into the farthest alcoves of her mind. Although she laughed along with her playmates and tried to pretend it didn't bother her, she suffered agonizing humiliation each time another child commented about her brace. Her shame was searingly intense with each awkward step in the hallway between classes or on her way to lunch.

The stroke left her with significant loss of motor function on the right side. Her right eyelid drooped slightly, her shoulder sagged, her right hand was clenched in a permanent fist, and she required a brace on her right leg in order to walk. While still in the hospital she'd heard the doctors tell her parents she would always suffer from a "claw hand" and "claw toes" on the right side of her body.

"Oh, Mommy!" she'd screamed, "Am I going to grow claws?"

How do you explain to a five-year-old that "claw" toes means spasticity of the metatarsal phalangeal joints?

Her first day back at school was nightmarish. While she awkwardly maneuvered her cumbersome prosthesis down the hall, her peers gawked with unabashed curiosity.

"Look! C'sandra's got a wood leg!"

"T'aint neither wood, it's plastic!"

A kindly teacher had disrupted the "show" by ordering the other children outside to play, but as the group had laughingly exited, Cass heard the cruel singsong of their voices echoing in the frosting February air:

"C'sandra's got a brace leg.

C'sandra's got a brace leg."

Ten years have passed since that first dreadful day back at school, but it could easily have been ten minutes. The memories remain lucid—revived with each step she takes. Now the carefully camouflaged limp of adolescence replaces the awkward shuffle of the six-year-old. She lifts, twists, swings, and drops her right leg with the grace of a ballerina.

Yet deep inside she still feels naked, exposed; knowing that others notice even though they no longer ask those awful "What-happened-to-you?" questions. Though her right foot drops quietly, with an almost imperceptible twist, to Cassandra each step sounds like an air hammer in a cathedral. Walking is like being lead drummer with a rock group. The shameful thump, thump, thump, she "hears" whenever she walks nearly bursts the inside of her head. Like most people who are noticeably "different," Cass lives suspended between outward "niceness" and inner rage.

Nearly every moment of every day Cass struggles to work out an existence that allows her some expression of rage without completely cutting off her social life—not an easy balancing act. When she was younger, she often indulged in revengeful fantasies against children who ridiculed her. She dreamed of hurting them in slow torturous ways. Her favorite fairy tale was Hansel and Gretel—with slight modifications. When she came to the part where Gretel pushed the wicked witch into the oven and slammed the door, she imagined it was one of her "friends" who'd recently been teasing her that was locked in the oven slowly cooking to a crisp.

She savored stories like the Ugly Duckling and the Frog Prince where homely creatures turned into swans and princes. Now these favorite fairy tales have been replaced with fantasies of miracle cures, natural prostheses, and the winning of beauty contests.

Good-Me, Bad-Me

There are really two Cassandras. The private Cass is deeply humiliated, shameful, and *angry*. The public Cass is smiling, compliant, and *"nice,"* seen by others as "that sweet young girl with the limp." She is split down the middle, psychologically as well as neurologically. She experiences her left side—the side on which her motor functions remain unimpaired—as her "good" side. Her right side houses the "crippled" Cass, and is experienced as "bad."

Cassandra's case illustrates how powerfully shame and anger, when chronically present, can fracture the personality. A deep split develops between the public "nice" me and the private enraged me. This divided self is difficult to mend. The "nice" and angry selves do not naturally come together; rather, they drift father apart, widening the gap.

Like the obese person who feels compelled to be "jolly," the repeatedly ridiculed person is publicly pleasant, feeling there is no other choice. But chronic teasing and taunting often drives their private life into ever deepening hostility. Most persons with "shameful" handicaps seesaw between rage and "niceness."

Like Cass, children with seizure disorders, speech problems, severe acne, club feet, tics, or other publicly-ridiculed features are usually "nice and angry." The split may not be as dramatic as the left-right vertical split that accompanies Cassandra's neurological problems, but it is nonetheless real.

Stutterers experience a "good" (fluent) me and a "bad" (stuttering) me because children will always tease stutterers—guaranteed!—and it usually begins when the child enters school for the first time.

Leaving home is a difficult transition for most children, but the "different" child is particularly vulnerable to ridicule. The amphitheater for anxiety moves outside the body. Tensions no longer occur in the rhythms of eating, elimination, and diapering. What matters now is how many friends you have, or whether Teacher likes you. How well you read or whether you wear new clothes to school.

The struggle to succeed shifts from the cradle to the classroom, and the crucial ingredients become social not physical. Newly-formed friendships remain fragile.

Tragically, laughter and ridicule are nowhere more prominent and painful than among the child's own peer group, and it is often teasing by "friends" which is most devastating for the young child. Although a teacher may provide some limited protection, this is often at the cost of becoming "teacher's pet."

In these early school years anything unusual attracts "interest" (ridicule). Six-year-olds have not attained the social grace of not staring when someone with a handicap is present. Quite the contrary, differences arouse their unabashed curiosity.

This is the age at which children ask "Mommy why does that man keep shaking his head?" or "Daddy why is that lady so fat?" or "How come that man doesn't have hair on his head?"

Thus, the stutterer is doomed to hearing:

"Hey T...T...T...Tony! Bet you can't s...s...say P...P...Peter P...P...Piper picked a pack of pickled p...p...peppers."

One of the enigmas of children is the glibness with which they engage in verbal cruelty. Possibly, like adult gossip, ridicule serves to reduce personal anxiety about self by focusing on others. Like heat-seeking missiles, children sense vulnerable spots in one another and attack at that point. The obese child is called "Fatso," while the flat-chested adolescent girl is called "Ironing Board." The intellectually slow child is labeled "Retard," while the child with thick glasses becomes known as "Coke bottles," or, just "Coke" for short. Few children escape those early years unscathed because almost everyone has "defects"—none of us is perfect.

Ridicule Leads to Shame. Shame is not ridicule, it is the *result* of ridicule. Teasing and derision continue to reverberate as "self-talk" long after the actual incidents of torment have passed. Thus although shame originates as an interpersonal social experience, it quickly becomes *internalized* and is then experienced as part of the self.

Now the persecutors no longer need be present—even the *memory* of their words arouses shame. Now the anger is difficult to direct *outward* or *against* external oppressors because it *feels* as if the enemy is *me!*

Shame shrivels self esteem:

"I could have crawled into a hole and died!"

Shame surprises with suddenness:

"Everything was going just fine, until Cathy said, 'Look at the way Susie's nose wiggles when she talks—I never noticed that before!'"

Shame is experienced as a surge of awfulness that quickly rises from the abdomen to heat the back of the neck and further humiliate the self by blushing the face. There seems to be no escape and no way to hide one's humiliation from the observing eyes of others. This kind of inescapable intensity accounts for the tenacity with which shame and self become fused as the *shameful self.* Ridicule cannot easily be shaken off or displaced. It seeps inward, engulfing and permeating the developing sense of self.

Anger Defends the Self. Ridicule intrudes inwardly—engulfing the self with shame, but anger serves to protect the self by fighting back. The angry self seeks to destroy the tormenter and thus end the humiliation. Even when anger is suppressed and goes "underground" as bitterness, resentment, or hostility its goal is to remove the teaser.

The inner life of resentful persons is rich with revenge. Like Cassandra, most teased persons have vivid fantasies of harming and hurting their tormenters. Anger allows the shamed or humiliated self to "fight back." Instead of withdrawing into nothingness, it allows one to act powerfully— at least in fantasy—against one's persecutors.

Since shame and anger pull in opposite directions—shame shriveling the self, anger defending it—in normal circumstances anger can sometimes serve a healthy function, enabling the child to fight back; however this becomes almost impossibly difficult when an actual handicap is present. The child often has conversations with herself that might sound like the following:

"They're right. I deserve to be laughed at because I *do* stutter, [or have a "claw hand," or have seizures, etc.] I don't have a right to be angry. If I get mad, they'll just tease me more. The best thing is to laugh along with them."

Unfortunately, although such an approach buys the child a bit of temporary peace, it tends to perpetuate the cycle. Such children often act in excessively "nice" ways and take their handicaps "in stride." But by actively holding back their destructive rage, they inadvertently encourage more of the same. Other children noticing that the teasing is tolerated—even "enjoyed" by the other person, since they are laughing too—continue their destructive ridicule.

As such vicious cycles continue, the rage intensifies, making it even more impossible to express. Living this way can be infuriating, but since even mild irritation is not expressed by the target child, such fury never finds public expression, and the chasm between anger and niceness deepens.

Try to imagine the psychological experience of someone with a publicly obvious problem. Think how it might feel, if once a month you experienced a grand mal seizure and regained consciousness to find yourself lying flat on the ground—possibly in your own urine or feces—with a circle of frightened faces looking down at you. Consider how terribly humiliating it would be. Imagine how hard you would try to be "nice" the other twenty-nine days of the month to "make up" for such a "shameful" episode. And when the pale faces and frightened eyes slowly returned to the first-grade room, while you were whisked off to the ER, ponder how humiliating it would be to see them all again the next day.

Much of Cassandra's therapy involved my assisting her to get in touch with her seething rage and helping her to accept it as OK. As she began to share her fantasies of what she wanted to do to those who had teased and humiliated her, the repression dam burst, the rage came pouring out, accompanied by violent sobbing and vivid descriptions of painful revenge visited on her persecutors. This "nice" young girl, who apparently dealt so admirably with her problems, would have rivaled a Gestapo torture expert in her malevolent machinations.

However, once she began to recognize and talk about her anger she also began to heal. The gap between her niceness and her rage began to narrow. She learned that expressing anger doesn't negate goodness, that most people live with both pleasure and frustration. She became more comfortable with the co-existence of negative and positive emotions and allowed herself to express annoyance, irritation, and other anger-related feelings more easily. This caused some initial problems with her family and friends who had considered Cass someone whom "you could count on" to be "nice."

But she gradually traded in her attempts to be like Mother Theresa for a much less perfectionistic view of herself. This allowed her not only to express her anger, but to reduce the internal shame arising from her private world of rage.

But it's not just the Cassandras of the world who experience shame. It's not just people with handicaps, *ordinary* people seldom escape childhood shamelessly.

RECOGNIZING Shame in Ordinary People

What Makes You Ashamed? Most persons are ashamed of numerous *personal characteristics*. Shape or size of nose, color of eyes, thickness of eyebrows, distance between front teeth, angle at which ears are attached to the head, size of breasts or penis, presence of acne or birthmarks, these are the items people include on the list of "Things I don't like about myself." Although the list apparently changes and mellows with maturity, upon closer scrutiny it remains surprisingly similar; worries about acne replaced by worries about wrinkles—neither adolescent nor middle aged adult enthralled with her epidermis. Adolescents can't stand the color of their hair, middle agers abhor the absence of it. Nails are never right— depending on your age, sex, or stress level, they are either dirty, ragged, broken or chewed—but *never* right.

Ridicule and the resultant shame often target a particular part of the body which is seen as even slightly "different" (e.g., petite breasts, large nose, small genitals, etc.) This can sabotage one's pride of ownership. "I hate my body!"—a phrase which clinicians often hear from the obese or handicapped—occurs among the general population as well, often in a more subtle form, targeting specific bodily zones: "I hate my ears...crooked nose...chubby hands...complexion...eyebrows, etc."

Even *nonphysical characteristics* are singled out for "shame focus." The thick lenses required for clear vision, the hearing aid that's impossible to completely conceal, the size 46 trousers, the "ugly" shoes one has to wear in order to accommodate arch supports—all such accessories are experienced as liabilities and devalue the person in the eyes of self and others.

The average person is plagued by numerous "imperfections" of which they—more than others—are aware. Most suffer throughout life with a diminished sense of self because so few of these "blemishes" are repairable at reasonable cost. While orthodontia can revamp crooked teeth and contact lenses can remove "coke bottle" glasses, few people have access to more elaborate interventions such as face lifts, breast implants, "tummy tucks," and the like. Most suffer silently, their misery being continually exacerbated by comparison with more-perfect-than-life caricatures created by Hollywood, *People Magazine, GQ,* and television.

"Blemished" family members are often an additional source of shame for siblings or parents. Children are usually profoundly embarrassed by siblings or other family members whom they know are see by others as "different." Almost any child growing up with a "shameful" family member will, vicariously, share much of the shame.

The sibling with cerebral palsy or mental retardation; the obese or alcoholic parent, are but a few of the possible sources from which children absorb external shame and make it their own. Such shame-by-identification often eludes detection, sometimes surfacing years later.

Nicknames perpetuate shame. Far too many children are tagged with "nicknames." All such names ought to be carefully scrutinized for their harm potential, because nicknames are like flea collars and eye glasses— they simply become a part of those on whom they're placed. But unlike flea collars and glasses, they often destroy their carriers rather than assist them to achieve a better quality of life. It is their taken-for-granted, accepted-as-part-of-me quality which makes them so dangerous. They are subtle but insidious.

Nicknames need not be restricted to physical characteristics, they often derive life from the behavioral reactions of the targeted child. *"Bud-Susie"* was one such nickname. Johnny, a fourth-grader, gave his classmates the "scoop" on his little brother Patrick who was entering school for the first time:

"If you call him 'Bud,'" Johnny informed his friends, "he'll get mad, and if you call him 'Susie' he'll cry."

Thereafter Johnny's little brother Pat became known throughout the school as "Bud-Susie," a name that stuck with him throughout his elementary years.

"Peabody." A college student told me—with anguish—of his childhood struggles with nocturnal enuresis (night time bedwetting). The most distressing part of the experience was not the bedwetting, but the fact that

somehow the kids at school found out and nicknamed him "Peabody." This name, of course, remained long after he had conquered the enuresis, a constant reminder of her previous failures and humiliation.

Abuse Often Begins at Home. Now that we've seen how damaging ridicule can be to the developing child's personality, it ought to be the goal of every parent to eradicate teasing from the home. Tragic as taunting is when it occurs among one's childhood playmates, it is even more deplorable when parents or siblings are the source of such verbal abuse.

Family therapists are well acquainted with the many cases where a child is called "Shorty," "Bones," "Beefy," "Dumbo," "Meathead," etc. by other family members in "fun." ("Fun" in most such instances is a euphemism for *ridicule)* Even in the rare cases where such names are genuinely affectionate "pet" names, they often do not mean the same thing outside the family.

Self Quiz

1. Was I regularly called a negative nickname while growing up?

2. Do I have any physical features that my playmates have noticed and teased me about?

3. Do any of the members of my family have noticeable physical or emotional handicaps? Have they been ridiculed or teased about such?

4. Were the words "Shame on you!" used very often in my home?

5. Did I ever (or do I still) blush frequently?

6. Did my parents teach me to always try for "first place?" Were they disappointed in my school grades?

7. Was I taught to worship Jesus, God, Allah, or some other divine being *and* to *model my life* after them?

8. Did I always secretly know I was *far short* of the model?

9. Did I dread any kind of performance in front of an audience?

10. Have I often felt bad because I didn't feel I had *really* done my best?

11. Do I believe that almost anyone can accomplish almost anything if only they try hard enough?

12. Do I remember my Dad being "disappointed" in my athletic (dis)abilities?

13. Do I often compare myself to others and come up short?

14. Do I often find myself saying (either aloud or silently): "I can't relate to people." "I'm never going to amount to much." "I doubt I'll get that promotion, because the boss knows—as I do—that I don't have what it takes."

15. Was I negatively compared to a sibling or playmates? ("If you studied instead of goofing off, you could get good grades like Becky does!")

16. Was I often the target of ridicule or teasing as a youngster?

17. Do I often put myself down?

18. Do I idolize movie stars or athletes?

19. Do I often feel as if there are two selves inside me—the good me and the bad (shameful) me?

20. Do I regularly read *People Magazine?*—and compare myself unfavorably with the "stars" pictured there?

If you or your lover has answered "Yes" to many of these questions, it means you have a pretty wide streak of shame in your personality.

Next, we'll become acquainted with an *ordinary* person who suffered not from seizure disorders, limping, or a learning disability, but was ridiculed just because he was taller than average.

Shyness and Shame in Ordinary People

String

"String Bean" is what he'd been called for most of his childhood and adolescence, but as he grew to adulthood it was shortened to simply "String." Though awkward in most sports, his lanky 6' 6" frame was a natural for basketball. When parked under the hoop, blocking shots and grabbing rebounds, being tall seemed briefly OK. Otherwise his spindly frame was a constant source of embarrassment to him.

It was in the second grade, on St. Patrick's day, when he wore a green shirt with matching green trousers that he was "discovered:"

"Hey look!" one of the other students excitedly exulted, "Billy looks like a string bean!"

The children had burst into laughter, Billy had responded by blushing crimson, and that was it. His destiny was sealed. In that single searing moment his future was fixed. From then on, he would be known as "String Bean," "Jolly Green Giant," "Bean Stalk," or "String." Prior to that he'd been called "Skinny" or "Boney Mahoney," after that one incident, the "green" names stuck—painfully, shamefully.

Even now, in his mid-forties, whenever an acquaintance from high school days runs into him, it's "How ya doing String? Long time no see!"

He doubts any of them know his name is actually William. He would gladly have traded Willie, Bill, or even William for one of his "green" names.

As he sat in my office, obese and depressed it was difficult to imagine this two-hundred-eighty pound man as a scrawny, skyscraping adolescent. He was extremely discouraged because his physician had recently told him he would soon need a knee replacement if he didn't lose at least a hundred pounds.

Bad medical news was not news to Bill. He'd been warned about risks associated with his chronic high blood pressure and other weight-related problems before, but in recent months the pain in his knees had become unbearable and he'd finally gone to a specialist to have it checked out.

Arthritis ran in his family, but the physician told him that the pain in his knee joints was being profoundly exacerbated by his weight. X-rays revealed very little cartilage remaining to cushion the joints and it seemed that a replacement was going to be inevitable.

Nonetheless, he'd been told he could put this off by losing weight. Furthermore, once the replacement had been done, it would have to be repeated if he didn't bring his weight down, because artificial joints wear out just like the original ones.

Bill was confident that he could lose the weight, but ironically, it frightened him. Although most people remember their "skinny" days with longing—"I wish I weighed what I did when I got married." or "I wish I weighed what I did in high school!"—not so with Bill. He had consciously tried to gain weight in order to put behind him forever the painful memories associated with being a "string bean."

Now, however, faced with the dire prospect of knee surgery, he was psychologically stymied. He knew he must lose weight—he consciously said he *wanted* to lose weight—but a deep unconscious part of him was terrified at the prospect of becoming slender again, and this paralyzed him.

It was only through intensive psychotherapy, combined with hypnosis that Bill was able to comfortably imagine himself slender again. Once he got past this psychological hurdle, the actual process of losing the weight wasn't as difficult as he'd imagined. Bill lost 94 pounds, and still has his original knees.

Monitoring the Environment to Lower Ridicule Emissions

Parents and teachers ought to do all they can to eliminate shame-producing ridicule which occurs in the form of teasing, name calling, and other home and school unkindnesses. The following are guidelines:

1. NEVER SPEAK DISPARAGINGLY ABOUT ANYTHING WHICH CANNOT BE *EASILY* CHANGED:

   [OK] "That green shirt doesn't go with those blue pants."

   [Not OK] "If you keep gaining weight, those slacks are going to split."

   [OK] "Eating green apples may cause your stomach to hurt."

   [Not OK] "Please talk more slowly, or you'll never get over stuttering."

2. FOCUS ON BEHAVIOR *NOT* PERSONALITY:

   [OK] "When I find toys strewn around the house—broken because they were not put away—I get really upset!"

   [Not OK] "Why are you so messy?"

   [OK] "I'm irritated that grape juice got spilled on the carpet. This wouldn't have happened if the 'house rule' about not eating in front of the TV had been followed."

   [Not OK] "You spilled your juice again—for the life of me, I can't figure out why you're so clumsy!"

3. DO NOT USE OR ALLOW OTHERS TO USE NEGATIVE NICKNAMES: This is a bit tricky, because attention is usually reinforcing and if you make a "big deal" out of occasional teasing by siblings or playmates, it can backfire and worsen the ridicule. It's almost impossible to "police" the playground, hallways, or locker rooms, which is where name calling often occurs; but at the very least, the child's home (and home room) ought to be ridicule-free environment.

   [OK to allow] "Slow poke, slow poke, I bet I can eat my lunch faster than you can!"

   [Not OK] "Debbie is a dumbo, Debbie is a dumbo!"

   "Freddie is a fatso, Freddie is a fatso!" "Dougy is a klutz, Dougy is a klutz!"

   The sound of sing-song rhyming should capture the attention of parents and teachers as vividly as the sound of screeching tires followed by shattering glass gets peoples' attention at an intersection. In both instances someone is likely to be hurt—badly.

4. TEACH YOUR CHILDREN NOT TO TEASE: Young children do not realize how damaging words can be. They really believe that "sticks and stones can break my bones, but words will never hurt me."

When two-year-old Matthew pulls Fido's ears and bursts out laughing because the dog yelps, he is not so much cruel as uninformed. He doesn't realize he's hurting the dog, so he has to be instructed about why the dog yelps.

Children need to be taught kindness in words as well as in behaviors. It isn't something they pick up naturally. A couple generations ago, the teaching of "manners" was considered at least as important as the three R's, but today it seems to have dwindled in importance. The wise man said it well:

"Pleasant words are a honeycomb, sweet to the soul and healing to the bones."—Proverbs 16:24 NIV

5. TEACHERS, DON'T LET CHILDREN "CHOOSE UP TEAMS" FOR ANY GAMES—BEING CHOSEN LAST IS SOMETHING A CHILD MAY CARRY THE REST OF HER/HIS LIFE: Instead, line children up and count off odd-even teams. Or assign teams on the basis of the alphabet. *Do not* allow them to choose among themselves on the basis of skill, because this will be affirming only for the first couple or three chosen, after which it will become progressively discounting, ending with profound shame for the "last one chosen."

An appropriate goal for parents and teachers would be the total eradication of shame from the lives of all children. Doubtless this will never be achieved, but just as we seek to save our natural environment by reducing pollutants, we ought to strive to drastically "toxins" like shame in the social environment.

We've examined some of the many ways shame is caused from outside oneself, but there is a more subtle shame generator—inside ourselves. Let's look briefly at how we might reduce shame from within.

REORGANIZING Expectations of Yourself

Reducing Shame From Within

Ideal Self & Real Self. Recall that when we discussed narcissistic lovers, we spoke of the *false* self—that self which the narcissist developed to please their parents, but which was not really who they were. In the case of shame-permeated personalities, we typically see them striving excessively to achieve an *ideal* self. This *perfectionism turned toward self* too often turns into a *self-inflicted personality wound.*

Unlike obsessives, who try to do things perfectly in order to maintain control of the world, shame-permeated persons try to become *perfect people* in order to be liked-as an attempt "make up" for their handicap. Of course they fail! Nobody can ever live up to their own idealizations—especially "blemished" people. Ironically, such valiant attempts at living up to one's ideals, causes even greater *disparity between the ideal self and the real self,* and this *disparity* generates *shame* from within.

The ideal self is the repository of our dreams and goals regarding the kind of person we would like to become—a kind of living blueprint we try to follow. It is similar to what we sometimes call "character" but perhaps not quite as moralistic in tone.

In fact, the ideal self is deceptively innocuous on first glance. It feels "user friendly" and unlike a severe conscience which punishes transgressions, the ideal self is concerned not so much with wrong doing as with achievement. And what could be so bad, after all, about trying harder? What could possibly be wrong with setting high goals? Why not "shoot for the stars?" Even the army encourages us to "Be all that you can be."

But there's a catch. When we fail to achieve our ideals, we feel disappointed or embarrassed. If the gap between who we *are* and who we *ought to be,* is substantial, we often feel ashamed, embarrassed-chagrined that we've failed, convinced that we could be OK if we tried harder.

Failing to meet our own idealism, we try even harder—subsequently failing even worse. In this way, the *ideal* self easily becomes an impossibly *grandiose* self.

The Grandiose Self. Clinicians writing about shame sometimes refer to a "grandiose self-representation" or to an "omnipotent self." In one form or another, these all refer to an *inflated ideal self;* an ideal self that strives to be "perfect," an ideal self that can never be "good enough." Such self-inflicted perfectionism inflates the ideal self to gargantuan proportions, creating a chasm between the ideal self and real self which becomes impossible to cross.

Michelle

Michelle was extremely ashamed. Unlike Cassandra and Bill, however, she had rarely been ridiculed, and she had no handicapped siblings. Her parents were well-educated, "sharp" people and she had no apparent blemishes or disabilities of her own. In a word, she'd grown up in a "perfect" home.

Though her father was a busy oral surgeon, he limited his practice to four and a half days, spending Friday afternoons and week-ends with his family. Mom was a traditional homemaker, who'd stayed at home with "Baby M" until kindergarten, and then worked mornings at the dental office.

Although the roots of Michelle's shame were obscure, the expressions were distressingly obvious. Michelle was a blusher. Like everything else she did, she was a "superb" blusher. No gentle sunrise pink-on-the-face here, no transient tinge of red that swiftly dissipated; when Michelle blushed everyone knew it. Her face and neck, even her shoulders, would turn deep crimson and stay that way for hours—or so it seemed to her. In reality, of course, it was only a few minutes—only as long as it took her to escape from the situation and from her dreadful self-generated agony.

Michelle worked as a programs analyst for a consulting firm and often found herself in new situations, translating "computerese" into terms that administrators and middle managers with little computer training could understand. She was highly competent, well respected, and generally articulate.

However sometimes in the middle of a presentation she would blush for no apparent reason. This sometimes even happened when someone else was up front doing the main presentation and she was merely a panel member or discussant.

The out-of-the-blue suddenness with which the blushing struck further fueled her anxieties about when it might next occur. She increasingly felt like she was living on the edge of an active volcano that could erupt at any moment without warning.

Of course, this only made matters worse. Like the male with erectile difficulties whose worries about performance cause the very "failures" he dreads, Michelle constantly worried about blushing thereby greatly increasing the frequency of these humiliating episodes.

Initially, treatment focused on relaxation training, and reassurance regarding the "seriousness" of blushing. I gently kidded her, using a careful "so-what?" attitude.

"Blushing isn't a felony," I joshed.

"I don't think it's even a misdemeanor."

Of course, to her it was no laughing matter, so I had to be careful not to appear insensitive. Nonetheless, a bit of humor, I thought would be helpful. Michelle gained relief from the combination of relaxation training and my refusing to treat her blushing as a life-and-death matter. I was able to convince her to take herself less seriously, i.e, not to try so desperately to live up to her *ideal* self. She made remarkable progress in just a few sessions.

Popular wisdom has it that if you feel ashamed, you'll work harder to improve. Wrong! If you feel ashamed, you'll want to hide, you'll avoid taking chances and you'll be less creative and less free to try again. Self confidence, not shame is the engine that drives creativity and productivity.

Social Impression. Shame propels people to hide. Sometimes in the first seconds or minutes of contact with a shame-based person, you have the feeling they would rather be elsewhere. The classic description: "I could have crawled in a hole!" expresses the urge to escape the situation. The body posture is also consistent with cutting off or reducing communication. Tomkins describes it well:

"The shame response is an act which reduces communication. It stands in the same relation to looking and smiling as silence stands to speech and as disgust, nausea and vomiting stand to hunger and eating. By dropping his eyes, his eyelids, his head and sometimes the whole upper part of his body, the individual calls a halt to looking at another person, particularly the other person's face, and to the other person's looking at him, particularly at his face. The child early learns to cover his face with his hands when he is shy in the presence of a stranger." (1963, p. 120)

Shame-permeated people project a lack of confidence, manifested either in the attempt to withdraw as described above, or in its polar opposite, hyperfriendliness which has a sycophantish, bootlicking quality about it. They are either shy saying nothing or puppylike "kissing up" to everyone.

Most often, however, people with shame-based styles are seen as shy or withdrawn, though friendly if others initiate social contact.

Psychological Style. If you spend several hours or days with such persons, you become intuitively "careful" not to criticize them. They disparage themselves so malignantly that you hate to add more, and find yourself subconsciously attempting to build them up by not agreeing with their self-derogatory remarks.

Although it sometimes becomes wearisome constantly propping up someone's else's self esteem, being around a shy/shameful lover is not repugnant—especially if they keep their rage hidden and behave "nicely" most of the time. In fact, until you tire of trying to inflate their sagging self esteem, being around them may even be gratifying, because you never feel put down by comparison. Around a narcissist you could feel threatened by their arrogance and a sociopath might cause you to be hypervigilant in order to avoid being "taken," but shame-based people usually feel safe— very safe.

Persons with shame-based styles are often seen as *shy*. Behind this shyness, however they yearn for friendship. They avoid social situations not because they distrust or dislike people, but because they fear saying something inappropriate or behaving in a way that appears foolish. They require assurances before becoming socially involved, needing to feel certain they will be liked ahead of time.

Although such persons are easily hurt by criticism or disapproval, they usually react to such disapproval by withdrawing, not by angry counterattacks as does the narcissistically injured person.

People permeated by shyness and shame are pervasive in our competitive compare-yourself-to-the-stars society. Our culture values performance more than character, athletic prowess over kindness, and entrepreneurial excellence above empathy.

We strain to see ourselves in media-created mirrors wondering how *we* might look on the covers of *People Magazine* or *GQ*, or on a huge screen with surround sound. By comparing ourselves to the "beautiful people," and to the larger-than-life facsimiles of persons that TV and Hollywood project into our lives, we always come out losers.

This produces distorted images of ourselves, like the ones we see in those S-shaped mirrors at carnivals or fun houses. Compared to almost anyone projected into our line of vision by media moguls, we are either too fat, too poor, too awkward, too old, or all of the above. If that's not enough of an affront, the televangelists are determined to convince us that we're too sexual, too miserly, and too self-satisfied. Further billions are spent to convince us that our breath is too stale, our armpits too pungent, and our skin too rough.

There seems to be no end to being reminded of our multiple short-comings—all shameful! Never before has comparison to "superior" beings been as near as the flip of a TV switch. Never before have a few media moguls so easily shamed the masses. If Churchill were living he might say: "Never in the field of human relations was so much shame, inflicted on so many, by so few!"

RECOGNIZING Shame-Permeated Lovers

Roxanne

Roxanne was in her late twenties when she first consulted me about what she described as a "sexual problem." Attractive and intelligent, relaxed but poised, she seemed to be one of those people who "has it together." However, almost as soon as she seated herself on my couch and began telling me of her unhappy marriage, her composure vaporized.

"I hate sex!" she sobbed. "It's...it's so messy!" She continued, haltingly, sandwiching her phrases between convulsive sobs.

"And whenever Jack gets turned on, he starts that deep kissing stuff. Yuk! I can hardly stand it. I wish when we had sex he would just do it and get it over with I might be able to put up with it, but that French kissing along with it, makes me almost gag!"

Although they'd been married less than six months, she and Jack were on the verge of breaking up over their sexual incompatibility.

I arranged for Jack to come in with Roxanne for a couple of joint sessions, hoping to pick up some clues as to what was going wrong in the relationship. However it only baffled me more because Roxanne and Jack seemed to genuinely care about each other.

I found this puzzling because for most couples sex is a barometer of the relationship. Sexual problems are usually the surface manifestation of deeper issues. Just as the classic argument about the correct way to squeeze a toothpaste tube is only the tip of the relational iceberg, sexual problems are often symptoms of deeper relationship conflicts. Usually little genuine progress is made until the deeper disagreements are understood.

The joint sessions perplexed me because I couldn't seem to turn up any clues. Roxanne and Jack enjoyed each other's company, even kidded around a bit during the sessions, and seemed like a very happily married couple, *except* for the fact that Jack wasn't interested in celibacy, and Roxanne wasn't interested in sex. Their courtship had been short and intense, and the fact that Roxanne didn't like deep kissing hardly seemed reason enough to call off their engagement. During the honeymoon, however, as sex became increasingly "messy," the seriousness of their differences began to dawn on both of them, but it was too late to do anything about it.

Since our joint sessions hadn't proved very useful, I decided to see Roxanne for individual psychotherapy. A few sessions into treatment, as she was talking about her childhood, I discovered that she had always been terribly embarrassed by Roger, her mentally retarded brother.

When I asked for her to describe Roger, the first image that came to her mind was his drooling mouth with that perpetual silly grin she hated so much. She vividly recalled his messiness at meals and the sound of him "chomping" his food with his mouth open and saliva running down the corners.

Roxanne was both shocked and pleased when I pointed out the similarity between her descriptions of sex and her first thoughts of Roger. She instantly made the "messiness" connection and understood without further explanation that her ardent aversion to messiness was because such events unconsciously reminded her of her brother, whom she had urgently wanted to distance herself from.

"What a relief!" she laughed, "finding out it's my brother, not my husband that turns me off!"

Once Roxanne understood this, her obsession with keeping the kitchen squeaky clean became less intense and her sexual problems subsided. She began to tolerate, even enjoy, "messy" sex. She never did develop much of a taste for deep kissing, but Jack said he could live with that.

Subsequently their marriage improved considerably and a few weeks later, she finished therapy. I now hear from her at Christmas each year when she unfailingly sends me a photo greeting card of her growing family.

Revitalizing Your Sexual Relationship

If you or your lover struggle with shyness or shame, don't give up hope. This is not like sociopathy or some other personality style that is deeply destructive to your relationship. Shy/shameful lovers feel awfully uncomfortable at times, but they don't typically bring destructiveness or suffering to the relationship, as is the case, for example with sociopathic partners.

Encouragement, reassurance, and comfort are the ingredients for successfully assisting a shame-permeated lover to blossom. It also helps to debunk some of the mythology surround sexuality. Shy/shameful lovers are especially likely to be adversely affected by such nonsense.

Taking Out the Trash

From the earliest recorded writings, the perfectly normal event of *menstruation* has been surrounded with folklore and superstition—mostly negative. Feminists have suggested that men, fearful of women's power, instilled shame and self-hate in them regarding their periods. As early as A.D. 60, the Roman historian Pliny said that menstruating women will cause new wine to sour, fruit to fall from trees, and seeds to become sterile.

But mythology surrounding menstruation isn't limited to ancient Romans or first-century historians. Indeed, the following myths were collected from present-day college students living in various parts of the country:

(a) Dogs fed by a menstruating woman will develop worms.

(b) A menstruating woman's hair will not "take" a permanent wave, and kinky hair cannot be straightened during the menstrual period.

(c) Well-trained domestic animals will not respond to directions from a woman who is menstruating.

(d) Shaving armpits or legs during menstruation will cause the woman to become weak and listless and will result in a difficult menstruation.

Notice most of these are not positive myths. Consequently, shy/shameful lovers are especially susceptible to many of the myths surrounding menstruation, because of their chronic shame and their tendency to degrade themselves.

Shy/shameful lovers also worry about many of the same myths that plague narcissistic lovers. Like narcissists, shy/shameful lovers worry about physical proportions: breast size, penis size, circumcision, shapeliness of legs, dimensions of one's derriere, shape of the nose, etc. These are of primary importance—*but in the opposite way!* Whereas narcissists worry about physical deficiencies in their *partner(s),* shy/shameful lovers worry about the self-same kinds of deficiencies in *themselves!*

In addition to all the myths surrounding menstruation, breast size, penis size, and other body parts, shy/shameful lovers are prone to the following sexual myths:

MYTH # 1: Sexologists agree that there are two kinds of orgasms: a *clitoral orgasm,* which is somewhat superficial and not quite satisfactory, and the *vaginal orgasm,* which is attained by mature, sexually adequate women.

TRUTH: Today, thanks to careful physiological studies by researchers, it is a well-accepted fact that orgasm is a total bodily response, and that it makes little difference how one reaches climax. Research indicates that "an orgasm is an orgasm is an orgasm." It seems to make little difference whether orgasms are reached through self stimulation, partner stimulation, clitoral stimulation, or vaginal penetration. Each is a valid experience and the actual point of stimulation doesn't much matter.

MYTH # 2: Regular douching is necessary to keep the vagina clean.

TRUTH: Douching is actually unnecessary because in a healthy woman natural secretions keep the vagina clean. If, however, a woman prefers to douche after intercourse for purely aesthetic reasons, she should use water alone, not lemon juice, vinegar, or commercially marketed products. Frequent douching can destroy beneficial bacteria that normally inhabit the vagina, leaving the woman more vulnerable to vaginitis.

Since worry about body odors frequently plagues shame-permeated people, they are likely to be overconcerned with such matters and vulnerable to over use of douching products.

MYTH # 3: Frequent masturbation during adolescence can lead to mental illness or maladjustment in adult life.

TRUTH: As is the case with menstruation, there is extensive folklore regarding the alleged harmful effects of masturbation. *None* have been shown to be true! However, shy/shameful lovers are especially prone to all masturbation myths, because during their own adolescence—typically short of sexuality because of their shyness and shame—they likely engaged in frequent solo sex.

MYTH # 4: Masturbation can cause a number of physical manifestations, including warts, hair in the palms of the hands, pimples, acne, poor eyesight, memory losses, stunted growth of genitals, and a host of other maladies too numerous to list.

TRUTH: Medical science has ascertained that *no dire consequences* accompany masturbation. *NONE* of these alleged effects are a result of masturbation.

There are undoubtedly numerous other myths that shy/shameful people are vulnerable to believing, but these illustrate how shame in the personality predisposes a person to believe negative things about herself. Whether the myths are about menstruation or masturbation, whether the person worries about breast size or penis size—or both—the common element is that shy/shameful lovers believe *"I'm inadequate."*

In this chapter we've seen several vivid examples of how shame, beginning in childhood, eventually permeates the lover's personality. This chapter, perhaps more than any other, has been for *ordinary* lovers. Shame is not restricted to persons designated to have mental problems, it is indeed a populace neurosis, an awfulness most of us have experienced more times than we wish to recall. Sadly, shame and sexuality have too often been bedfellows.

In the next chapter we will discuss a sexual style which shares much in common with shame-based styles. People who feel "one down," weak, or vulnerable, often resort to *indirect styles* because it is one of the few ways in which they are able to maneuver in a world that seems dominated by the mighty. Children, the handicapped, the uneducated, the poor, the religiously subservient, are the kinds of people who often engage in indirect expressions of their needs.

Chapter 7:
Indirectly Angry
Lovers

"Daffodils?...You sure?...They looked like milkweeds to me."

INDIRECTLY ANGRY LOVERS

Understanding Passive Aggressive
Personality Styles
or
Don't Pout When He Mows Down Your
Petunias Instead of the Grass

T he people you'll meet in this chapter are experts in bringing about great discomfort—even pain—in others by doing *nothing at all.* Through "forgetfulness," silence, withdrawal, lack of emotions, and lack of opinions, they *indirectly,* but effectively accomplish what others achieve through anger, fury, rampage, confrontation, and other direct methods.

These strategies—often mastered during childhood to deal with powerful adults—persist into the adult years in a form known as *Passive Aggression.*

In the *bedroom* the passive aggressive lover brings displeasure to his partner by what he *leaves undone,* rather than in any direct way. Thus, if the man ejaculates before his mate climaxes, if he is passive aggressive, he will put forth little or no effort to provide additional tenderness to his partner using his hands, mouth, or other stimulation.

In the *kitchen* his most ferocious weapon is the morning paper or the Wall Street Journal, behind which he spends most of the meal, thereby communicating rejection without any irritable words ever being spoken. Other weapons in his arsenal include the computer, television, home repairs, sports, friends--anyone or anything which keeps him isolated from his partner.

Francis

He was a problem even during the blurry months of intrauterine life—an annoying embryo. When Maggie discovered she was pregnant, at thirty-eight, she wasn't much pleased. The bothersome bouts with nausea and the painful breached birth amplified her irritation at the prospect of having to rear another child.

Maggie was emotionally fatigued. Having already gotten three active boys through infancy, childhood, and nearly through adolescence, she urgently needed to make something special out of this prospect of yet another child.

She began to see the "hand of God" instead of failed birth control as the reason behind this pregnancy. She envisioned this child would be a special gift--a kind of divine "workman's compensation" from the God she'd faithfully worshipped and relied upon during the long, difficult childrearing years.

She was confident her reward would be a daughter; a quiet, pretty little girl who would be her cohort in the kitchen, and to whom she could teach the many culinary skills she'd learned from her own mother. She would teach her to can and freeze, and show her how to make pasta and bake exquisite pastries. What fun it would be shopping for dolls and purses instead of rubber swords, plastic pistols, and toy tractors--buying blouses with lace and pretty ribbons instead of warrantee-wear denim jeans with brass rivets.

She could almost hear girlish giggles and the nearly inaudible sound of little feet practicing ballet steps, instead of the shrieks and bangs of cowboys and Indians, cops and robbers, and Star Wars.

Maggie had developed her own method of self hypnosis which allowed her to become "hearing impaired." She could balance a checkbook, make a shopping list, even read when the noise level was in the range doctors say causes permanent damage to the ears.

But worse even than the incessant noise were the mind-numbing repetitive routines: breakfast dishes were cleared away to make room for lunch, which in turn allowed one to serve supper and clean up so that breakfast could be served again. Her brain seemed almost destroyed by the mindless treadmill of dull, demanding routines that brought only fatigue, not fame. You couldn't very well plant an American flag atop the Everest of diapers that got changed, washed, and folded in the early years of three boy's lives. And when the bottles-and-bib part of the journey had been navigated, she found the ensuing "adventures" of the elementary school years just as hectic but no more fulfilling.

Getting married and having a family had turned out to be such a disappointment. It was the loneliness and isolation of it that got to her most. She sometimes compared parenting to hiking across North Dakota and eastern Montana with a heavy backpack; just a lot of hard work and very little in the way of scenery.

Even her "disasters" lacked excitement. Though she frequently found herself in the emergency room with one of the boys, seeking aid for broken limbs, injured eyes, or loosened teeth, she often sat for hours, waiting her turn. Compared to cardiac arrests, drug overdoses, and severed fingers, her emergencies were deemed less important and she waited while other "serious" accidents were treated.

Frank wasn't a bad man—when he was around. Things could have been much worse. He wasn't an alcoholic, he didn't gamble, he didn't chase women, and he always sent his checks home. He had only one major flaw—his job. He was a truck driver, and since he'd bought his own rig, he was home even less than when he'd been driving for J.B. Hunt. On holidays, he might be home for twenty-four hours, but most often it was only for six or twelve. This wasn't a time when the burdens of parenting could be shared, however, because after two or three weeks on the road Frank would be primarily interested in "S & S" as he referred to it--sex and sleep—in that order.

He wasn't your stereotypical truck driver—boots, grubby jeans, hair in need of shampoo, ample stomach from too many greasy meals on the road. No, it was hard to picture him even turning the steering wheel of the massive Peterbilt he owned. A small milksoppy man, he seldom squabbled with Maggie. His vocabulary at home was comprised mostly of "Yes honey," and "Right away dear."

If Maggie became intensely angry attacking him viciously, he would simply shrug his shoulders, turn his palms outward in a conciliatory gesture and mumble "No problem, it won't happen again." Then he'd start studying his motor carrier maps, and within an hour he'd be on the road again. You had to wonder if he chose to be on the road because of the way she was, or if she was overbearing from the years of being both father and mother to three rambunctious boys.

Francis' birth changed nothing. Maggie knew she was beginning another trek across the flatlands of single parenting, and she fought desperately to wrench some meaning out of this disaster. Brittle with fatigue she construed her world according to her pressing unconscious needs. The doctor's words "It's a boy!" failed to penetrate her ears or infiltrate her benumbed psyche.

Maggie's early choice of a name reflected her deep inner need for a little girl. Within hours of discovering her pregnancy she'd picked "Francine" for her daughter. There was already a Frank Jr.—"Little Franky" they called him—and Jeffrey, and Michael. Her daughter would have a name with class, something that bespoke sophistication and culture.

"Francine" was French, she liked it a lot. Now even her sophisticated name must go and she begrudgingly adopted the masculine form—"Francis." But it would take more than a name change or circumcision to dislodge Maggie's dreams of having a daughter.

She dressed him in the most delicate things she could find at the baby shops, and cooingly referred to him as "Fancy Francy." His development would be shaped by Maggie's unconscious needs for a daughter. Although his birth pre-dated the development of psychoendocrinology—the study of the how psychological influences regulate glandular output—even his androgen levels seemed regulated by Maggie's craving for a daughter.

Francis remained soft and effeminate throughout childhood. Absent was that rough-and-tumble toughness that comes so naturally to many boys. His growth spurt was late in coming, and he was nearly twenty before he began shaving. Though his effeminism was exacerbated by inheriting Dad's diminutive frame, it was really Maggie's yearnings that overrode her son's Y chromosomes. He became the quintessential mamma's boy, shaped more by circumstance than by genes, deriving his destiny more from Maggie's dreams than from Muhammad Ali or Joe Namath.

Tragically, the name "Francy" stuck. Although it carried affection from Mom, and was tolerated by the rest of the family, among his peers it was an everpresent vehicle of ridicule. The mere mention of his name brought sadistic smiles to their freckled faces. Life at school was chronic agony for the velveteen boy with blonde curls known laughingly as "France-e-e-e-n-e-e-e." They loved to mockingly draw out those E's.

Increasingly Maggie became his umbrella from the "mean boys" and other harsh realities that awaited him not only on the school playground, but among the neighborhood children. He spent more and more time with her, and she taught him all the culinary skills in her domestic portfolio. By the time he was twelve, Francy could cook an elegant dinner of tortelleni in romano sauce, steamed artichokes, and Caesar salad.

His skills on the piano were equally impressive as he ably interpreted DeBussy, Tchaikovsky, or Chopin. Whether creating baked Alaska in the kitchen or Clair de Lune on the keyboard, Francy was impressive—almost prodigious.

He'd indeed become a "special" child, but it was a tragic specialness, a mutant madness that derived from Maggi's deep wish for a perfect daughter. Separated from his three older brothers by a decade and a half, he was psychologically an "only child." Sensitive and soft, he fulfilled his mother's deepest needs.

Amazingly his brother's grew up relatively normally, in spite of, or perhaps because of, their endless quarreling. Through their constant squabbling and competing, they learned from each other and from peers what it meant to be a boy, and later a man.

But by the time Francis was born they spent most of their free time with adolescent friends, so without brothers to bicker with or a father to model, Francis was skilled in the kitchen but abysmally inept among his peers. He remembered clearly the disgrace of being beaten up by one of his playmates in the third grade. Losing the fight had been embarrassing enough, but the fact that he'd been punched out by a *girl* was mortifying!

Ann

Even late into adolescence Francy thought of other boys as "rude and crude," and he would likely have remained with Mamma indefinitely, or decided his differentness meant he was gay, had he not met Ann. They met at the Olive Garden where he applied for work in the kitchen. She was the week end manager and had hired him as one of the assistant chefs.

Late one evening when Francis was cleaning up the kitchen after closing, Ann came and began to visit with him. She confided to Francis that she was an ACOA (adult child of an alcoholic) and regaled him with tales of abuse and mistreatment at the hands of her drunken father. He listened with a mixture of astonishment and sympathy—a combination that won her heart. In those early days of romance they seemed perfect for each other, fulfilling each other's deepest unconscious needs—his for another mother to please, hers for a safe father.

When I first saw Francis in therapy, he and Ann had been married for seven years. He was deeply angry with her but could not describe why. On the surface, their marriage seemed OK.

During the first couple years of marriage, Ann had worked full time while Francis had completed a 2-year business degree. He now worked long hours at a local CPA firm doing what he described as "shitwork"— unending columns of tedious calculations which no one else wanted to do.

Somehow these jobs always found their way their way to his desk while other partners managed investment portfolios and did the "fun" jobs.

Ann still worked the late shift at the Olive Garden, but—it seemed to Francis—did little else. Her large frame now supported enough flesh to be classified "obese" and he wondered what he had ever seen in her. She was asleep every morning when he left for work, but would somehow manage to awaken in time for Oprah, Geraldo, All My Children, and The Young and the Restless. She lived in a world of drama while he labored at a tedious job he despised.

In addition to working long hours, he brought home groceries, cleaned the house, and did all the cooking. They "shared" laundry duties, which meant that he washed and dried the clothes and she folded them while watching "her shows."

His rage was buried beneath layers of obsessive compliance and only emerged a bit at a time. Psychologists function as archaeologists of the psyche, brushing off a piece of pottery here, examining an arrowhead over there; searching among the shards for artifacts that are part of a larger motif—reconstructing the past in order to enrich the present.

Working with Francis was like that. It took several months before I began to understand his anger, because it was so deeply submersed that it came out only rarely and then *indirectly*. The first clue was subtle, but to an archeologist of the mind, unmistakable. It was embedded in a matter-of-fact description of one of their many squabbles. They had been arguing about his mowing the lawn. Ann had been nagging Francis for several days, asking him if he was going to do it, or if she was going to have to hire someone else. Francis related that he stomped out of the house. Then added, "She ended up wishing I hadn't mowed the lawn after all."

"Why?" I inquired.

"Because," he said, "I mowed down her flowers yesterday...by mistake."

I said nothing, but sat quietly picturing the incident in my mind. Francis, reacted to my contemplative silence as if I had criticized him.

"It was an accident...how was I supposed to tell the difference between the weeds at the edge of the lawn and her *precious* petunias?"

He bitterly savored the word "precious".

I suggested that he felt unfairly used. He admitted that it bothered him that *he* was expected to mow the lawn, even though they'd bought a riding mower specifically so she could do it while he was at the office.

His unspoken conviction that she was lazy, exploitive, and intellectually shallow, permeated the remainder of the session. But it did so in elusive ways. Francis never really said anything *directly* against her. He never openly disparaged her or bluntly belittled her. Instead there was a between-the-lines dissatisfaction that was so camouflaged with compliance he fooled even himself.

But the flowers had given it away. In his unconscious mind, he *did* want to mow them down and it *did* give him inexpressible delight to do so.

The "flowers incident" as it came to be known, was an important turning point for Francis. Continued therapy brought about a metamorphosis that gradually freed him from his cocoon of compliance and allowed him to be honest with his feelings and real in his relationships. The metamorphosis from milktoast to man took many months, but it did occur.

When I last saw Francis, he had been promoted to partner in the firm—after threatening to leave if he wasn't given responsibilities more in keeping with his abilities. For some time it seemed like the marriage would not survive his psychological growth and consequent honesty. He and Ann separated for several months; both finding to their surprise that their bonding ran much deeper than either had imagined. When they got back together it was with renewed interest since each of them had grown in the interim. Ann had lost weight and was attending the community college studying management/food services.

Although many of their unconscious attractions still remain intact, it is no longer at the expense of personal autonomy. Francis still likes to fix dinner occasionally, but he no longer feels coerced to do so. Ann finds going back to school and holding a full time job drama enough, and seldom watches TV anymore.

Ann still enjoys managing, but longer tries to micro-manage Francis, who for his part still appears a bit effeminate, but has developed a strong sense of self. More often than not, he chooses to do what he wants to instead of complying with everyone else's wishes. Although the humiliation of his "Fancy Francy" years still haunts him from time to time, he has developed a sense of pride in his career and only occasionally experiences the shame that was once such an unrelenting part of his life. On Saturday evenings he plays piano in a nightclub and enjoys it immensely.

The indirect style seen in Francis' life is commonly seen in males with dominant mothers, but it is by no means restricted to them. Children can be maestros at indirect frustration as most parents know. Anyone in a close relationship with a more powerful person such as a parent, employer, or too-significant other, will necessarily use indirect means to express anger. You just don't tell your boss to "drop dead," or a state trooper to "kiss my grits!" Likewise you don't tell your parents that you think they're "stupid"— at least not until you reach adolescence.

Aggression is the most common emotion that is detoured in the presence of powerful others. This occurs with such regularity that even ordinary people are apt to label others as "passive aggressive," a favorite term in the helping professions.

This, however,masks the fact that nearly all emotions can be expressed indirectly. "Shy" describes someone who has difficulty in being direct about positive feelings. "Procrastinator" often depicts a person who preserves a sense of independence in the presence of a tyrant, by agreeing to perform a job, but being "slow" in getting it done. Like mowing down flowers, such "delay tactics" simultaneously serve several purposes. It frustrates the taskmaster, but more importantly it preserves the dignity of the laborer. Thus the father who domineeringly shouts at his son to weed the garden "Today!" all but necessitates that the child will be weeding by moonlight—in order to comply with "Today!" yet not be "giving in" to the old man.

"Jerry"

"Homer Jeremiah Slocum Ph.D." The name on his diploma seemed etched in day glow, and the Doctor of Philosophy below it looked diminutive even though the type style was identical. "Jerry" as he had billed himself all through college and graduate school had tried desperately to flee his roots.

To Jerry—and to the rest of the world, he assumed—"Homer Jeremiah" might as well have been spelled HILLBILLY, and tacking a Ph.D. onto it didn't make his sow's-ear signature into a silk purse.

What a name! He thought, *Why didn't my parents just name me "Dumbo" or "White Trash?"*

In Jerry's mind the name "Homer" conjured up the image of a country boy with the face of a hog and a room temperature IQ, while "Jeremiah" was a good Old-Testament name that told the world you were a "believer." But it didn't indicate *what* you believed in, and Jerry knew what his family believed in.

They believed in God and country—especially *country!* They believed in the Bible—sort of—or at least they believed in Brother Jimmy (Swaggert) when he wept and railed against sin, and when he was scandalized for having a bit of illicit sex on the side, the mountain folk understood that things like that happen.

Mostly they believed in homebrewed moonshine, hand-rolled cigarettes, and frequent sex—not necessarily limited to one's spouse. They believed in Mail Pouch tobacco, and one of the earliest visual-motor skills learned in the hills surrounding his childhood home was how to spit a string of golden brown tobacco juice with the pin point accuracy of a toad spitting his tongue at a hovering mosquito.

Jerry hated his name (he thought) but it wasn't so much his name he hated as it was himself. Although his SAT scores and athletic prowess had brought a steady stream of recruiters to his Applachian trailer home, he'd never really shaken the past. An athletic scholarship took him from his 12 X 50 trailer deep in the hills of West Virginia to Duke University where he studied psychology and eventually received his Ph.D., but he still felt like a fraud.

His love for moonshine, squirrel hunting, and pork rinds, contrasted sharply with the tastes of his more "intellectual" counterparts, who spent their time discussing Broadway plays and operas.

But Jerry's loathing was much deeper than his shame about his name or family origins. It had more to do with his physical disability and how his mother related to it, than his with his appellations or Appalachia.

Born with a club foot Jerry might have been blessedly unaware he was "different"—at least while still a toddler—had his mom not been so eager to display her son. As it turned out, his earliest memories were of Ma calling him from his bedroom, where he would retreat whenever company came to visit:

"Homer!" her voice would have an edge of excitement, "Come show your aunt Naomi how you walk!"

Then, an animated commentary to accompany his pitiful promenade:

"See! He's got no ankle! See how his foot turns out when he walks?"

Finally:

"OK Homer, you can go back to your room and play now."

Not surprisingly, such antics—circling slowly about the room like a circus bear—left Jerry feeling like a spectacle, but unsure why. The sympathetic responses of the spectators left him feeling not only different, but damaged. The solicitous cluckings of aunts and other of his mother's lady friends drove this sense of damage deep into his psyche.

Fortunately, Jerry received innovative surgical procedures which left with him with almost no limp, and very little noticeable physical deformity, but the damage to his psyche was much more extensive. He grew up with the feeling that "There's something wrong with me." No, it wasn't only his name. That would have been escapable. In fact omitting Homer and simply signing his name as "H. Jerry Slocum, Ph.D." was his attempt to escape, but it hadn't worked. How do you escape from yourself? From your damaged, often-pitied self?

Education was another way he'd tried. His excellent grades in school and stellar performance as quarterback of his small high school football team had attracted the attention of several recruiters from distant universities. However, even his graduate degree—he was one of the few kids from the small appalachian town to graduate from high school, and finishing college was almost unheard of! But now, even the letters Ph.D. weren't enough to erase "HILLBILLY" from his mind.

After earning his doctorate in clinical psychology, Jerry had interned for a year at the Menninger Foundation in Topeka Kansas, working closely with other psychologists, social workers, and psychiatrists, as well as analysts in training. He never felt completely comfortable with the other professionals, but the analysts were the worst.

These aspiring shrinks wore their almost-regulation tweed jackets and puffed their designer pipes with a seriousness of purpose that amused Jerry. And while they discussed the Broadway plays they were missing while stranded in Kansas, he found himself fantasizing of his glory days as quarterback at Southeastern High. He cared little for these snobs from "The Big Apple" or Boston, who felt their artistic sensibilities were being insulted by having to live in Topeka.

Jerry's life illustrates a mixed style—one with about equal amounts of the shy/shameful style and the indirectly angry style. Now, although his mother no longer parades him around the room for relatives and neighbors to gawk at his club foot, he still feels stressed around certain groups of "hoity toity" people, and whenever he finds himself in such circumstances, he feels like escaping *inward*. This drives his indirectness. He still doesn't feel worthwhile enough to tell someone off *directly*. He didn't still doesn't feel entitled to be angry. *Directly* telling someone that they irritate you requires power, status, self esteem. You have to feel you *deserve* to express your feelings. Jerry doesn't.

His marriage is in trouble too, because Sandra has gradually taken over his space. Since he doesn't feel entitled and she does, he gradually finds his territory shrinking to accommodate Sandy's expansionism. Early in the marriage they'd each had an equal portion of the large walk-in closet in the master bedroom. But Sandra insisted that her numerous dresses and shoes required more space than her "fifty per cent share" of the closet provided, and since his minimal apparel occupied only a small portion of his, it was only "natural" that she began to use most of his allocated space for her things.

This seemed to work OK for awhile, but even Jerry had his limits, and when he came home one evening to find all his clothes and shoes crowed into half of a small hall closet to "make room" for the baby's things, he was enraged-but still not enraged enough to confront Sandra *directly.*

Instead he "suddenly remembered" he'd forgotten to dictate a report at the office. Leaving supper on the table he started to drive to the office but stopped at a bar instead. Sometime later—much later—he called Sandy and, with slurred words, inquired:

"Hey Shandra! wanna be my deshignated driver?"

He was so wasted he could hardly walk to the car. Nonetheless, he never told Sandy about his frustration with her for encroaching his space. Instead:

"I jesh had a shudden urge for a beer" he told her; "sho I shtopped at the Watering Hole (his favorite pub) and nexshthing I know, they're locking up."

As a child, whenever Jerry had gotten really angry, he'd felt as if his boundaries had collapsed on him—felt like he was being squeezed into a tiny ball from which he could not escape. During such times he felt like he was entangled in a steel trap or being compressed in a garbage compactor into a tight little sphere from which he could neither escape by moving more tightly inward, or by running away.

Anger pushes most people to erupt outwardly—*directly*—but it only pulled Jerry more deeply inward. While others exploded, he imploded. This centripetal pull inward was a knee-jerk response to intense feelings of any sort, but especially anger. This reflex, learned as an early toddler now covered his entire emotional spectrum.

He recalled how as a little boy he often feel asleep clinging to the wall. As he would lie in bed recalling a painful or shameful experience of the day, he would find a small degree of comfort by wedging his club foot between the mattress and the wall, while boring his head into the envelope created by the wall and his pillow.

Somehow, this cloistered posture afforded him a degree of comfort he could find nowhere else. It was escape *from* the world *into* the self, the clearest enactment of "I could have crawled in a hole and died!" With his face flat to the wall, the warmth of his own breath comforted him. Moist, warm, and rhythmic, it soothed him. Sometimes he would augment the feedback by gently rolling or banging his head against the wall. He sometimes licked the wall and wasn't surprised when in his graduate training he learned of inner city children who had significant levels of lead in their bodies as a result of eating the paint off their apartment walls. When his classmates would incredulously ask "Why would a kid eat paint?" Jerry said nothing, but he knew why.

Little children use what psychoanalysts call "transitional objects"—favorite blankets, dolls, or Teddy bears—to comfort themselves in times of stress, or when going to sleep. Jerry's wall clinging was his transitional object—his own giant Teddy bear. If you had been able to sneak into his dark bedroom and had seen him sprawled flat against the wall it might have reminded you of climbers on the face of Half Dome in Yosemite Park. Jerry clung to his "safe" wall, most children cling to their beloved blankets or special dolls, but cling we must—everyone needs comfort.

As he became older the complexities of his world increased and the satisfaction he derived from his self-soothing bedtime routines decreased. He now sought chemical assistance to escape inside. The warmth of his breath returning off the wall, was increasingly replaced by the warmth of double shots sliding over his throat and down his esophagus like a sluggish roller coaster. As he moved into middle life, Jerry drank more and more and, as a result, liked himself less and less.

I never saw Jerry as a patient. We became acquainted in Hawaii where, serendipitously, we were both attending a week-long workshop on shame. During the long flight home—complete with meals (and drinks for Jerry) he disclosed to me his own personal sources of shame, and his indirect ways of dealing with his feelings.

It wasn't so much my listening skills as the anonymous atmosphere and numerous cocktails that allowed him to share his usually-deeply-hidden self. Although we talked of "keeping in touch," somehow we both knew it wouldn't happen. It seemed almost part of our unspoken contract that we wouldn't see each other again. Although Jerry was a professional helper himself, he was a wounded healer. He needed the safety of a small plane seat, altitude, and anonymity, in order to feel safe.

Sometimes when I find myself flying at 35,000 feet, soaring, godlike, through the night darkness, above fluffy white moonlit clouds, I wonder how many little children below me are clinging to their blankets or to their bedroom walls in an attempt to escape anxiety or forget shame. I wonder for how many the darkness is filled with the terror of sexual or physical abuse instead of the tenderness of good night kisses and quiet lullabies. And I remember Jerry. I wonder if his life is going better now. If he's drinking a bit less alcohol and dealing a bit more directly with his anger.

Indirectly angry or passive aggressive styles. In the first few minutes of interacting with indirect persons you might see any one of a variety of faces. The could be angrily sullen or shamefully shy. They sometimes withdraw, but at other times manifest a toogoodtobetrue compliance. Since indirect styles are often used to cover up aggressive feelings, a variety of scenes share common elements:

A parent is pacing between the breakfast nook and dining room, periodically shouting "Hurry up! You're going to make me late for my car pool!"

A parent agitatedly squirms in the driver's seat of the family van—motor revving, radio blaring, shift in the drive position, puffing a cigarette with machine gun rapidity—simultaneously a child slowly saunters down the sidewalk finally, almost triumphantly, opening the car door with:

"Well, I was hurrying as fast as I could—my hair just wouldn't do what it was supposed to."

Another common scene is an adolescent mowing the lawn and "missing" numerous spots of grass around the edges and on turns in an otherwise-fastidious yard.

Indirectness is typified by the student or conference participant who asks "questions" in the attempt to show how smart she is:

"Professor Harris, I very much agree with your point, but I noticed in my reading that Silverton and Brach's 1991 study took a slightly different tack. Do you think their study is significant, or did it turn out as you would have predicted?"

If the same person were more hostile and wanted to put the professor down instead of show off, they might refer to the Silverton and Brach study and end by asking:

"Doesn't that pretty well disprove what you've presented here today?"

Indirectly angry lovers seem, at first, to be calm, pleasant, and tolerant. Yet, over a period of days or weeks, their repressed anger begins to surface in a variety of *indirect,* but noticeable ways. Whenever they "botch" things up, "forget," or otherwise cause life to be difficult for their partners, they are quick to apologize, offering various explanations and excuses which seem plausible in any single instance, but which occur with such high frequencies as to cause even gullible co-dependents to become skeptical.

The regularity with which indirectly angry persons "forget", run out of gas, own alarm clocks that fail to go off, possess cars that won't start, or operate computers that crash, leads even the most trusting partner to become suspicious.

Like other insecure lovers with shame-based, dependent, or co-dependent styles, indirect lovers live two lives—while the public "nice" self acquiesces to the wishes of others, the private *real* self seethes with rage or smolders with resentment, but only expresses this in indirect ways, such as "forgetting," or failing to show up for appointments.

Embittered over the many unappreciated jobs or chores performed for those who routinely take them for granted, they get even, but in subtle ways. Indirectly angry persons typically have fantasy lives rich with revenge and full of instances where they tell others to "shove it." But they're only direct in fantasy—in real life they only procrastinate, forget, or make "mistakes."

Lovers who express their anger indirectly, often tend to be indirect when expressing *positive* feelings as well. Not surprisingly, indirectness fails to work very well with feelings of eroticism or attraction either. The indirectly expressed signals are sometimes misread by the intended recipient while more direct suitors become winners. Even when picked up and responded to by a receptive person, indirectness communicates anxiety or insecurity.

To sum it up, indirectness seldom works well, but it is sometimes difficult for such persons to obtain the help they need. Unfortunately many mental health professionals have marketed a kind of audacious assertiveness which has alarmed many of the people who need it most.

It is important that shy/shameful or otherwise indirect lovers learn that one can be *direct* without being *obnoxious* or *nasty*. Even romantic cat-and-mouse games, one can be direct without spoiling the mood. Romance can be creative, subtle and nuanced, yet remain direct. One can send flowers accompanied by a note which states *directly:* "Darling, beautiful flowers remind me of you, and of how much I love you," instead of *indirectly* "These flowers are a symbol of my feelings for you."

RECOGNIZING the Indirect Sexual Style

Those who worry about hurting their lover's by being too direct, need to be reassured that it is possible to be sensitively direct, gently straightforward, kindly candid. They need to realize that "telling it like it is," has fallen into disfavor because so many people let angry feelings accumulate until they *explosively* (and directly) erupt. If they can feel psychologically secure and emotionally safe in the presence of their lover, they will be able to risk being authentic. To be genuine is to be direct.

Self Quiz

1. Do I usually state my opinions by beginning with "Don't you think that...?" (Thereby encouraging agreement before I start)?
2. Do I feel like a child (uneasy, nervous—maybe even sweaty palms or butterflies in my stomach, etc.) around authority figures such as teachers, parents, bosses, police?
3. Do I usually *not* say how I really feel if I think it might offend someone?
4. When I feel intensely, do I pull my feelings inward and shut the door after me? i.e., do I *implode* instead of *explode?*
5. Even when my moods are not very intense, do I tend to not express them, preferring to just keep them to myself?
6. Do I feel I usually deserve what I get—even (or especially) when things turn out badly?

7. Do I usually interact with others in "stereo"—private & public channels—with each channel playing a different tape?

8. Do I usually feel like a social dwarf?

9. Do I constantly use the verbal crutch "Ya know?" (which really means "Do you agree with me?") to reassure myself that others like what I'm saying each step along the way?

10. Am I "sort of aware" that I'm going to "forget" an appointment that I'd rather not keep, or that I'm going to be "late" for a meeting I'd rather skip?

11. Do I have difficulty meeting deadlines at work? Have I ever been fired because I couldn't get my job assignments done on time?

12. Do I resent it when my boss or work associates make suggestions as to how I can become more productive?

13. Do I find myself scornful and critical of people in positions of authority?

14. Do I purposely slow down at work when I'm given jobs I dislike?

If you or your lover answered "Yes" to most of these questions, you probably have a significant streak of indirectness in your relationship.

REORGANIZING Your Expectations

Suppose you're convinced that your lover is indirectly angry much of the time, can you do anything to improve things? Probably. Try some of the following suggestions. Add some of your own. Bottom line, read their behavior *patterns* over the long haul, and don't take too seriously their verbal denials: "I'm not mad!"

(1) Try to "get the cards on the table." This is not always easy with an indirectly angry partner, but if you understand what's going on, you may be able to persist in discussing things until they begin to own their anger. This requires maintaining a delicate balance between persisting in discussing an issue but not becoming overbearing or authoritarian.

If you become too insistent, you guarantee that your partner won't respond directly, because you've just re-created the very conditions that frighten him/her in the first place. So you have to *gently* invite her to share with you what *really* is bugging her. Don't accept superficial answers, but don't insist on analyzing something to death.

(2) Suppose your partner insists that "I just *forgot!* I don't know why you're trying to make a big deal out of it." Or, states angrily, "I wasn't mad, I'm only mad that you keep trying to make a big deal out of nothing. I was *late,* so what!"

Don't come across like you're trying to "play shrink," rather you might say "Well, honey, I've just noticed a *pattern* that every time you forget something, it seems to be one of the things you don't really like to do. Don't you think that's interesting? Want to talk about that?

Another tack that might work is to inquire about how they handled *not* doing certain jobs they disliked when they were children: "How did you handle it when you were a little kid and your Mom asked you to do something you didn't want to do?

Then you may find out that there is a similar pattern. i.e., he used to "wait until the last minute to do it," or "do it the next day, so I felt like I was doing it on my own terms."

You might then be in a good position to notice and comment upon parallels between such childhood incidents and the present circumstances:

"That sounds kind of like what happens when I ask you to mow the lawn, doesn't it?"

(3) Even after you've had some of these discussions, however, it's possible that your partner's deeply-ingrained habits of indirectness may persist. Then it becomes important to use your understanding, not to assist him in changing, nor to nag him into admitting that he really is angry, but rather in helping you to cope with his devious ways.

(4) You may find it helpful to *Reorganize* your expectations, and simply "translate" your partner's indirect expressions of anger ("forgetting," procrastinating, "botching" a job, etc.) into *direct* confrontations:

"Honey, I notice that each time I ask you to unload the dishwasher something gets broken. That leads me to think you resent doing it. Is that the case? Does it seem unfair to you that I ask you to help me in the kitchen—since we both work? Is there something you would rather do besides put away dishes?" etc.

(5) Ever notice that kids tend to forget their math books but not their roller blades or skate boards? Isn't it curious that Suzanne is often late to Sunday school, but always a few minutes early to the movies?

It doesn't take a rocket scientist to figure out that kids "forget" homework assignments or math books in order to avoid having to do school work in the evening. Too often we assume that what adults verbally tell us is truth, when in fact, we sometimes need to ignore the actual words, and look for the pattern. If your partner *consistently* forgets, shows a *pattern* of tardiness, or somehow manages to *never complete* certain tasks, you need to look beyond his words and assume you're dealing with some *indirect* resentment, anger, or frustration.

REVITALIZING Your Sexual Relationship

It is essential that you try to relate to your partner in a *mutual* way. An indirectly angry lover will often *feel* and *act* like a child in the presence of a powerful parent, teacher, or some other authority figure. Fearing they might offend you, they will never be *straight* with you. However, as we've seen in the case illustrations, this doesn't work *over the long haul.* Consequently, it is essential that you work at keeping the relationship Adult-Adult rather than Parent-Child.

With some couples, a Parent-Child relationship works OK, because one partner wants to be parental while the other desires dependency. But in the case of indirectly angry partners, such a coupling seldom works, because it repeats the same situation (powerful parent-weak child) which led to the indirectness in the first place.

Consequently, although *mutuality* is *desirable* in most sexual relationships, when one of the partners is indirectly angry, *mutuality is a must!* You must avoid becoming the "parent" to such a partner.

This has implications for all aspects of your sexual relationship, from who initiates sex, or who decides "What we'll do this time," to who provides whom an orgasm, or in what order.

Evaluate your sexual relationship, being especially aware of the balance. Are your interactions pretty much 50-50? Is there generally a good balance between the two of you regarding, initiation, who's on top, and all those other little subtleties that comprise the sexual relationship?

You don't have to strive for a perfectly balanced 50-50 relationship (unless, of course, you're an obsessive compulsive), but if your relationship tends to be 70-30 or 80-20 with one of you consistently being the "parent," taking care of the other, assuming responsibility for setting aside the time to be together, etc., then you need to re-vamp things for more balance.

Taking Out the Trash

MYTH # 1. All women love anal intercourse and the only reason my partner refuses to accommodate me is that she's a prude.

TRUTH: Many women do *not* enjoy anal sex, and it's not prudish to avoid sexual maneuvers which aren't appealing. If the male is insistent on anal sex as the primary way his partner can prove her love for him—even though she clearly states her opposition to it—it is likely that he has some *indirect* anger or hostility either toward his specific partner, or toward women in general.

Some radical feminists have claimed that intercourse is *always* a "pure, sterile, formal expression of men's contempt for women." For example, in her controversial 1987 book *Intercourse,* Andrea Dworkin contends that men use intercourse to "occupy," "violate," "invade," and "colonize" women's bodies. Dworkin concludes that since this is a world ruled by men who hate women, women cannot freely consent to any act of sexual intercourse.

I strongly disagree with such a bitter view of intercourse, and I would argue that although intercourse may *sometimes* consist of a male "colonizing" a female's body, that would be more accurately described as *rape,* not intercourse. In terms of our present discussion, I would suggest that if either partner *insists* on engaging in a sexual activity that is distasteful to the other—whether that be oral sex, anal sex, bondage, etc.—this could be an indication of *indirect* anger.

MYTH # 2. If I initiate sex, and my partner is disinterested, it proves that I'm not very attractive.

TRUTH: When your partner isn't interested in sex it can be the result of many different factors. She may be genuinely tired. He may be stressed over problems at work. She might be preoccupied with the fact that one of the children is failing fourth grade. He might be worried about losing his job.

There are many different causes for lowered libido, so don't immediately assume that it's related to your personal attractiveness—or lack of it. Usually it's not.

However, if your partner is prone to indirect expressions of anger, it is possible that his lack of interest in sex *might* be an *indirect* expression of anger. There are few ways of "getting even" or punishing your partner that are more effective than refusing to become involved sexually when she's wanting you.

But even in that humiliating circumstance (you want him—he doesn't want you) you must be careful that you don't experience this as primarily a commentary on your attractiveness or lack of it. It probably has more to do with indirect anger, lack of libido, or lack of honest communication, than with your attractiveness.

Imagine, for a moment, that you got off work early and decided to surprise your lover by making dinner. You stop on the way home, buy fresh veggies, a prime cut of beef, and plan a scrumptious meal, complete with silver, china, candlelight, wine—the works. He, meanwhile, knowing nothing of your planned surprise, is running a bit late, figures you will have already eaten, and drives through Arby's on his way home. He's pretty hungry so he eats while he drives and arrives home with two Arbys Roast Beef Deluxes tucked into his tummy.

You would likely be disappointed, irritated, maybe even angry, but would you feel *unattractive?* Would you feel that he had *purposely* rejected your cooking? Would you be enraged and accuse him of not wanting your food anymore? Probably not.

But that's the difficult thing about sexual relationships, it is so easy to *personalize* any lack of interest. It is so easy to feel rejected because your partner's libido is at a low ebb for reasons having nothing to do with you.

I'd like to close this chapter with a case study that illustrates how the indirectly angry style sometimes persists over a long period of time.

"Daddy Insisted That I Graduate From Harvard"

Doreen (Irish for "sullen") was prophetically named. She seldom smiled. She didn't have much to be happy about. She'd dropped out of college the final semester of her senior year, she'd been unable to become pregnant, and her marriage was failing. A far cry from the sparkling sorority queen she had once been, her green eyes, seldom danced with happiness anymore, and her lightly freckled face, surrounded with cinnamon hair, seldom broke into smile wrinkles. Mostly she talked in terse, angry sentences about how her husband Greg was "always gone."

"Either he's working late at the construction site," she complained, "or he's playing softball, basketball, or racquetball!"

Doreen McAllister's Irish eyes were *not* smiling because her marriage of nearly five years had filled her with more bitterness than joy-or at least that's how she saw her problems. She felt Greg was mostly to blame because he was "never home," but she did acknowledge that her own resentment might have played a role in "driving him away."

The breakthrough came several sessions later, when Doreen was talking about her educational experiences.

"I mostly hated the Harvard University," she admitted. "Even though it seemed like all Daddy ever talked about, from the time I was a baby, was how *wonderful* Harvard was. It was simply taken for granted that someday I would graduate from Harvard, just like he had, just like his father had. When I was a senior in high school and other kids were trying to decide where they would be going to college, it was never even discussed in my home. Everyone *knew* I would be attending Harvard."

Doreen's facial expression and body language bespoke anger rather than pride. As if she had been sentenced to four years in the state penitentiary.

"All I ever heard during high school was 'Better keep up your grades, or you won't get into Harvard!'" Seems like that was about the only time Daddy and I ever talked about anything. Mostly he didn't say much to me, but whenever my semester grades came out, he would say something like "Good girl, Doreen, those A's are your ticket to Harvard."

"Of course Daddy had season tickets to all the Harvard games, and I don't think we ever missed a single game during my entire childhood!"

I must have looked slightly dubious, because Doreen spontaneously added,

"I'm serious, I'm not exaggerating, we *never* missed a Harvard home game!"

Then she bitterly concluded, "the only time I can remember our entire family together at meal times was when we were tailgating before and after Harvard home games."

It became increasingly clear to me that Doreen and her father had a very poor relationship, seldom speaking, and mutually distrusting one another's motives. I won't discuss all the details and reasons for that, except to note that Doreen *indirectly* expressed her anger against her father by not graduating from Harvard.

Doreen's intense animosity against her father was displaced onto his beloved alma mater.

"I hated Harvard from the day I first arrived in Cambridge. I don't know why, really, I just didn't like it there."

Doreen seemed to have no clear sense of why she hated Harvard. Although she was in touch with the *intensity* of her feelings, she couldn't seem to formulate a clear focus for her anger or offer any logical explanations regarding *what* about living in Cambridge was so offensive to her. Whenever I tried to get more details or clarification, she would only offer vague generalizations:

"I don't know, kids weren't very friendly."

Or, "Winters were too cold, I probably should have gone to UCLA or Berkeley."

Amazingly-in a remarkable example of cutting off your nose to spite your face--Doreen dropped out of college in the final semester of her senior year. Up until that time she had apparently been quite successful. She grudgingly admitted to me that by her senior year she had even grown to "like" Harvard. Her cumulative GPA at the beginning of the second semester of her senior year was 3.64. Daddy was proud! That was the problem!

During Christmas vacation of that year, he had, according to Doreen "gone on and on about graduation." Sitting around the Christmas tree after opening presents, he had told everyone, "When Doreen gets her diploma, I'm going to throw the biggest graduation party this town has ever see!"

Doreen said that she had the feeling "as usual, this was all for Daddy, not me!"

"He as much as said so," she sighed.

He was pacing around the room saying stuff like "Three generations of Michigan graduates! Now that's something to celebrate! Your Grandpa, your Mom and me, and now *you!*"

But like most children of narcissistic parents, Doreen sensed that attending Harvard, her high GPA—everything about the experience was going to be used to aggrandize Daddy. *He,* not she, would be the center of attention—even at her own graduation party.

"That was it!" she said. "That was the final straw! I can still remember it as clearly as if it had happened yesterday--Daddy strutting around the Christmas tree, bragging about how smart Doreen was, what good brains she had inherited, how "magnificent" it would be when she received her diploma from Harvard."

And I decided right then and there," she reported-her Irish resolve tingeing her face pink-"that I would *never* graduate from Harvard University!"

And she didn't. Doreen, who had until then been an honor student, began partying on a nearly full time basis. She skipped classes, failed examinations, and ultimately flunked out of college a few weeks prior to commencement.

After a couple years of weekly psychotherapy, during which we thoroughly examined her troubled relationship with her father, Doreen was able to become more direct in expressing her bitterness. As she emotionally worked through years of stifled anger, the bitterness that had nearly destroyed her marriage started to recede. The sullen cynicism that had suffocated her inner life was slowly being replaced with happiness.

Greg started spending more time with her and less on the basketball court. Doreen returned to school (Michigan State University this time) and completed her degree with honors. Finally, Irish eyes were smiling.

Summary

In the last few chapters we've looked at various styles which share in common excessive development of the *inner* life, at the expense of direct outward-directed expression. Shamefulness, shyness, dependency, co-dependency—even narcissism, all tend to focus inward at the expense of outward involvement or direct expression.

In our final chapter, we will briefly consider a few sexual styles which are seriously dysfunctional, paying special attention to one which has come to be known as "sexual addiction." We'll discuss whether sexual "addictions" exist, and if they do, how they are similar to chemical addictions and how they differ.

Many dysfunctional styles have an addictive component. We've just seen, for example, how Jerry used alcohol to facilitated his escape inward. People come to depend on certain ways of coping with anxiety or stress, relying on certain tried-and-true rituals for producing pleasure or reducing stress, such routines become interwoven with the fabric of their lives in self-perpetuating ways cycles which lead them to ignore other alternatives.

In addition to sexual addiction, we'll look at alcohol and drug addictions and consider a number of other serious conditions as well. You'll learn how to decide whether you or your partner suffers from paranoia, schizophrenia, depression, mania, or bipolar mood disorders, and you'll be better able to decide if you or your partner could benefit from professional help.

As you read, perhaps you'll notice that in most of them, what is lacking is the *corrective experience* of social interactions. In these more serious conditions, there is often an excessive focus—an *isolative* focus—on self.

The alcoholic or drug addicted lover is excessively attuned to his internal state and attempts to fix it with chemicals that crowd out most of the psychological relationships of life. The depressed lover lacks the energy to get very far away from her own centralized misery. Even the paranoid, whom we usually think of as being persecuted by *others*, is really in a state of excessive self focus—worrying moment by moment about who is trying to do *him* in!

Chapter 8: The Mentally Ill Lover

"Why does everyone think I'm a sex addict?"

WHAT TO DO IF YOUR LOVER IS A SEX ADDICT

How To Decide Whether You Need a 12-Step Program or Psychotherapy or Neither!

How can you know if your lover is a sex addict? Let me begin by suggesting—even without knowing you or your lover—"He's probably not." Or, "I don't think she is."

I know, it may seem foolish for a shrink to diagnose someone he's never seen, but sexual problems are almost always communication problems—relationship problems—*not* addictions. Even the word *intercourse* has several meanings: coitus, copulation, love-making, spring to mind, but intercourse also refers to communication, conversation, and discourse.

Put in the form of a mildly bad joke, you ask your friend:

"What is a four-letter word for intercourse that ends in "k"?

Your friend thinks, then hesitates to say the "F" word, so you nonchalantly continue:

"Talk."

The joke may not be very funny, but it makes an important point. Bad sex is about bad talk, not disease or addictions.

We live in a labeling culture and it seems that everyone everywhere is an expert in diagnosing and labeling. From Jenny Jones to Geraldo everyone has gotten in on our national pastime *diagnosis*. Even President Clinton "feels your pain."

Besides the alphabet soup of *educational* labels (ADHD, LDL, EMR, etc.), *psychiatric* labels (OCD, PTSD, MPD, etc.) the *recovery* movement has created an entire new cottage industry by adding the word "addiction" to almost any problem you can think of and offering a 12-step program or support group to help you cope.

Currently, it's trendy to be "addicted" to things besides those "old" substances—cigarettes, booze, or drugs. But not to fear, in place of such passe things comes a whole new wave of addictive substances. Today you can legitimately be "addicted" to nearly anything that fits into your mouth: chocolate, cheesecake, ice cream, donuts, Twinkies; or any activity you find enjoyable: work, tennis, racquetball, running, etc.

A whole new class of "patients" has been created by simply adding *"holic"* to whatever people like to eat, drink, or do—especially if they eat it or do it with what society thinks is too much intensity. Nowadays we have support groups and twelve-step treatment programs not only for alcoholics (boring!) but for workaholics, chocolaholics, gamblaholics, *sexaholics*—even *paperholics!*

A recent article in *Redbook,* entitled "Are You a Paperholic?" advised readers how to sort through the unwanted clutter of paper and concluded with information on how to contact the local chapter of *Messies Anonymous,* a self-help support group for *paperholics.*

Pop addictionologists have created a diagnostic circus by including virtually the entire range of human problems under the big tent of the *recovery movement,* and offering slightly-altered twelve-step programs as the "cure" for each new "addiction."

Since many societal problems today are at least correlated with, if not directly caused by, the misuse of drugs, it is hardly surprising given the tidal wave of illicit drug use, alcohol-related traffic fatalities and smoking-related health problems, that there has arisen an accompanying plethora of "experts," and drug "czars" of various stripes and colors.

Almost overnight, and often with little or no graduate training in their proclaimed fields of specialization, "experts" have diagnosed and treated all manner of "addictions" with a calm authority that beguiles a desperate public into believing.

Self-help is as American as apple pie, appealing to the average person because: (1) they bypass those ivory-tower professionals, (2) they allow one to self-diagnose—a very egalitarian process, (3) they legitimize forming social groups with other persons intensely involved with similar activities—be it sex, gambling, fundamentalist bashing, or handwashing, (4) and—most importantly—they allow one to be indefinitely "in recovery"— which is to say you never really need to resolve your problem just so long as you're "working your steps" and attending your weekly support group.

This lifelong "recovery" process can be reassuring to people for many reasons. It offers structure, goals, companionship, acceptance, even dating opportunities in a community of believers.

Few social entities in America today can compete with such powerful incentives. The barn raisings, quilting bees and church picnics of the past have been replaced with the countless support groups of today. Such groups doubtless fill an important social vacuum, but they do so by redefining loneliness as sickness. The friendless or forlorn become "patients" who are seen to suffer from an almost limitless variety of problems which are now called "addictions."

Why I Don't Believe in Sex Addiction

I will limit myself to three problems arising from treating sexual problems as addictions, though many more could be discussed.

(1) *Defining* the complexities of sexuality in addictionology jargon blurs important distinctions. For example in popular writing, a "sex addict" is someone whose sexual behavior has become vastly more important than other significant relationships including family, friends, work associates and others. According to the National Association of Sexual Addiction Problems, some 14 million Americans are sexual addicts. Astounding as that might seem, it probably *underestimates* "sex addicts" if one takes seriously the following definition of sexual addiction offered by one of the leading proponents of the notion:

"The fact remains that a significant number of people have identified themselves as sexual addicts: people whose sexual behavior has become 'unstoppable' despite serious consequences. These consequences include the physical (self-mutilation, sexual violence, disease, unwanted pregnancy), occupational (large financial losses, job losses, sexual abuse and harassment, withdrawal of professional licenses), and familial (loss of relationships, impaired family functioning, sexual abuse, sexual dysfunction). In addition to these problems, one of the most frequent mental health complaints of sexual addicts is suicidal ideation." (Carnes, 1986)

If we followed Carnes' definition it's likely that instead of 14 million sex addicts we might have 64 million! For starters, we could include a large portion of adolescents—most of whom would admit that sexual fantasies often seem "unstoppable." Then add the huge number of cases where sexual difficulties *accompany* but do not necessarily *cause* such problems as job loss, impaired family relations and depression with concomitant suicidal ideation and we're talking about enormous numbers of troubled Americans.

But do we actually *understand sexual problems better* if we apply the label "sex addict" and encourage such persons to join other self-diagnosed addicts in twelve-step programs or support groups? I don't think so.

Most "facilitators" of such groups have no training in psychology or the social sciences—their claim to "expertise" being that they are "in recovery." Even professional addictionologists often have little training in diagnosis, psychotherapy, or psychiatry. Consequently, they are *not* prepared to understand or treat the various personality styles we've discussed earlier in this book.

For example, the "paperholic" referred to in *Redbook* is really an obsessive-compulsive hoarder, and the wise clinician will be better informed by consulting the relevant literature in that area than in re-naming the paper collector an "addict" of some sort.

Sexual relationships are infinitely more complex than decisions regarding keeping or throwing away papers, and any attempt to label complex sexual conflicts as "addictions" is a serious mistake.

(2) *Treating* sexual problems as addictions trivializes sex. Klien (1989) observes that encouraging people to admit that they are "powerless" functions to avoid confrontation with the guilt, shame, and darker aspects of individual sexuality. He contends that the expression "That's my addiction talking!" which has crept into popular vocabulary really means "Don't confront or puncture my defenses."

Klien further notes that competent therapists are prepared to confront rather than collude with the client's dark side, and in so doing facilitate genuine growth. To buy into the self-identified "addict's" diagnosis is counterproductive because (a) It encourages people to externalize their "bad" sexuality, (b) it makes a disease out of what is often within reasonable limits of normal sexual behavior—i.e., high levels of masturbating are not *always* a sign of malfunction, (c) it doesn't teach people about complex sexual decision making, often substituting a "Just say No!" approach.

Planned Parenthood's Faye Wattleton aptly puts it this way: "Just say no!" helps people abstain from self-destructive behavior about as well as "Have a nice day!" helps people deal with depression.

(3) *Professional psychotherapists and sexologists* are being replaced by "addictionologists" as the relevant experts in treating sexual problems. Addictionologists typically have little or no training in diagnosis, psychotherapy, or sexology. They are often "in recovery" themselves (which is a euphemistic way of saying that they have unresolved sexual or impulse control problems).

These "in-recovery" addictionologists are the new high priests of the "emerging discipline" of sex addiction. That is downright scary, but is powerfully driven by the twelve-steppers themselves--lay people who are too often "addicted" to recovery! Maybe we need to start some support groups for "recoveryholics."

In summary, if you or your partner feels *obsessed, driven,* or *compelled* by sexual urges so powerful they tend to overwhelm you, or make a mockery of your family commitments, or social boundaries, you might want to consult a professional therapist to help you evaluate if these urges are normal or aberrant. If your libido is unusually intense or if you worry about losing control, a professional can help you sort through this. This doesn't make you an *addict,* it just means you might benefit from consultation with a professional. Your sexuality might be intensive and somewhat obsessive compulsive, but treating it like an *addiction* won't help.

SUSPICIOUS LOVERS

"Sure...You Were Working Late at the Office!"
or
If You Were Bowling, How Come My Private Detective Couldn't Find You?

If your lover is paranoid, you will notice some of the following characteristics:

(1) He will suspect—without real basis—that others are out to do him in.

He will be convinced that others are trying to exploit him or harm him. This may not be "way out" as in people trying to poison him or assassinate him. He may only figure that "You can never trust others, because given the chance—sooner or later—they'll do you in."

(2) She is often preoccupied about matters of "loyalty." Suspects that her friends talk about her behind her back. She is reluctant to confide in others because she suspects that anything she says "may and will be held against her." It makes "sense" (to the paranoid) that if others are trying to harm you, it's wise *not* confide in others.

(3) He holds grudges—is unforgiving of perceived insults, injuries, or slights. This is also consistent, because if you believe people are *usually* out to harm you, then forgiving them *now* doesn't make much sense because they'll just do it to you again later.

(4) She *reads hidden meanings into nearly everything.* If you can understand this, you will grasp the essence of the paranoid personality. Suspicious people don't usually "make things up." They don't simply *imagine* things. They don't see things that aren't there. In other words, they don't hallucinate—see pink elephants, or hear voices in a quiet room. In fact, suspicious lovers are usually keen and penetrating observers.

Paranoid partners see all the same things you and I see. Suspicious lovers hear the same sounds we hear. What *is* different is the *meaning* they attribute to what they see and hear. In other words, what is paranoid is their *interpretation* of events.

Hector passes someone on the street. They briefly make eye contact and the other person smiles at him. (an innocent gesture of friendliness) But since Hector is *prone to be suspicious,* he cannot accept this gesture simply as a smile of friendliness—he seeks to find deeper, hidden meanings in the smile. His inner suspiciousness causes him to *interpret* a simple smile as meaning that this stranger knows something special about him or has heard something unusual about him and is laughing at him.

At the very least, Hector is convinced that as they passed each other this stranger *noticed* something about Hector that looked stupid, silly, or funny—maybe this person thought the way Hector parted his hair made him look like a wimp!—and he was chuckling to himself *about Hector!*

Such are the thought processes of suspicious lovers. Paranoid partners always have something on their minds. They are preoccupied with *preventing* harm by *anticipating* it. They display a quality clinicians describe as *hypervigilance.* Always searching, persistently probing, they keep the world, and the people in it, under constant and careful scrutiny.

Whereas obsessive compulsives scrutinize the world for *facts* in order to be in control of things, or in order to buy the "best" car, paranoid people search for *clues* in order to anticipate and be prepared for danger. And, since the paranoid person frequently feels himself to be caught in some sort of important life or death struggle, his *hypervigilance* is continuous. Suspicious attention is intense and persistent.

In psychotherapy, for example, paranoid patients seldom *really* listen to the therapist, but rather *watch* and *scrutinize* the therapist in an attempt to figure out what he is *really up to!* Suspicious people are always looking for *deeper meanings, hidden motives,* and the like.

Such incessant, unrelenting scrutiny typically causes problems in the area of sexual relations, most often showing itself in the form of *jealousy*— unreasonable, persistent jealousy. Since the suspicious lover feels that the world is a dangerous place, is convinced that everyone is out to do him in, it's hardly surprising that your paranoid partner *suspects* you are having an affair. He will notice *any* smile you exchange with a stranger and will *interpret* such interchanges as probably a chance encounter with your secret lover.

He will insist on such phone services as Caller ID and will often hit the re-dial button on the phone when he first arrives home to "check" out whom you last called. Unbeknownst to you, he may have a wiretap on your line and be recording your conversations. At some point in your relationship, he's likely to have hired a private detective to follow you, or—to save money and reassure himself (you can't necessarily trust detectives, after all)—he's probably followed you and observed you himself.

Paranoid lovers have a *pre-existing internal bias* to distrust, so your partner finds it difficult to reassure himself, once and for all, that you *don't* have a secret lover. After all, just because he surreptitiously followed you to work and back doesn't mean you aren't having an affair. Your lover probably just happened to be out of town for a couple days!

Living With a Paranoid Partner

Living with a suspicious lover isn't easy. And getting your partner to "seek help," is almost impossible. Mutuality and trust are crucial components of psychotherapy, and since paranoid personalities find it so difficult to trust, they seldom seek treatment. Here the adage "You can lead a horse to the water, but you can't make him drink," requires modification.

If the "horse" is paranoid, it's often almost impossible to get him to the water. And, if perchance, with his feet planted you've been able to *drag* him to the water, there's no way he'll drink anyway, because he knows the water has been poisoned!

Sorry to sound so pessimistic, but in thirty years of clinical work, I've seen very few paranoids change much. Most are highly resistant to change. Usually their partners tire of the constant accusations, the unrelenting suspiciousness, and eventually leave them, often saying "Since he was always accusing me of having an affair, I decided I might as well have one!"

Your Choices

If you're convinced your lover is paranoid, you may decide to get out of the relationship. If you do, you need to be wise in how you handle it. If your partner is severely paranoid, it could be dangerous. He might stalk you, and finding you with a new lover, you both could be in danger.

Better to get out of the relationship gradually, possibly even to re-locate if it's not too disruptive to your life. It's probably best to wait a few months—even a couple years—before you begin seeing someone else. This will allow your paranoid ex some time to cool off and get used to the idea that he no longer owns you and to focus his rage over rejection on someone else.

These are the kinds of situations in which Personal Protection Orders are frequently filed. Unfortunately they do little to protect you *ahead* of time. If you've been married to a paranoid and had children together it becomes even more messy because unless he's a raving lunatic (paranoids usually aren't), he can look good in court while being quite severely maladjusted. This means he'll probably be allowed access to the children, who will be at risk for "catching" his paranoid perception of the world.

It's not a pretty picture. The best you can do in such circumstances is to consult a good therapist who can help you cope with the many difficulties that arise in such situations.

Living With Larry

On a brighter note, if your partner is only *slightly* or *moderately* paranoid, you can sometimes learn to live with it. Over time, a good marriage often has a healing effect on a mildly suspicious partner. As the years roll by and he *doesn't* find you in bed with another lover, he'll begin to worry less.

In the television sitcom *Dharma and Greg,* Dharma's father (Larry Finklestein) is portrayed as mildly paranoid. Larry's suspicions, however, usually focus on the IRS and other governmental agencies so he doesn't typically accuse his partner of sexual unfaithfulness. Although one can't pattern life after sitcoms, *Dharma and Greg* portrays how an entire extended family "works around" one person's paranoid style and offers a playful example of how to live with a mildly paranoid partner.

If you choose that route, you will frequently find yourself walking that middle ground between taking his suspicions seriously and simply ignoring them or laughing them off. You can't be too cavalier or he'll be angry that you don't take him seriously, but on the other hand you can't move into his paranoid world with him either. Living with a paranoid partner isn't easy, but it can be done—sometimes.

PSYCHOTIC LOVERS

"I'd Like to Have Sex, but My Insides are Rotting"
or
"Voices Have Been Telling Me That Sex is Evil."

A lthough we've spent most of this book learning that personality problems are just a more intense version of normality, I want to briefly outline what to look for if you think your lover may be *seriously mentally ill.* This isn't intended to be a substitute for seeking professional help; rather it will assist you in knowing if your partner has crossed the line.

Neurotic lovers have emotional problems that cause *inner turmoil or conflict in social relations.* Neurotics feel anxious, distressed, unhappy, conflicted or in other ways emotionally upset and this often leads them to seek out a therapist with little coaxing or coercing from others. The key notion here is that the neurotic knows that something is wrong. There is *no significant distortion of reality.* For example, the claustrophobic patient, who is afraid to ride the elevator to her forty seventh-floor office *knows* it's irrational, *knows* she is excessively afraid, but *doesn't know* how to cope adequately.

Psychotic lovers, on the other hand experience severe *distortions of reality.* The term "psychotic" generally refers to a mental impairment that severely interferes with the capacity to meet ordinary demands of life. Psychosis always involves a *gross impairment in reality testing.*

Whereas people with personality problems or neurotic conflicts are sometimes seen as "a pain in the butt," *psychotics* are seen as "crazy." A droll definition puts it this way: The psychotic thinks that 2+2=5, the neurotic knows that 2+2=4 but *worries* about it!

When Your Lover is Psychotic

If your lover is *psychotic,* there will be *distortions of reality.* He or she will probably exhibit some of the following characteristics:

(1) hallucinations (sensory experiences—sights, sounds, smells, etc—in the absence of external stimuli)

(2) disorganized or grossly thought and speech

(3) grossly disorganized behavior or posture.

If your partner suffers from the psychotic condition known as *schizophrenia* you should notice two or more of the following five signs: delusions, hallucinations, disorganized speech, grossly disorganized behavior, or flat emotions. Schizophrenia is further divided into several types:

In the *Disorganized Type,* disorganized speech, disorganized behavior and flat or inappropriate emotions are always prominent.

In the *Catatonic Type,* at least two of the following are prominent: motoric immobility or excessive motor activity, resistance to movement and the maintenance of a rigid posture, extreme resistance to instructions, bizarre movements or posture, echolalia (copying spoken words) or echopraxia (copying movements of others).

In the *Paranoid Type* there is preoccupation with one or more delusions and frequent auditory hallucinations. But disorganized speech, disorganized behavior or inappropriate emotions are *not* present.

Such persons are much like the paranoid lovers we've already discussed, except that their delusions are more severe and are often accompanied by hallucinatory voices as well. In the case of paranoid *schizophrenics* there is a genuine *distortion of reality*—not merely a *misinterpretation of meaning.*

If your lover suffers from *Delusional Disorder,* you won't notice any of the bizarre behaviors noted above, but your partner will be consumed by a delusional idea and will be unshakably convinced of the reality of this delusion. Unlike the *paranoid personality style* we discussed earlier where there is no distortion of actual facts, only a *misinterpretation of meaning,* in the *psychotic delusional disorder* your lover may be absolutely convinced that he is being followed or poisoned or that you are having an affair with a secret lover.

Delusional Disorder is subdivided into the following types:

In the *Erotomanic Type* your lover will be unwaveringly convinced that another person—usually someone of higher status—is in love with him.

In the *Grandiose Type* your lover will have delusions of inflated worth, knowledge, power, or influence and this will sometimes manifest itself in a distorted belief of a special relationship to God, some other deity or a famous person.

Lovers of the *Jealous Type* are fervently convinced that their sexual partner is being unfaithful.

Lovers suffering the *Somatic Type* of delusional disorder are convinced that they have some physical defect or general medical condition—in spite of medical tests to the contrary. There are also people known as *hypochondriacs* (a neurotic condition) who *worry* about health, but their concerns are not so bizarre—do not fly flatly in the face of reality. The hypochondriac for example might worry about some sort of malignancy and schedule a complete physical every six months in order to be assured of early detection. The *psychotic* might believe his stomach is slowly rotting away—which is confirmed he feels each time he passes wind. If encouraged to see a doctor to have it checked out, he would shrug it off saying "There's nothing they can do anyway."

In summary, if your lover is psychotic, there is no choice but to seek competent professional help. Since these lovers are absolutely convinced that their view of the world is reality-based, you cannot try to adjust to "things as they are." If you did, you yourself would have to become part of their "crazy world." Then, *you* could be diagnosed as suffering from a *Shared Psychotic Disorder*, also known as *Folie a Deux*. In rare instances, clinicians see a delusion develop in an individual who is in a close relationship with someone who has an already-established delusion.

If your partner is delusional, seek help, don't become part of a *folie a deux!*

DEPRESSED LOVERS

"I'm Too Tired"
"Besides, Why Would You Want Sex With a Loser Like Me?"

F or the most part the schizophrenic and delusional disorders we've just discussed have involved *thought* disorders. The massive distortion of reality was in the realm of *thinking* bizarre thoughts. Now we look at conditions in which the prominent feature is a disturbance of *mood*. If your lover suffers from one of the following conditions, she will experience problems in how she *feels* not in how she *thinks*.

Dysthymic Disorder will cause your lover to feel depressed for most of the day much of the time. Although his mood may not be *extremely* depressed, he will be "blue" more often than happy.

This condition may develop gradually and may occur over a period of years, so you may not have noticed a *sudden* change. Often you will have gotten so used to it that you won't expect anything different. But take a moment and look carefully at your partner's behavior and see if she exhibits several of the following signs:

(1) either poor appetite or overeating

(2) insomnia (trouble sleeping) or hypersomnia (sleeping too much

(3) feelings of hopelessness

(4) low energy

(5) low self esteem

(6) poor concentration or difficulty making decisions. You'll recall that obsessive compulsives have difficulties making decisions, but it's not because of lack of energy as is the case with dysthymics.

(7) increased irritability

(8) lowered libido

In summary, dysthymics suffer chronic but milder depression than full-blown depressives. Theirs is not the kind of depression that usually leads to hospitalization or electroshock therapy, but it is nevertheless takes a significant toll in their lives *and* in the life of anyone trying to be a sexual partner.

If your partner suffers from this kind of chronic, moderate depression with its accompanying *lowered sex drive,* you will often be left feeling unattractive, unsatisfied and angry. Don't despair—this condition usually responds well to a combination of psychotherapy and medication.

Encourage your lover to seek professional help and don't just settle for Prozac or some other antidepressant without including *psychotherapy* along with it. Otherwise, you may see the mood temporarily lift, but you will not have dealt with the underlying issues. This leaves you at high risk for recurrences.

There is a lot of talk in medical circles these days about how mood disorders "re-cycle," but that occurs not because mood disorders are some kind of biological rhythm, but because they are so often superficially treated—only with drugs.

Drugs are like duct tape, they might temporarily hold you together for a while longer, but they don't solve the underlying problems. Unhappy marriages, unruly children and nasty work supervisors can only be temporarily mollified with drugs. You can do better than that. Don't settle for Dupont's slogan: "Better Living Through Chemistry."

If we don't believe that adolescents should try to settle their turmoil by smoking pot, why should adults attempt to solve relational problems with Valium or Prozac?

Major Depressive Episode or *Major Depressive Disorder* are quite similar and I'll discuss them together. The main difference is one of *duration*—the *depressive episode* usually has a more abrupt onset and often lifts more quickly, whereas *depressive disorder* often begins gradually and lasts for a long time.

If a depressive *episode* hangs on for a long period of time, it becomes diagnosed as depressive *disorder.* In either case about five or more the following signs will be present:

(1) depressed mood most of the day, *nearly every day.* Either your partner will report that she feels sad, empty, useless or the like, or you will observe weeping and other signs of sadness.

(2) your lover will show a markedly reduced pleasure in nearly all activities most of the day, nearly every day.

(3) she may experience weight loss (when not dieting) or weight gain.

(4) he experiences insomnia or hypersomnia nearly every day.

(5) your partner shows either slowing down of body movements or agitation.

(6) he complains of fatigue or energy loss nearly every day

(7) she experiences feelings of worthlessness or excessive and inappropriate guilt nearly every day

(8) your lover has difficulty thinking or concentrating and is often indecisive

(9) your partner may experience recurrent thoughts of death or even suicide—but without suicide attempts or a clear plan of how she will do herself in.

Before leaving this discussion of depression, it's important to note that depression occurs in degrees and that the major differences between the various diagnostic categories is primarily one of intensity. Thus, depressive disorders differ from *dysthymia* primarily in *intensity* and *duration.* In *major depressive disorder,* for example, the depressed mood must be present most of the day *nearly every day,* whereas in *dysthymia* the depressed mood occurs for most of the day *for more days than not.*

Depression is widespread in our culture and many people at some time in their lives will struggle with depression. It shouldn't surprise you to discover that depression is a common ingredient in sexual difficulties.

Good sex between lovers ought to be playful and sparkling with excitement. Obviously if one of the partners is depressed (even moderately) it is difficult to create this *joie de vivre.* If you're having sexual difficulties, it's crucial that you make certain depression isn't the culprit. If it is, seek professional help. A *combination* of psychotherapy and antidepressant medications usually proves to be quite successful in dealing with these disorders.

Next we consider the opposite pole of mood disorders—when the mood is *too* happy, when excitement runs *too* high. Known as *mania,* such moods can be almost as debilitating to good sex as depression.

MANIC LOVERS

"What Do You Mean? You Don't Want
*Sex **Again!***"
*We've Had **Two Hours** of Sleep!*
or
"How Could You Turn Down Sex With
the Greatest?"
or
"Baby, I've Got to Get It Somewhere,
Please Don't Drive Me to Another Lover!"

L ike depressive disorders, excited moods vary in duration and intensity. In *Hypomanic Episodes* moderate excitement generally lasts for at least four days. In *Manic Episodes* intense excitement lasts at least a week or more. Since both have similar features, differing primarily in intensity, I'll discuss them together.

Manic Lovers show the following features:

(1) grandiosity or inflated self esteem

(2) decreased need for rest—often sleeping only two hours a night.

(3) extremely talkative with pressure to keep talking

(4) racing thoughts

(5) highly distractible

(6) increased goal-directed activities at work, home, or school—during manic episodes there seems to be unlimited energy

(7) excessive involvement in pleasure-seeking activities that have high risk for painful consequences: gambling, buying sprees, foolish business investments, unrestrained sexual activity.

In manic disorders the mood intensity is frequently so high as to interfere with occupational and social functioning. Sometimes it becomes necessary to hospitalize such persons to prevent them from harming themselves or others.

The intense hyper-active sexuality of lovers suffering from a manic disorder is probably what led to the terms *nymphomania* and *satyriasis*.

Although these terms are not used professionally by clinicians today-such terms are still bandied about in fraternity houses and on the street. Most males (especially during adolescence) fantasize about encountering a *nymphomaniac*—a woman whose voracious sexual desires drive her to seek fulfillment again and again. The male condition *satyriasis* is the mirror image—a man whose voracious sexual hunger is almost insatiable.

From our previous discussion, you could probably guess that these terms have been replaced by the ubiquitous term "addict." Yesteryear's nymphomaniac is today's female sex addict. Yesteryear's male who suffered satyriasis is today's sex addict.

More appropriately, excessive sexuality can be understood in terms of sociopathic personality, obsessive compulsive disorder or, as we've just seen, manic mood disorders.

In closing the discussion of mood disorders, I should point out that in addition to *depressive* and *manic* episodes or disorders, we sometimes see a *combination* of these.

In *Cyclothymic Disorder* we see a chronic pattern of fluctuating mood swings involving numerous *hypomanic* symptoms which alternate with *depressive* symptoms.

In *Mixed Episodes* or *Bipolar Disorder* we see more severe mood swings which alternate between *manic episodes* and *major depressive episodes*.

WHEN YOUR LOVER ABUSES DRUGS OR ALCOHOL—OR YOU!

"Honey, I'd Sho' Like Shom Shex, But I'm Shlightly Mellow!"or "If You Don't Quit Bitchin' 'Bout My Drinkin' I'll Hafta Rough Ya Up!"

C linicians make a distinction between substance *abuse* and substance *dependence*. Both are serious conditions, but in the case of *dependence* there is development of *tolerance*—meaning the user requires higher and higher levels of the substance to get a buzz. Additionally, the user will experience *withdrawal* if denied access and usually engages in *compulsive* drug-taking.

Alcohol—the most widely abused drug—is simply a special case of substance abuse. Consequently, most of the signs of substance abuse or dependence also apply to alcohol.

Your partner is a *Substance Abuser* if:

(1) recurrent substance use results in failure to fulfill her obligations at home, school, or work. Signs include excessive and repeated absences, poor work or school performance, neglect of household or children

(2) chronic substance abuse occurs in situations where it is physically dangerous (e.g., operating machinery or automobiles)

(3) recurrent legal problems arise from substance-related problems (e.g., arrests for driving under the influence or for disorderly conduct related to substance use)

(4) continued substance use in spite of experiencing recurrent social or interpersonal problems (e.g., arguments with your lover about finances or other problems related to substance use)

When the above signs are accompanied by *tolerance, withdrawal, or compulsive use,* a diagnosis of *Substance Dependence* should be considered.

How can you spot *withdrawal?* It depends on what drug your partner is dependent upon. Manifestations vary, but in general you'll know that something is going quite wrong.

Amphetamine or Cocaine Withdrawal usually results in fatigue, vivid and unpleasant dreams, increased appetite, motoric agitation or retardation, and insomnia or hypersomnia.

Nicotine Withdrawal usually results in depressed mood, insomnia, irritability or anger, anxiety, difficulty concentrating, restlessness, decreased heart rate, increased appetite or weight gain.

Sedative-Hypnotic-Anxiolytic (anxiety-relieving) Withdrawal usually results in two or more of the following developing within several hours: increased autonomic activity (e.g., elevated pulse >100 beats/minute, sweating) increased hand tremor, insomnia, nausea or vomiting, transient visual, tactile, or auditory hallucinations, motor agitation, anxiety, grand mal seizures. Most of these same symptoms are seen in *Alcohol Withdrawal.*

Sometimes these signs are difficult to recognize in your lover, because drug abuse tends develop gradually, over long periods of time. Few people become immediately *dependent* on alcohol or other drugs. Instead there is typically a long period of *use* that only gradually turns into *problem drinking,* and finally, *abuse or dependence.*

Nonetheless, alcohol-related problems cause so much misery in families that it is worth being alert. Be brutally honest about *why* you or your partner drinks? If you enjoy a glass of wine with dinner, or if a cold beer while mowing the lawn "does it" for you, you're probably not on the road to addiction. However if after drinking one or two you *nearly always want more,* you are at high risk for substance abuse. If beer is for you like potato chips are for most people (few people enjoy *one* or *two* potato chips) you are at risk.

Consequently, in evaluating how you or your lover use substances, don't just look at the signs of serious abuse that I've outlined above. Sometimes *tolerance* is so great that people can hold an amazing amount of liquor without actually looking or acting drunk.

I once interviewed a man who man who drank a *case* of beer *each day!* That's right—24 cans of beer a day! And the more amazing part was that he did *not* get drunk. He worked in a body shop, doing satisfactory work, but always with a beer near by.

I interviewed another alcoholic who was on welfare. Since he couldn't purchase alcohol with food stamps, he used his food stamps to buy soft drinks. Then, pouring out the pop, he returned the bottles to the grocery store for a ten-cent refund on each bottle and took the cash to a liquor store to buy his booze!

To summarize, study your lover's and your own substance-use patterns paying more attention to *why* you drink than to the *number* of drinks you consume. If you or your lover drinks primarily to get "buzzed," you're at risk. You might want to seek help in learning to cope with life without chemical assistance.

Violent Lovers

Violent Lovers often cycle back and forth between "wonderfully nice" and dangerously violent. Contrary to the popular scenario of a brutish husband beating his helpless wife, it turns out that violence within marriage is equally likely to be directed against *either* gender. Straus (1980, p. 685-686) reports that the annual incidence of violence by husbands was only negligibly higher: 12.1 per 100 husbands, compared to 11.6 per 100 wives.

Often—but not always—alcohol is part of the equation. Dutton (1988) reports a case where Robert and his wife were attending an office party of about thirty people. According to Robert, his wife disappeared (i.e, he could not find her in the large unfamiliar house). About ten or fifteen minutes later he finally found her and insisted they leave the party. He recalled feeling nothing at that point. They drove home, she went to bed, and he began to watch television. His next memory was of seeing her lying in a pool of blood, severely beaten. Realizing that he had severely beaten her, he called relatives and police.

It's not clear from this case study whether Robert was intoxicated or not, but in many such cases, alcohol, jealously and a history of violence conspire to make it a very dangerous situation for the "offending" spouse. Usually the assaulting spouse reports feeling a "build up" of anger which suddenly erupts into a violent attack.

Typically, a period of calm follows violence. During this time the assaultive spouse becomes increasingly ashamed, embarrassed and powerless—especially if the partner presses charges. Often during this time the victimized spouse begins to feel more powerful and this is reinforced by the (temporarily) contrite and loving behavior of the now-embarrassed spouse.

Walker (1979) describes the reversal of power which women often feel while in the hospital:

Within a few days they went from being lonely, angry, frightened and hurt to being happy, confident and loving... These women were thoroughly convinced of their desire to stop being victims, until the batterer arrived. I always knew when a woman's husband had made contact by the profusion of flowers, candy, cards and other gifts in her hospital room. (1979, p 66)

Dutton elaborates further:

The batterer throws himself on his victim's mercy, reversing the power relationship between them dramatically. He places his fate in her hands; he will be destroyed—lost—if she doesn't rescue him by returning to the relationship. (1988, p. 111)

In closing, I want to put this all in perspective. We spent the first seven chapters of this book exploring the many ways in which increased understanding of your lover can enhance your relationship. We considered how to **R**ecognize your lover's style, **R**eorganize your expectations and **R**evitalize your relationship-all ways to *accommodate* the small peculiarities and minor idiosyncracies in your partner. But this chapter has been written to alert you to the fact that you *cannot* and *must not* put up with everything.

If after reading this chapter you're convinced that your lover is mentally ill, abusing substances, or violent, you ought to seek professional help. If your partner refuses to participate in treatment or fails to benefit from therapy, you may have no choice but to end the relationship. If you plan to "work things out—no matter what" by "trying harder," please re-read chapter three. Now!

Epilogue:
"Mars and Venus"

"Your wife's had a baby. Federal regulations prohibit us from telling you its race or gender, but I can tell you it weighs a little over six pounds, is bald, and seems to be in good health."

"IF MEN ARE FROM MARS, AND WOMEN ARE FROM VENUS," HOW ON *EARTH* CAN A GUY BE A *REAL* MAN?

What is a Man?

Apparently "Everything I Learned in Kindergarten" was sexist, racist or otherwise politically insensitive. The Three Blind Mice we callous kindergartners sang about were visually impaired rodents who were victimized by an agribusiness owner's co-equal partner.

In kindergarten, I thought it would be as easy as 1,2,3: a boy "grows up," "learns to behave," and "becomes a man." Well, I've accomplished number 1, but just how does a man behave?

In the "good old days" answers to such questions seemed more clear. "Real men" fought wars, built log cabins and brought home the bacon, while the "earth mothers" to whom they were married waited for them to return from war, cleaned the cabins their men had built and fried the bacon they brought home.

Please understand, I'm not arguing for a return to those rigid role definitions which kept women from enjoying equal opportunities and allowed men the smug illusion of superiority, but after kindergarten, things get complicated. These days it's not easy figuring out how to get along with your girlfriend or your wife—for starters you shouldn't have both. But what about role models? Anyone out there?

The other day I stumbled onto a real nineties man—not some gravel-voiced, weatherbeaten John Wayne, but a world class photographer. I met him in the pages of *The Bridges of Madison County* where, in his search for covered bridges, he drove his pickup truck into the world of Francesca Johnson, Iowa farm wife.

Robert is a *real* man. The adventure begins as follows:

"He stepped in behind the wheel, [of his pickup] lit a Camel...Kincaid wore faded Levi's, well-used Red Wing field boots, a khaki shirt, and orange suspenders. On his wide leather belt was fastened a Swiss Army knife in its own case." (p.2)

"His razor caught the sunlight, where it lay on cement beside the pump, and she watched him soap his face and shave. He was—there's the word again, she thought—hard. He wasn't big-bodied, a little over six feet, a little toward thin. But he had large shoulder muscles for his size, and his belly was flat as a knife blade. He didn't look however old he was, and he didn't look like the local men with too much gravy over biscuits in the morning." (p. 44)

Now that we know how a real man looks. He smokes Camels, has a flat belly, wears orange suspenders, and carries a Swiss Army knife. But how does a *real man* talk to a woman? The answer comes after he's made love with the farmer's wife:

"This is why I'm here on this planet, at this time, Francesca. Not to travel or make pictures, but to love you." (p. 108)

Then, Kincaid gives his romantic talk of "falling in love" a Shirley MacLaine-spin:

"I have been falling from the rim of a great high place, somewhere back in time, for many more years that I have lived in this life. And through all of those years, I have been falling toward you."(p. 108)

Apparently it's important that *real men* have jobs that afford flex-time— none of this boring milking cows twice a day, or baling hay when it's not raining. Kincaid has the kind of job that allows for romance:

"Robert Kincaid gave up photography for the next few days. And except for the necessary chores, which she minimized, Francesca Johnson gave up farm life. The two of them spent all their time together, either talking or making love." (p. 111)

Francesca describes her husband Richard (who is off with the kids at the livestock fair for the week) in the following words:

"Richard could never get his arms around this; he doesn't think in these terms. He doesn't understand magic and passion and all those other things we talk about and experience, and never will. That doesn't necessarily make him an inferior person. It's just too far removed from anything he's ever felt or thought about. He has no way of dealing with it." (p. 113).

In other words, in modern parlance, Richard isn't the faithful husband who takes the kids to the fair, he's a bore, he "doesn't get it," he's "clueless."

Graciously, Francesca explains to Kincaid why she can't run away with him:

"Yes, it's boring in its way. My life, that is. It lacks romance, eroticism, dancing in the kitchen to candlelight, and the wonderful feel of a man who knows how to love a woman. Most of all, it lacks you. But there's this damn sense of responsibility I have. To Richard, to the children.'" (pp. 115,116)

But this is all really preface. Our hero is about to describe the characteristics of a *real man:*

"I'm one of the last cowboys. My job gives me free range of a sort. As much as you can find nowadays. I'm not sad about it. Maybe a little wistful, I guess. But it's got to happen; it's the only way we'll keep from destroying ourselves. My contention is that *male hormones are the ultimate cause of trouble on this planet.* It was one thing to dominate another tribe or another warrior. It's quite another to have missiles. It's also quite another to have the power to destroy nature the way we're doing. Rachel Carson is right. So were John Muir and Aldo Leopold."

"The curse of modern times is the *preponderance of male hormones in places where they can do long-term damage.* Even if we're not talking about wars between nations or assaults on nature, there's still that aggressiveness that keeps us apart from each other and the problems we need to be working on. *We have to somehow sublimate those male hormones, or at least get them under control.*

(pp. 101,102) [Italics mine]

Ah, at last! With the help of Rachel Carson, John Muir, Aldo Leopold and Robert Kincaid I finally find out what's been wrong with me all along! *Male hormones.* That's why we have war, famine and poverty. Too much testosterone! Too little estrogen. And this "insight" doesn't come from an angry feminist like Andrea Dworkin who writes that intercourse is "the pure, sterile, formal expression of men's contempt for women." Who claims that men use intercourse to "occupy," "violate," "invade" and "colonize" women's bodies. No, Robert Kincaid is of my own gender. He's the sensitive guy who's tender lovemaking and perceptive insights cast a long shadow from the mid sixties to the late nineties.

Now, if Kincaid has put his finger on the problem—*hormones!*—what is the solution? *Androgen* Replacement Therapy? Castration instead of circumcision? Eunuchs uniting for world peace? Should we require all males to take Prozac—calm things down a bit? Is the ubiquitous "biochemical imbalance" behind sexual dysfunction as well as depression?

I don't think so—in fact I think *hormones* have little to do with sexual problems and I don't believe in solving interpersonal problems with psychoactive chemicals.

Sexual problems are usually *psychological problems* and it is *psychological insight* not *hormones* that will help you understand the other gender. A *real man* aspires to get inside a woman's brain before he gets inside her bra. So if there's one truth I'd like you to take from all the preceding pages it is that *sexual behavior involves a complex interaction between two unique personalities.*

Too often our culture portrays sex as a behavioral act with a limited goal—orgasm. Too often we've strip sexuality of intimacy, spirituality, romance, or love, contenting ourselves with "doing it." Because biological sex has a clearly definable climax we are prone to describe this multifaceted psychobiosocial interaction in cryptic, goal-oriented terms: "doing it," "making it," "scoring," "the sex act." But to speak of a complex social interaction between two unique personalities as "doing it" trivializes the relationship.

Even driving an automobile frequently gets more attention in our culture than love making. Motoring from one place to another is not portrayed as simply "doing it" or "the driving act." What could simply be a way of transporting ourselves from point A to point B, is celebrated, glamorized and invested with additional meaning. We're told that "Americans have a love affair with automobiles." People spend enormous amounts of money in making the trip from A to B exciting exhilarating, and stylish.

When it comes to sexual relations however, what ought to be frosting on the cake of intimacy too often is only an empty ritual, a bitter aftertaste of unfulfilled dreams. This is because our society has things backwards. The "Hugh Hefner Myth" has convinced us that happiness is being surrounded by "bunnies." We have been led to believe that sex leads to the good life.

Like little children who believe that Mickey Mouse is the carrier of all good things and Disney World is Paradise Found, too many adults believe Hefner's fantasy: exciting sex with a variety of partners would bring ultimate happiness.

Nothing could be more backwards. The best sex takes place between people who deeply love and understand each other—first! The finest sex is based on shared laughter and tears, common financial struggles, mutual anxieties about a sick child, joint pride at graduations and myriad shared memories which form the bedrock of a solid psychological relationship.

I hope that in reading this book you've discovered a deeper understanding of your partner and of yourself, because deeply loving your partner is the real secret of sexual success—not variety, not aphrodisiacs, not the latest in sexual gimmickry, not erotic movies, *not hormones.*

Love and *psychological understanding* are the keys to good sex. When your lover is also your most intimate friend, you will experience fine sex, The BEST SEX = FRIENDSHIP ON FIRE!

In a word, there are three things that last forever: faith, hope, and love; but the greatest of them all is love. —I Corinthians 13:13 NEB

References

Abrahamsen, D. *Confessions of Son of Sam.* New York: Columbia University Press, 1985.

Carnes, P. "Progress in Sex Addiction: An Addiction Perspective." *SIECUS.* 1986, Vol. 14, No. 6. New York.

I Corinthinans 13:13. *New English Bible.* Oxford University Press, Cambridge University Press, 1961.

Cleckly, H. *The Mask of Sanity.* (5th ed.). St. Louis: Mosby, 1976.

Dutton, D.G. *The Domestic Assault of Women: Psychological and Criminal Justice Perspectives.* Boston: Allyn & Bacon, 1988.

Dworkin, A. *Intercourse.* The Free Press, 1987.

Frank, G. *The Boston Strangler.* New York: New American Library, 1966.

Harrison, K. *The Kiss.* New York: Random House, 1997.

James, M., & D. Jongeward. *Born to Win.* Reading, MA: Addison-Wesley, 1971.

Klein, M. "Why There's no Such Thing as Sexual Addication--And Why it Really Matters," *Annual Meeting of the Society for the Scientific Study of Sex.* November 1989.

Kohut, H. *The Restoration of the Self.* New York: International Universities Press, 1977.

Landers, Ann. *The Herald Palladium.* St. Joseph, MI., Sept. 15, 1994.

Massie, R. K. *Peter the Great: His Life and World.* New York: Knopf, 1980.

Meloy, J. R. *The Psychopathic Mind: Origins, Dynamics, & Treatment.* Northvale, NJ: Jason Aronson, 1988.

Merkin, D. "Eros Redux." *The New Yorker,* Dec. 27, 1993.

REFERENCES

Michael, R. T., J. H. Gagnon, E. O. Lauman, & G. Kolata. *Sex in America: A Definitive Survey*. Boston: Little, Brown, and Company, 1994.

Michaud, S. and H. Aynesworth. *The Only Living Witness*. New York: New American Library, 1983.

Nash, O. *There's Always Another Windmill*. Boston: Little, Bown, and Company, 1967.

Offit, A. *The Sexual Self*. Northvale, NJ: Jason Aronson, 1995.

Proverbs 16:24. *New International Version Study Bible*. Grand Rapids, Michigan: Zondervan.

Salzman, L. *Treatment of the Obsessive Personality*. Northvale, NJ: Jason Aronson, 1987.

Shapiro, D. *Neurotic Styles*. New York: Basic Books, 1965.

Straus, M.A. "Victims and agressors in prnaritall Violence," *American Behavioral Scientist*, 1980, 23, (5) 681-704

Sullivan, H. S. *The Interpersonal Theory of Psychiatry*. Edited by H. S. Perry and M. L. Gawel. New York: W. W. Norton, 1953.

Tompkins, S. S. *Affect, Imagery and Consciousness , Vol. 1 & 2*. New York: Springer, 1963.

Walker, L.E. *The Battered Woman*. New York: Harper and Row, 1979.

Walker, RJ. *The Bridges of Madison County*. New York: Warner Books, 1992

Wishnie, H. *The Impulsive Personality*. New York: Plenum, 1977.

About The Author

JOHN MICHAEL BERECZ, PH.D., A.B.P.P. received his Master's Degree in Counseling Psychology from American University, Washington, D.C. in 1966. He attended Indiana University, Bloomington as a U. S. Public Health Fellow in Clinical Psychology, completing his doctorate in 1970. The following year was spent as an intern at Children's Hospital Medical Center, Boston, a Harvard Medical School teaching hospital.

Since 1971 Dr. Berecz has maintained a private practice in Clinical Psychology as well as teaching at the University level where he holds the rank of Professor of Psychology. In addition to over two dozen articles and research reports that have appeared in various professional journals, he has authored two previous books: *Understanding Tourette Syndrome, Obsessive Compulsive Disorder, and Related Problems,* published by Springer Publishing Company, New York, NY, and *Beyond Shame and Pain: Forgiving Yourself and Others,* published by CSS Publishing Company, Lima, OH.

Dr. Berecz is licensed as a Clinical Psychologist as well as a Marriage and Family Counselor by the State of Michigan. In 1979 The American Board of Professional Psychology awarded him the Diploma in Clinical Psychology, and in 1994 he was elected a Fellow of the Academy of Clinical Psychology.

In addition to his teaching and psychotherapy practice, he has served as a supervising psychologist at Battle Creek Hospital, and as a clinical consultant to the D. C. Cook and Palisades Nuclear facilities.

Dr. Berecz has taught a Human Sexuality course at the University level for more than fifteen years.